PENGUIN BOOKS

BURN THE ICE

Kevin Alexander is a James Beard Award–winning food journalist and recipient of the Society of Professional Journalist's Mark of Excellence Award. His work has appeared in *Esquire*, *Elle*, *Men's Journal*, *The New Republic*, and *The Boston Globe*, and he is a 2018 Association of Food Journalists Award winner. He was born in Texas, grew up in New England, and now lives in Northern California.

Praise for *Burn the Ice*

"Mr. Alexander is an admirably thorough researcher. He conducted hundreds of hours of interviews for the book, meeting with some of his subjects dozens of times and revisiting most at least once to chart the arc of their careers. This groundwork allows him to bring us deeply into their worlds, probing their motivations, backgrounds, flaws, and virtues, writing with authority not just about public perceptions but also about private moments. . . . The book provides an entertaining and informative picture of the American restaurant scene over the past dozen years. Just dipping in and out of it pretty much guarantees learning something new." —*The Wall Street Journal*

"Kevin Alexander makes a fascinating case that we've witnessed the most exciting and creative time for food in recent history, but now, the golden age has passed. It's a bold idea, and one that'll get you thinking hard about what's next." —*Plate*

"[A] well-researched, witty food industry history . . . Alexander's sharp wit keeps the narrative moving. . . . This astute reflection on an era of American food culture will give foodies a new perspective on the restaurants they love and the dining experiences they've grown to expect." —*Publishers Weekly*

"Kevin Alexander is such a fluent and engaging writer that I was several chapters in before I realized how gimlet-eyed his view of the American culinary world is (and by 'gimlet' here I mean the thing that pokes holes in other things, not the one that's a mix of gin and Rose's lime juice). We need this book."

—David Wondrich, author of *Imbibe!: From Absinthe Cocktail to Whiskey Smash, a Salute in Stories and Drinks to "Professor" Jerry Thomas, Pioneer of the American Bar*

"This is a big American story, essential and gripping. Kevin Alexander shows how our culture fought and lost a battle against a creeping suburbia. *Burn the Ice* is modern anthropology about the physical and spiritual implications of what and how we eat. I loved it."

—Wright Thompson, author of *The Cost of These Dreams: Sports Stories and Other Serious Business*

"In his direct and spirited way, Kevin Alexander builds a swirling, deeply reported narrative about the American culinary scene. He digs into so many stories, shaping a detailed picture of how and what we've been fed in restaurants for the past twelve years. For anyone who follows chef and restaurant culture—and anyone who likes to eat out—*Burn the Ice* is a juicy, satisfying read."

—Erin Byers Murray, author *Grits: A Cultural and Culinary Journey Through the South* and *Shucked: Life on a New England Oyster Farm*

"Crucial reading for food lovers, social anthropologists, and cultural historians, alike. Kevin Alexander takes the great rabble of kitchen slave misfits, backwoods foragers, and tattooed food truck savants who turned the old gourmet dining culture on its head during the early years of the new millennium and brings them vividly to life."

—Adam Platt, *New York Magazine*'s restaurant critic

"If you've noticed that food has become especially central to the American consciousness today, you're not alone. Kevin Alexander takes a fresh and original look at the whirlwind of circumstances—cultural, legislative, and economic—that have laid the groundwork for food's precarious ascendance. *Burn the Ice* is captivating, concerning, and—most of all—inspiring."

—Danny Meyer, CEO, Union Square Hospitality Group; founder, Shake Shack; and author of *Setting the Table*

"All revolutions end—and let's face it, they're kind of exhausting. Progress in the restaurant craft has now relaxed into evolution, which of course every industry needs to prosper. With instructive, hilarious, and sometimes harrowing stories from the greatest minds in America's culinary trenches, *Burn The Ice* offers an authoritative preview of what's next."

—Ted Allen, host of Food Network's *Chopped*

BURN the ICE

The American Culinary Revolution and Its End

KEVIN ALEXANDER

PENGUIN BOOKS

For Wendy, Annie, and Peter

In the American din, that small thing was everything.

–George Packer, *The Unwinding*

PENGUIN BOOKS
An imprint of Penguin Random House LLC
penguinrandomhouse.com

First published in the United States of America by Penguin Press, an imprint of
Penguin Random House LLC, 2019
Published with a new afterword in Penguin Books 2020

ISBN 9780525558040 (paperback)

THE LIBRARY OF CONGRESS HAS CATALOGED THE HARDCOVER EDITION AS FOLLOWS:
Names: Alexander, Kevin (Food writer), author.
Title: Burn the ice : the American culinary revolution and its end / Kevin Alexander.
Description: New York : Penguin Press, 2019. |
Includes bibliographical references and index.
Identifiers: LCCN 2019006584 (print) | LCCN 2019016459 (ebook) |
ISBN 9780525558033 (ebook) | ISBN 9780525558026 (hardcover)
Subjects: LCSH: Cooks—United States. | Creative ability in cooking—United States. |
Food industry and trade—United States.
Classification: LCC TX649.A1 (ebook) | LCC TX649.A1 A44 2019 (print) |
DDC 641.50973—dc23
LC record available at https://lccn.loc.gov/2019006584

Printed in the United States of America
1   3   5   7   9   10   8   6   4   2

Book design by Daniel Lagin

CONTENTS

2009

2013

2017

Introduction

On November 4, 2011, a restaurant opened in San Francisco.

AQ—an acronym for As Quoted—was the venture of first-time restaurateur Matt Semmelhack and veteran chef Mark Liberman, and it featured an almost fanatically seasonal menu plus a design component (including bar tops and waiters' uniforms) that changed along with the food. It was experimental and ambitious and in a Mid-Market neighborhood in San Francisco that had been all but abandoned by the restaurant industry. Minutes before their "friends and family" night kicked off, they'd been recruiting said friends and family to sweep construction debris off their stoves. The gas was turned on just hours before. The kitchen staff had not yet used the equipment. They may not have yet had a health permit. And then the next night they opened this jumble of hopes and dreams and money to the public. Like most opening nights, it was both incredibly euphoric and rewarding and also completely terrible.

That euphoric honeymoon lasted exactly one month. Then they had to pay all the bills from the build-out. Despite being incredibly organized and a compulsive planner, Semmelhack somehow hadn't realized they would have to cut a separate check to pay sales tax. One day, an hour before service was meant to start, he was with his wife, Robin, a professional ballerina with the

Smuin Ballet in San Francisco, at the printer getting new menus. When they got back in the car, Semmelhack sat at the steering wheel, and wept. They were out of money, he told Robin. This was all a very bad mistake.

When he finally pulled himself together, he took a hard look at what the restaurant was doing. Shortly after launching, AQ had lunch, dinner, and brunch service seven days a week. That was unsustainable (and also insane). They shortened dinner service to five days a week, and cut lunch service, which meant laying off some daytime staff. Semmelhack feared that was just the beginning. But then, by the grace of Michael Bauer, they got their first review in the *San Francisco Chronicle*. Bauer, the longtime *Chronicle* critic, gave them three and a half stars for food and three overall.

A few minutes after midnight on the night it came out, Semmelhack had gone to the convenience store two doors down and bought the paper. He brought it back, and he and Liberman read it together seated at the chef's counter. It was glowing. They both cried, and then Semmelhack went back to the store and bought a dozen more.

Overnight, the restaurant went from the verge of closure to rousing success. Whereas they'd been averaging about 75 covers a night (or one "turn" of a table), a few months later they were getting 250. National reviews started pouring in. They were James Beard Foundation finalists for Best New Restaurant in America, and appeared on *Esquire*'s 2012 Best New Restaurants list. They'd gone from a neighborhood restaurant to a national dining destination. In keeping with their newfound reputation, they pivoted the menu, making it a little fancier, increasing the price of entrées, trying to serve fewer people a night but charge them more.

In early May 2012, Semmelhack, Liberman, and their wives flew out to New York City for the James Beard Awards. Nicknamed "the Oscars of food," the Beards are the biggest night for the industry, and they had been getting increasingly competitive and visible as the country got more and more smitten with its food stars. Semmelhack was blown away to be there. Though they didn't win, later that night they went to Gramercy Tavern and saw Union

Square Hospitality Group CEO and legendary restaurateur Danny Meyer and his wife standing in the door. Meyer's restaurants had won several awards, so they were in a festive mood. Semmelhack, a huge fanboy of Meyer's, nervously stood in a line of well-wishers waiting to shake his hand. When it was finally his turn, Semmelhack stammered out that he was inspired by Meyer and his book *Setting the Table* to open his own restaurant. Then he turned to Meyer's wife and said, "And this must be Audrey."

Meyer looked at him, laughed slightly, and then asked the name of his restaurant. "AQ," Semmelhack told him. "It's a restaurant in—" Meyer cut him off. "I know exactly who you are." Ever the master of his domain, Meyer then turned to Semmelhack's wife. "And this must be Robin." For the rest of the night, Semmelhack was floating.

On the plane back, Liberman and Semmelhack plotted their next move. In under a year, they'd managed to build a successful, profitable, nationally acclaimed restaurant. Things were looking up from there. The hip coffee roaster Four Barrel had just moved into a space next door and they were planning to open a café. It seemed that a sea change was afoot, and Semmelhack and Liberman had money in the bank. They were in the perfect position to take advantage.

They'd open a more casual restaurant on this block, they said, something to compliment AQ. This time, they'd do things differently: come up with a realistic budget, raise money properly, train the staff well, and plan it all carefully. The first one was hard; this one would be easy. There was an energy they couldn't quite explain. Everything was changing so quickly. It felt like a revolution.

THE UNITED STATES OF AMERICA is no stranger to revolution. For the better part of four hundred years, it's stubbornly refused to stand still. Perhaps more than any other nation in history, it's constantly in a state of reinvention, and nowhere is this truer than when it comes to what, where, and how we eat. But for the last twelve years, the change has accelerated, reaching previously unseen speeds, and it has been incredible, a—perhaps *the*—golden age of American dining. And it may already be over.

If you've spent the past decade covering the national restaurant scene, as I have, this ridiculously grandiose statement may not come as a surprise. To those of us immersed in that world, it's been clear for some time a bull market was raging, with the stakes constantly being raised as outside money kept pouring in, right up until the market saturated and everyone began white-knuckling their grip on whatever piece of the pie they had left. But if you're just an everyday American who casually enjoys eating nice and sometimes new foods and drinking refreshing and sometimes alcoholic beverages outside your home in an effort to delay the existential dread of an examined life, you may not have registered changes taking place, even as you enjoyed the benefits of the transformation. Like a fishing trawler sitting out at sea when a tsunami rolls by seismically deep below, almost entirely undetected, we are all capable of living through something remarkable without quite realizing it, until it's over and suddenly people start asking each other where they were.

That, on some level, is what I'm trying to do here. I'm trying to set down on paper the story, or a story, or several competing stories, of this particular culinary explosion, and maybe bottle some of the madcap energy of the past decade before it fades. Because it is fading—like so many halcyon moments before it—inflated, then consumed by its own success, a victim of impossible standards. Perhaps the wheels didn't have to come off so abruptly, but as the Blood, Sweat & Tears song states, what goes up must come down. And there was nothing to suggest the American food industry would defy gravity. And yet, just for the briefest of moments, at the height of the food crazes, it did seem as if American culinary glory would last forever.

And God, was it glorious: chefs bringing extinct crops back from the dead; bartenders finding ancient cocktail tomes in haunted attics and re-creating the recipes found within; tiny farms and distilleries and breweries blossoming from Montgomery to Montpelier; food trucks run by French-trained chefs creating singular, perfect foodstuffs; cheeseburgers becoming fancy and then purposefully not fancy again; a Vietnamese immigrant's small hot sauce company threatening ketchup's place as condiment king while spending zero money on advertising; obscure cuts of meat becoming celebrated by butchers; butchers becoming celebrities in their own right; hotel bars and restaurants turning into genuine destinations rather than necessities; regional pizza styles (Detroit!) becoming national icons; bars making everything with fresh juices and better ingredients; third-wave coffee shops reshaping coffee's identity into something to be savored; airport food becoming palatable and, in some cases, downright good; new delivery companies increasing the quality and scope of food you can get at home; European-style food halls flourishing in every city; more diverse cuisines being celebrated and reimagined to take their place in the culinary mainstream; bakers merging together croissants *and* donuts.

It's been a veritable food Valhalla. And very quickly, as is our habit, we, the American people, have adjusted our expectations and palates during the food world's tectonic shift over the last decade. Make it new, we scream with ever-increasing frequency and volume. So much so that it is very easy to forget our current food reality is still, in fact, very much a new reality. Mostly coming from unlikely locales.

For generations, culinary creativity in the United States basically came out of two places: New York City and the Bay Area. New York City had the longest culinary family tree, stretching back to the original Delmonico's (largely believed to be the first restaurant in America to let you order off a menu) in the early nineteenth century, but chefs at the best restaurants in New York were almost always from France (think Pierre Franey and Jacques Pépin at Henri Soulé's Le Pavillion or André Soltner at Lutèce), or followed French technique, first from legendary French culinary writer Escoffier, then in the realm of "nouvelle cuisine" as practiced by world-famous Lyonnaise chef Paul Bocuse. It wasn't until restaurateur Joe Baum began opening restaurants in the 1950s and 1960s that an "American" style really began to develop, culminating with the 1959 opening of the Four Seasons restaurant in the Seagram building in Manhattan. Though his opening chef was the Swiss-born Albert Stockli, Baum hired a team of some of the finest American culinary minds as recipe testers, including James Beard, Barbara Kafka, and Mimi Sheraton, and ordered them to scour "books and magazines for seasonal foods." In 1979, Larry Forgione took this seasonal ethos even further when he took over the River Café in Brooklyn and began connecting with local farmers and serving their bounty (famously coining the term "free-range chicken").

The West Coast started developing its own style in 1971, thanks to Alice Waters, who opened Chez Panisse after a revelatory trip to France. Her obsession with only foraging for local vegetables and buying from local farms cultivated the first idea of the farm-to-table restaurant, but when she hired the Harvard-educated, eclectic food savant Jeremiah Tower as chef, the combination of his encyclopedic knowledge of cookbooks and food history combined with her strict adherence to local products produced a sort of new French-countryside-meets-Bay-Area hybrid that became known as California Cuisine. Chez Panisse itself became an incubator of talent, producing class after class of impressive cooks like Judy Rodgers of Zuni Café, Coyote Cafe's Mark Miller, and Jonathan Waxman (more on him in a minute).

There were exceptions to this rule, but they tended to be exceptions that proved the rule. In the early to mid-eighties, Los Angeles had a major culinary moment, initially spurred by Michael McCarty opening Michael's in 1979 in Santa Monica and that young chef from Chez Panisse, Jonathan Waxman, taking over its kitchen four months in. Waxman's signature dish, a roasted half chicken with tarragon butter and fries, became his international calling card. Another Michael, Michael Roberts, opened the unfortunately (or presciently, depending on how you look at it) named Trumps in 1980 in West Hollywood, where he reveled in weird combinations, such as his famous brie-and-grape quesadilla and lobster with vanilla sauce, which seemed purposefully designed to piss off traditionalists. Add in Bruce Marder's West

Beach Café, Susan Feniger and Mary Sue Milliken's City Café, and Wolfgang Puck's Spago and Chinois on Main (which, alongside 385 North and Chaya Brasserie, helped kick off the first Asian fusion movement) and throw in a bunch of drugs and silly eighties celebrity money, and it seemed like LA's spin on the original California Cuisine moment (same local ingredients, more grilling and using fruit in a savory-sweet combination) would last forever. But the combination of Waxman moving to New York to open Jams, Puck expanding his empire outside the city, the stock market crash, and the revelation that cocaine might not be great for you helped end the era.

New Orleans experienced a similar trajectory, thanks to Louisiana chef Paul Prudhomme, who originally revitalized New Orleans standby Commander's Palace in the mid-seventies doing elevated takes on the Cajun food he'd grown up with, cleverly marketed as "Nouvelle Creole," before opening his own restaurant, K-Paul's, in 1979. One dish in particular, blackened redfish, became such a national craze in the early eighties that the redfish population in the Gulf of Mexico was in danger, and as Prudhomme graced the covers of national magazines and did cooking demos on television and toured the country doing what might've been the first-ever version of a pop-up restaurant, Cajun dishes like jambalaya and gumbo entered the national lexicon.

Finally, Dallas (and really all of Texas) had its moment in the culinary sun in the late eighties and early nineties. It started when a Dallas culinary consultant and cookbook author named Anne Lindsay Greer put a who's who of young Dallas chefs, like Stephan Pyles (Routh Street Cafe) and Dean Fearing (the Mansion on Turtle Creek) together with young Houston chefs like Amy Ferguson (Charley's 517) and Robert Del Grande (Cafe Annie), had the foresight to recognize they were all doing interesting things with local ingredients, and started to publicly talk about their collective styles as "Southwestern." Savvy with the press and lauded by James Beard Awards in the early nineties, the Dallas chefs became the face of a national Southwestern cuisine craze, as goat cheese quesadillas, lobster tacos, and things glazed with cactus pear took over menus in California, Colorado, and New York City, before eventually fizzling out as fads.

Each of these cities' earlier culinary movements came on with a fury that suggested they would be the arbiters of systemic change and possibly cement themselves into permanent Important American Food City status, but each time the trend had run its course or a particular chef left, the momentum receded, and the torch was sheepishly handed back to New York City and the Bay for safekeeping.

But in 2006 this all changed, when Portland, Oregon, jumped out of the culinary backwater and became the new face of American gastronomy. Portland's rise was almost as unexpected as the style that accompanied it. Young, fearless chefs were making bold, challenging dishes (sautéed lamb's brain with mustard crème fraîche, foie gras profiteroles) with locally sourced foods, served to you in a no-bullshit, rough-hewn space on chipped plates by mostly laconic servers with myriad tattoos. It wasn't clear whether the DIY aesthetic helped to spawn the menu or whether the menus being written called for a new kind of restaurant space, but a feedback loop came into being, and with it a playbook for young chefs in what had previously been second-tier culinary cities. Almost overnight, "the next Portland" became shorthand for smaller cities that were, all at once it seemed, and on relatively shoestring budgets, sprouting exciting food scenes. Places like Austin and Charleston and Nashville suddenly had something they hadn't come in contact with for a while: national buzz.

Looking back today, it might be possible to connect dots and make a case for explaining the etiology of the food virus that infected all in its path, but at the time there was no grand theory or interventionist god telling chefs what to do. It was more like something had been poured into the water supply. But it quickly became clear that the food world's collective unconscious was aflame, and among the folks involved, it seemed as if an omniscient zeitgeist was orchestrating the openings of ramen shops and Neapolitan pizza spots and pre-Prohibition cocktail joints all over the country.

The symptoms of this mania were remarkably consistent, but a few stood out above all: for one, an obsession with the idea of Paying Homage. This meant honoring those things that came before you, and it showed itself in everything from naming the restaurants and bars (Alden & Harlow's "name itself is a nod to the history of the building. . . . It refers to the architects of 40 Brattle Street"), to the interior, which had to use elements of the historical structure either in their original form ("original tin ceilings") or repurposed in a creative way ("salvaged wood paneling"). Drinks didn't just pay homage; they were often actual historical artifacts themselves, as the cocktail movement suddenly became infatuated with an earlier "golden" era, giving us the return of the Cobbler and the Rickey.

There was also an idea, especially as it related to food, that as more and more of life took place digitally, crafting something by hand became an especially revered profession, especially by the hipster movement's rural-chic (big beards, lumberjack flannels and work boots, folkish music from groups named after animals, etc.) practitioners. Thus, everything had to be hand-crafted. Hand-distilled spirits. Hand-butchered whole hogs. Hand-churned ice cream. Hand-pickled . . . pickles.

Coupled with that was the quest to find or learn things in the most "authentic" manner possible. If you were going to do ramen, you better go to Japan and learn noodle techniques from Yuki Onishi at Tsuta. Neapolitan pizza? Get certified by the Associazione Verace Pizza Napoletana. Molecular gastronomy? Travel to Spain and grovel at the feet of Ferran Adrià. Fermentation? Foraging? Nordic Cuisine? Do the same with René Redzepi. In the past, American chefs seeking this sort of culinary enlightenment would almost always travel to France, but now, as you saw David Chang return from Tokyo to open Momofuku or Andy Ricker come back from Thailand to do Pok Pok, there was a groundswell of interest in going almost anywhere that something culturally distinct and specific was happening, and as much as anything, this was because competition was getting fierce and it was taking more and more effort to stand out from the crowd. Authenticity inflation was high: what was authentic today might very well be shamefully derivative tomorrow.

Part of this obsession with authenticity was a reaction to the late 1990s and early 2000s, which had been defined by a reckless, dangerous, shark-jumping fusion fetish. Seeds of this can be traced back to LA's aforementioned eighties culinary moment—Wolfgang Puck at Chinois on Main and Roy Yamaguchi at 385 North and later Roy's—but other celebrity chefs pushed it further into the limelight again, especially with Jean-Georges Vongerichten's Vong and Spice Market, Rocco DiSpirito's Union Pacific, and Ming Tsai's Blue Ginger. As with most trends, however, the elevated, nuanced food being showcased by masters took on a distinctly different form when it was hijacked and subsequently dumbed down by the mainstream, and suddenly every new restaurant claimed to be Thai-Irish or Vietnamese-Finnish, and lemongrass mashed potatoes, yuzu martinis, and lots of different things involving warm kiwi proliferated on menus from San Francisco to Savannah.

Now fashion went back the other way. Foods were unpacked and simplified and reduced to their core elements. The ingredients were the narrative: where they came from, who made them, and what they did during the process. You could hardly order a protein without hearing its "origin story." The method mattered as much as (if not more than) the end product. You didn't want the biggest, reddest strawberry; you wanted the sweetest, most local strawberry, the one that had undertaken the most precious journey. At Husk in Charleston, Sean Brock was bringing back nearly extinct legumes and grains and only serving products made below the Mason-Dixon Line. In Portland, John Taboada's restaurant, Navarre, put out a menu that changed daily based on whatever farmers dumped on his doorstep. Daily-changing menus and scratch kitchens (where everything is made in-house) became ubiquitous, as did the idea of serving them in an ultracasual setting.

A creative culinary influenza seemed to afflict entire swaths of America, as more and more people began to obsess over, glorify, and fetishize food, just as the culture at large had done with love in the 1960s and money in the

1980s. In a way, this moment was a long time coming, the culmination of decades of gradual social change as public life had tilted away from the suburbs and back toward cities, but there was something unique about the sudden rush toward food enlightenment in the mid-aughts that wasn't matched elsewhere in society.

Eschewing standard cooking demonstration fare, food television got markedly better. Anthony Bourdain's *No Reservations* (and later *Parts Unknown*) gave viewers a knowledgeable, refreshingly respectful, unpretentious, yet still truly epicurean look at other country's culinary worlds, both elevating the travel/eating narrative and triggering renewed interest in underexplored cuisines, whether he was eating fermented shark in Iceland, documenting the privileged doldrums of waiting out a war trapped in a hotel in Beirut, or discussing modernization in the mountains of Oman. Reality competitions like *Top Chef* expertly interplayed the dynamics of reality television (grudges! heroes! villains! people crying into the camera!) with the tension and pressure of a competition show, affirming the now unremarkable idea that cooking is a means of identity creation. You are not just what you eat but what you serve. This made for a previously unseen hybrid that elevated competitors into legitimate marketable stars, securing them investments for their own places; serving as a launchpad for a slew of now nationally known chefs like Carla Hall, Tiffani Faison, Stephanie Izard, Richard Blais, and Kristen Kish; and driving a frankly incredible increase in culinary school applications during the mid and latter aughts.

Food media and criticism became a 24-7 proposition in earnest with the rise of blogs like *Eater* and *Serious Eats*. *Eater*, as it was originally envisioned by creators Lockhart Steele and Ben Leventhal in 2005, was essentially the *Gawker* of food. Just as *Gawker* (originally) covered the traditional New York media world as if the people writing celebrity profiles for *New York* magazine were in fact the celebrities themselves, *Eater* did the same for chefs and restaurateurs. The "we are all famous to ourselves" spirit of the age had come to food. Starting in New York City, and eventually making its way into more than twenty American cities, *Eater* churned out daily content discussing restaurant openings and closings, chef world gossip and drama, and other fare that helped turn chefs into public figures to a degree that had been previously reserved for actors, athletes, and politicians (i.e., people who chose to lead a public life). *Serious Eats*, started in 2006 by Ed Levine, was more of an amateur food nerd's paradise, a place for roving correspondents to post reviews of burgers or pizza, or share technical tips on the best Japanese knives to purchase, or how to sous vide steak, the Web 2.0 version of the Chowhound and eGullet message boards.

Alongside the blogs came the e-newsletters. Sites like *DailyCandy, Thrillist, Tasting Table*, and the unfortunately named *UrbanDaddy* sent out e-blasts five days a week, often covering whichever bars or restaurants were opening in the specific city you'd signed up for. Because these entities needed daily content and were in competition with each other, they were not picky about coverage, providing new avenues of exposure for restaurants and bars with limited marketing budgets that might not get a chance to entice the traditional food media gatekeepers, what I will from here on out refer to as the New York Food Mafia (aka NYFM). Like the actual mafia, the NYFM consisted of about five families (er, publications) mostly based in NYC (*Bon Appétit, Food & Wine, Saveur, Gourmet, The New York Times*), alongside a handful of restaurant critics at NYC-based men's and general-interest magazines (*GQ, Esquire, New York*), who more or less enjoyed hegemonic power in dictating the national food narrative. But the rise of the food blogs, e-newsletters, Yelp, and then social media threatened to topple this monopoly, as restaurants and bars entered into Faustian bargains with these new enterprises in exchange for coverage.

At its peak, this movement—this social upheaval—was truly beautiful to behold, a serious step forward in connecting Americans with the food on their plates and educating them in what it would mean for their health and that of the planet too. The idea of "foodies" being some tiny niche population of wealthy, retired couples excitedly standing outside suburban strip mall

Thai joints, holding marked-up copies of *Zagat* and Michael and Jane Stern's *Roadfood*, became increasingly outdated, as entire swaths of upwardly mobile twentysomethings, with their knowledge squeezed from *Eater* Heatmaps and *Thrillist* Eat Seekers and Yelp and Infatuation ratings, considered finding good food so obligatory that it no longer registered as a defining characteristic of one's identity. It became intrinsically cool to care about where things were grown, and to know if restaurants got their Cornish game hens from small farmers, or made the bar they built out of discarded ceramic tubs by hand.

After all, these were the sort of businesses and crafts that the utopian ideal of pre-Big-Box America was built on, a memory of a kind of city life that revolved around an aesthetically pleasing main street lined with an artisan butcher and an artisan baker and an artisan candlestick maker, all conveniently located next to each other and within walking distance of your surprisingly spacious and affordable apartment (with an original tin ceiling!) and eternally punctual, almost Swiss public transportation. Because this revolution took over neighborhood by neighborhood, you got a sense that hip prelapsarian villages were being rebuilt, matryoshka doll-like, within the greater confines of a big city's structure and that living (or at least eating and drinking and buying your small-batch gin) in those little townships-within-a-city made you truly feel like part of an intimate community. And then it all began to fall apart.

Over the past few years, in city after city, I've sat drinking small-batch gin and tonics and eating self-consciously retro bar snacks and talked about the last twelve years with chefs and bartenders and pitmasters and line cooks and waiters and farmers and food writers and thinkers and activists, and I've discovered that many of the very factors that caused this era to explode are causing its downfall. Most of those independent, chef-owned, casual fine-dining restaurants that came to define the last decade of dining have proven difficult to sustain as chefs burned out, rent and food costs increased, and the labor pool, especially in the back of the house, dwindled to near catastrophically low levels. The 24-7 food media, which for so long published fawning profiles of mostly male, white, mercurial chefs and bartenders, has come to realize during the #MeToo movement's awakening that male, white, mercurial chefs and bartenders are an imperfect, often highly troubling vessel for deification. The social media that brought exposure to creative ideas without traditional gatekeepers now overexposes trends at lightning speeds while rewarding whichever bullies and copycats are willing to scream loudest into the void. The small-town feel of many of these neighborhoods has become an oversaturated marketplace controlled by hostile landlords and aggressive developers intent on capitalizing on past excitement while whitewashing a neighborhood's culture and history. The words "craft" and "artisanal" and "farm-to-table," once vitally important signifiers of the movement, have become so commonplace they've really stopped meaning anything at all—or, worse, have taken on a sneering, ironic edge in the mouths of cynics. Plus, there are too many *Top Chef* spin-offs.

But even as this golden age dims like the Edison bulbs in its signature restaurants, something new is appearing on the horizon. The last days of disco have come and gone, and yet we keep dancing. There will still be dinners out, and new, exciting minds in the kitchens and behind the bars. The food kings are dead, long live the food kings. But there's something unique to what has transpired over the past decade or so, and the people and places I chose to write about in this book were part of that. Some helped start it, some precipitated its fall, and some were just bystanders who inadvertently left their mark as the revolution rolled through.

In the kitchen, the term "burn the ice" means to melt down whatever remains in the ice machine at your station at the end of the night. At the bar, it's also used when someone drops glass into the well and you've got to burn off all the ice to find the glass. The first version suggests an end, a way to close; the second, a restart. Both meanings, I think, apply to the current culinary landscape.

And to that end, the choice to write about certain folks (and restaurants, and neighborhoods) was based around whether or not their stories, either symbolically or emblematically, could help tell a larger story about the shifts in that landscape. So we follow chef Gabriel Rucker as his small restaurant, Le Pigeon, unwittingly becomes the influential restaurant prototype for the Portlandization of American dining, and he fights to overcome addiction and keep his creative edge. We watch Indian immigrant Anjan Mitra and his wife, Emily, as their South Indian restaurant, DOSA, is first forced to battle against stereotyping from outside the Indian community and suspicion from within, and then later forced to evolve as the rest of the food world finally "discovers" and appropriates more and more non–Western European cuisines. We find Nashville's André Prince Jeffries paradoxically celebrated as a famous culinary legend for maintaining the legacy of her family's hot chicken restaurant and threatened as that hot chicken morphs into a city's calling card, then a national phenomenon. We behold grouchy Pittsburgh native Phil Ward as he finds his place in the world of bartending just as the craft cocktail movement has taken hold in New York City and beyond. We observe a single street in New Orleans as, over the course of a decade, it evolves from hurricane-ravaged into the clearest example of the complicated, gentrifying, new New Orleans. We regard Internet-famous stunt person Josh Ostrovsky, aka the Fat Jew, as he attempts to cash in on the rosé trend. All of this, I hope, adds up to a mosaic of the last decade's sprawling, mercurial, pyrotechnically creative culinary ecosystem and serves as a type of food world immersion software, an industry Rosetta stone.

But of course, for each one I write about, there are hundreds if not thousands of other figures out there who toiled away and laid an integral brick in the construction of an era. This is not an all-star lineup of the biggest names in food and drink. Some people in this book are famous. Others are food industry famous. And a few aren't really known at all (or are, as you'll see, purposefully and necessarily anonymous). To write about all the brightest lights would have been to tell the same story over and over again, and I didn't want to do that, and doubt you would have wanted to read it. To that end, I left out some incredibly influential people from the world of food and drink, like David Chang, Sean Brock, Danny Meyer, and many others. More often than not, these giants have had their stories told already so skillfully as to render me physically incapable of attempting it again.

But in the stories I did tell, I was struck by just how American they were. The hospitality industry is a mash-up of Americans of all stripes: entrepreneurs, actors, shut-ins, charlatans, visionaries, misanthropes, dreamers, and cynics. This has always been the case. But what made this last decade so compelling was that for a moment, it seemed—much like in the days following the election of Barack Obama, as people longingly and ultimately futilely questioned whether we might now be living in a "post-racial" world—that a hopeful, progressive future of food was upon us. Indeed, Michelle Obama herself, with her healthy school lunch push, did as much as anyone to make that future real. We were living in an Alice Waters fever dream, a time when it seemed possible that everyone not only should but could eat great, thoughtful food from local farmers and their own gardens, and that chefs and bartenders doing the most creative, progressive things would be the ones rewarded, and that 2006 Portland would live on forever in the hearts and minds of the true believers.

ON JANUARY 17, 2017, a restaurant in San Francisco closed.

The years following AQ's run of national accolades hadn't been kind to Semmelhack and Liberman and their Mercer Restaurant Group. Health and labor costs had increased dramatically. Since they'd opened, there'd been a 211 percent increase in the number of San Francisco restaurants. Michelin had inexplicably failed to give them a star, one that would've helped bring in more deep-pocketed international diners. Their follow-up to AQ, the more casual TBD, had been no less ambitious, with live-fire cooking, but the problem with live-fire cooking was that it involved a live fire, and after three unintentional extremely live and uncontained fires in the first few months, they pivoted into a non-live-fire, lower-cost Mexican concept before finally shutting the doors. External factors didn't help the cause. Tech companies that had moved close by, thanks to massive tax breaks, walled their employees off from interacting with the city through perks like in-house chefs serving three free meals a day. That Four Barrel café next door that was supposed to help revitalize the neighborhood never materialized.

Other projects, like their French brasserie, Bon Marché, and a Mission café, also fizzled out, but still they held out hope that their flagship could weather the storm. After a 40 percent drop in revenue from the year before, however, it became very clear that they had to do something. So that night in January 2017, Semmelhack and Liberman shut it down and threw a party.

When I arrived, around nine thirty p.m., you could see the energy shifting, ties loosening, hair being released from ponytails. By ten p.m., the last paying customers had settled their checks and were starting to filter out. Soon after, a makeshift open bar materialized on a table, blue Solo cups came out, rap music was turned on and up. Servers, managers, and cooks cliqued off into groups, clustering as at a high school party; young women in weekend dresses danced together; cooks with aggressive facial hair hung near the sharp knives in the open kitchen, sipping brown liquor and watching out of the corners of their eyes.

Many of the original team had come back for this night: the first sous chef worked the line; the original sommelier tried to sell some of her favorite bottles of wine still in the cellar. Regulars came in to pay tearful tributes and emotionally overtip. The lone walk-in couple, unaware they were seeing a legendary restaurant's last night, left no gratuity and wrote "disappointed" on the check. They'd expressed severe displeasure when, at nine thirty p.m., the server explained that, as the restaurant would not exist tomorrow, they were out of bread. Semmelhack took a picture of the check with his phone, almost wistfully.

A little past midnight, someone turned the music down and Liberman stood up on a table and gave a speech about ambition and how proud he was of the effort everyone had put in over the past five years. Semmelhack followed with a talk about the marriages, offspring, and new jobs that had come from this place. After he finished, they left the music off for another couple of minutes and offered anyone else a chance to speak, but perhaps the alcohol had yet to metabolize into bravery because no one did. Shortly after, Semmelhack and his wife got ready to go. An empty bottle of 2006 Volnay Clos des Ducs sat on their newly vacated table next to a white spatula, an overturned high chair, and a neatly folded server's shirt. As they walked out, there was a brief lull, then someone turned the music up.

Because they were going my way, I hitched a ride home with the Semmelhacks. As we drove through the desolate Mid-Market neighborhood, I noticed a plaque wrapped in bubble tape wedged between a child's car seat and two boxes. It was AQ's James Beard Award for Best New Restaurant in America 2012. "That," Semmelhack said, noticing me studying the frame, "feels like it happened a decade ago."

And a little more than ten years before is when this heroic, tragicomic, utopian story of American self-invention—the story of a culinary revolution—begins.

THE RESTAURANT RAT PACK? YOU CAN BET THAT CHEFS WOLFGANG PUCK, MICHAEL MINA, AND BOBBY FLAY WILL MAKE ATLANTIC CITY'S BORGATA THE NEXT HOT DINING DESTINATION. | Year-old Eater (eater.com) has become required reading for anyone who follows New York City's frenetic restaurant scene, thanks to its obsessed-with-getting-the-scoop founders Ben Leventhal, 28, and Lockhart Steele, 32. Now the enormously popular website is expanding to California. | **"When you have the Internet, who needs cookbooks?" said Amy Cisneros, an avid cook from San Antonio. "I look at all the different recipes, and then I make it my way."** | The next day, though, she happened to go on www.opentable.com and found a table at 7:30 p.m. Were there tables she could get on the web but not by phone? Had she received a straight answer the first time around? | **I had some terrific times at Dressler, in the Williamsburg section of Brooklyn, a borough whose dining scene kept getting better.** | *Sous-Vide (soo-VEED)—literally "under vacuum" in French, it's the fancy boil-in-a-bag technique that's sweeping the nation's high-end restaurants.* | The $40 entree, which first appeared in New York and Las Vegas, is appearing on menus across the nation. | **"THERE'S PORK FAT IN JUST ABOUT EVERYTHING AT MOMOFUKU."** | Popping a few CDs into a sound system isn't good enough for the best restaurants anymore. These days playlists are expected to show as much creativity as the menus. | *These gastronauts, who have fallen under the spell of Spanish chef Ferran Adria, consider the kitchen a laboratory and their experiments include "cooking" with liquid nitrogen, working with heat barely above room temperature, and of course serving everything with the now ubiquitous foam.*

2006

CHAPTER 1

Gabriel Rucker, Portland, Oregon, Part 1

The story of Portland's 2006 rise to national food-world prominence begins in 1990 with an old cookbook and a nine-year-old boy named Gabriel Cameron Rucker. Rucker's family lived in Napa—not the fancy part where wealthy women exhort other wealthy women to split cases of fruit-forward zinfandels, but the actual town. The son of a Travis Air Force Base machinist and an elementary school teacher, he liked to look through cookbooks, mostly at the pictures of finished dishes. During this process of discovery he found an old, tattered 1970s tome on his parents' shelf and made the simple pasta with tomato sauce recipe inside. Though the glory of a nine-year-old making dinner was truly something to behold, his parents, who liked the simple, sugary pleasures of dumping an entire jar of Prego over said pasta, could not abide the thin, homemade sauce he'd whipped up. "Gabriel," his mom told him once, gently, "enough already with that darn pasta."

In high school, Rucker got a job in downtown Napa at New York Bagels, run by two East Coast expats. The shop used an old New York taxi cab to deliver the bagels, and driving that retro ride while girls looked on longingly was considered the best high school job in the area, the Peach Pit gig of Napa. Rucker was excited to work there, at first, because it was hip, but soon became fascinated, not with the New York cab driving but by the process of making the bagels: the craftsmanship, the machine that rolled them, the reaction the dough had to the live yeast. He also liked that in the back, behind the cool high school kids making bad lattes, were real people with full, complicated, grown-up adult lives. So Rucker asked to help make the bagels. And he loved it.

The only problem was, he also loved tucking his giant JNCO jeans into his sneakers, throwing on a fairly tight polo shirt and some candy bracelets, taking shitloads of ecstasy, and spending entire nights caught up in the Bay Area rave scene, out at Homebase behind the Oakland Coliseum, or at Second and Jackson, or San Francisco's Maritime Hall, listening to Dyloot, Tom Slik, Nostrum, Mars & Mystrë, Tracer, and Thomas Trouble. And when you're spending an entire Saturday night liquid-hand-dancing your face off in the jungle and trance rooms with a glow stick attached to your earring, then heading back to a friend's house around eight a.m. to smoke hella weed and pass out, your ability to cook bagels at a high level suffers.

Rucker never does anything half-assed, and so he jumped drugs-first into the rave scene, spending as much free time as possible either rollerblading or hanging out at F-8 on Haight Street, learning to DJ acid and cyber trance. This didn't afford a ton of time for a stellar academic career, so when Rucker graduated from high school, he took his talents to Santa Rosa Junior College. A housing shortage on campus meant he lived twenty minutes away in Cotati's Sonoma State student housing, in the Jung house, a four-bedroom setup with two kitchens, two fridges, and two bathrooms. Through the glory of God, Rucker's three roommates happened to be two Japanese exchange students named Shinji and Musashi, who barely spoke English but had a fascination with rave music and weed, and a house DJ from LA. Their setup also included two sets of turntables, and a random pot dealer named Drew. It was quite a time to be alive.

On the second day of school, Rucker took a pre-algebra class in which the professor defined a "lab," which sounded like a code word for a shit ton of homework, something that would inherently conflict with the Jung house lifestyle. So he saw a counselor, a wizened old man with gentle, trusting eyes, who looked past Rucker's statements and into his soul, then handed him a list of vocational school topics and told him to point to one that interested him. As Rucker scanned the list, his finger stopped right in between Consumer Issues and Dental Assisting. Culinary Training triggered a Pavlovian response in Rucker's brain, firing up mental imagery of his time in the kitchen at home and at the New York Bagels shop, the hypnotic pleasure of making those bagels. It was decided: Gabriel Rucker would be a chef.

School, which had been hard for Rucker, suddenly clicked. A dormant fluency in food emerged, as if he'd known a language his entire life and only now people around him were speaking it. Intro to Professional Cookery made sense. Practical Professional Cookery made sense. Sanitation and Safety was boring. On the nights he wasn't focused on half-tobacco, half-marijuana bong rips, Rucker studied Thomas Keller's *French Laundry Cookbook*. But after a year burning béchamel and doing reports on the origins of the croissant for Baking and Pastry, Rucker was getting impatient. He remembers sitting in a class as someone made a joke about foie gras, and feeling stupid because he had no idea what that was. It wasn't enough to cook huge vats of chicken for the staff; he wanted to do it for real.

So he dropped out, and used a connection from high school to get a job at Silverado Country Club back home in Napa, under chef Peter Pahk. The original gig was not sexy: he was working nights for the garde manger chef (aka the keeper of the refrigerated storage area), and that usually consisted of squirting dressing on premade salads, cutting pounds of cantaloupe, and bugging his mentor, an older woman named Lorena, about the specifics of what they were doing. Lorena and some of the other older cooks took him under their wings and taught him fundamentals, like how to break down, sear, and roast a whole beef tenderloin. And how to whip up a batch of hollandaise for three hundred people. And how, if you're making risotto, you put the onions in and season them to build the base of flavor. Another cook, a French guy who went by the rather transparent moniker "Frenchie," gave him his first lesson in foie gras, showing him how to make torchon. This was a big deal. In traditional kitchens, eighteen-year-old nobody in-line skating enthusiasts stuck in the garde manger don't get near the foie. But here was Rucker, not only touching it but learning to clean it, devein it, make terrine, portion it, everything.

Other things stuck as well. Another cook lifer named Benjy, the type of guy who could've been anywhere from forty-five to seventy-five years old, who had lines on his face like tree rings and drank heavy cream out of the cartons while chain-smoking, had a thing for birds. "I love little birds," he'd say, his vocal cords scratching and thumping against each other like an inexperienced rugby squad. "Little birds with little bones." Rucker would watch him casually pick up an entire grilled quail and shove the whole thing in his mouth, smiling as the little bones stuck out of the sides of his cheeks.

Despite the learning, Rucker got bored hanging around his hometown and decided to move in with his girlfriend down in Santa Cruz. The older cooks at Silverado gave him a going-away present: a copy of legendary chef Auguste Escoffier's cookbook, signed by every cook he worked with. One of those cooks, Maynard, told him to go to page 167. If he could make that dish, Maynard wrote, he could really call himself a cook.

Rucker had asked Silverado's Chef Pahk if he could get him in at one of the best restaurants in the area, the Lodge at Pebble Beach, and Pahk said yes. To show he was serious—and because Pebble Beach drug-tested—Rucker quit smoking weed for a long time, a monumentally challenging feat for a person who smoked upward of three to infinity bowls a day. But when he got down there and showed up, Pebble had no idea who he was. Fill out an application if you want, they said, but no one's vouched for you.

So he did, and though he never heard from them, Rucker never really took to smoking weed again. Not high, Rucker was forced to wander around town, both to check out the best potential rollerblading routes and to apply for jobs. He came across Southern Exposure Bistro, a jack-of-all-trades restaurant making everything from lasagna to filet mignon with mashed potatoes out of a piping bag. Eager for a job, he popped his head in the front door and was immediately chastised. "Don't you know," the chef yelled at Rucker, "kitchen staff doesn't come through the front? Go the fuck around to the back."

Even with his faux pas, the chef put him on, first in a familiar role in the garde manger, but eventually he recognized Rucker's talent and let him make the specials. It wasn't hard work. Rucker had a routine: after cooking for about twenty-five people, he'd be home by nine thirty p.m., drink a bottle of Jack Daniel's, eat a couple of shitty corn dogs, play a couple of games of pool in the basement, and page through Keller's *French Laundry*. He'd lie on the double bed he shared with his girlfriend and dream about dishes he'd want to create. These weren't dreams about portions and ingredients—his brain didn't operate like that—but lucid, fully formed pictures, the finished product sitting there in his head like an open oven. His goal in the kitchen the next day would be to work backward from those pictures, and so he began experimenting, making things like duck liver and wild mushroom in phyllo dough, escolar with chorizo and zucchini, black bass with glazed cipollini onions in a David Bruce pinot noir reduction. Some of these were fucking delicious and would get him praised; others were shitty and would get him yelled at. When a dish didn't go his way and all of a sudden Rucker was behind the eight ball, he had another routine: he'd walk out of the kitchen and go behind the bar, where—in the very bottom left-hand corner—a liter bottle of raspberry Stoli was tucked away. He'd take a few quick pulls and walk back into the kitchen.

For two years, Rucker worked at the bistro in Santa Cruz. He got close with one of the other cooks at the bistro, David Reamer, a Jersey expat with an affinity for photography, and tiring of Santa Cruz, they started talking about moving to a bigger place with more action. San Francisco was out (they couldn't afford it), but Reamer told Rucker about a friend who'd moved to Portland and said it was pretty cool. Rucker, never one to meditate long on a decision, said fuck it, let's do it. That next week, during the summer of 2001, they packed up Rucker's 1997 blue Honda Accord and drove it up to Oregon, renting a four-bedroom house at Thirty-Ninth and Powell in Southeast with a gigantic porch and basement for $1,400.

For three weeks, Rucker sat around their new house, eating Stouffer's frozen lasagna, drinking the full repertoire of Safeway's Vendange wine collection, and unsuccessfully trying to learn how to play Pavement's "Shady Lane" on guitar. When he finally got his first cooking gig, working for a chef named Eric Laslow at his eponymous restaurant, Laslow's Northwest, it wasn't a great fit. This could've been because of Rucker's brash attitude, the young, dickish sous chef overseeing him, or sadness about his inability to master Pavement's oeuvre. Whatever it was, Rucker wanted out, and started to ask around. Then one day, another guy in the Laslow kitchen, Luis Cabanas, pulled him aside.

"You want to work somewhere legit?" he asked.

"Do Rollerblades have four wheels?" Rucker replied.

"What?" Cabanas asked.

"Never mind," Rucker said. "Yes, I do."

"All right, man," Cabanas responded. "Come on through tomorrow and I'll make an introduction."

"What's the restaurant called?" Rucker asked.

"Paley's Place," said Cabanas. "They're for real."

TO UNDERSTAND PALEY'S PLACE'S REALNESS, you need to go back further, to the seventies and eighties, when Portland was just a small, soggy, gray municipality barely clinging to its old shipbuilding past and still alarmingly reliant on the boom-bust cycles of the timber industry. Back then, if you wanted something other than a tavern with blacked-out windows or a middling diner, you only had a few options: in the seventies, there was Howard Waskow and Millie Howe's Indigine, a fiercely beloved sort of Chez Panisse knockoff that turned into an Indian restaurant named Cherie Kebaby on Saturday nights. Or you could opt for one of local cooking school despot Horst Mager's German joints. And then, for years, it was basically just Genoa, the fancy Italian anniversary and birthday joint. Or L'Auberge, essentially the French version of the very same thing. As Paul Prudhomme's new New Orleans cuisine swept the nation, Digger O'Dell's Oyster Bar & Restaurant hopped on the trend, offering up blackened catfish (for better or worse). If you went looking, you could find good dim sum in Chinatown at Fong Chong or Vietnamese at Mai or Thanh Truc, but most people didn't.

Then, in 1990, came Zefiro. On the edge of the Pearl District at Northwest Twenty-First and Glisan, with an iconic copper-topped bar, sponge-painted yellow walls, a lively, trendsetting bar scene, and a local, seasonal menu that switched up twice a month, it felt like a "big city" restaurant. And not for nothing: its co-owner, Bruce Carey, and chef, Christopher Israel, had both come from San Francisco, where they'd spent time at two of SF's legendarily influential restaurants: Square One and Zuni Café. Fellow co-owner Monique Siu had spent time in France and loved the Francophile idea of a menu heavily reliant on whatever could be found locally and in season.

Everyone in Rose City who could afford a pair of status jeans showed up at Zefiro to eat the legendary ricotta gnocchi, or salmon wrapped in grape leaves, or the Caesar salads you tore apart with your bare hands like a barbarian herbivore. They went to listen to Pink Martini's Thomas Lauderdale play midnight shows on Saturday nights. They went to drink non-pink martinis at the beautiful bar. You had Nike's top executives. Director Gus Van Sant and his actor buddies. Wieden+Kennedy's creative directors. Mid-level Nike executives. Mayor Vera Katz. The Intel people. Lower-level Nike executives. Everyone.

To the guys and gals from Zefiro, Portland was an extraordinary culinary jukebox, willing and able to play almost any comestible genre. Here was a place that lacked the intensity and competition of New York and San Francisco, but had even more of an incredible bounty, essentially untapped. The area had no real deep-rooted, historical culinary traditions that new chefs had to adhere to—unlike, say, the gumbo and crawfish étouffée of New Orleans, New England's clam chowder, or even the more modern nouveau regional cuisines that took hold in the seventies and eighties in California, New Orleans, and Texas. It was, as legendary Portland food critic Karen Brooks put it, "the culinary version of having your parents out of town forever. No one was judging, and that was great."

On top of that, Oregon's strict urban growth boundary law passed in 1973, forbidding big-box stores, malls, and housing developments from taking over farmland and forestland outside the boundary; limiting the normal suburban sprawl you see in places like California; and keeping the city more compact and walkable, and farmland close. The only issue was that most of these very local farmers were not selling their goods locally. The best cherries, peaches, apples, pears, and so on were going abroad, to places like Japan and Germany. Master French chef Philippe Boulot tells the story of how, before he moved to Portland in the nineties, he would buy chanterelle mushrooms from Germany while working in New York and they would come in a box that said "from Oregon." But in 1992, a crucial turning point: Portland Farmers Market opened downtown and a true farmer-chef relationship began to take hold.

Zefiro's resounding success put a new spotlight on food culture in Portland. Line cooks at Zefiro like Andy Ricker, Kevin Gibson, and Scott Dolich would later go on to be star chefs in their own right, but Zefiro's true magic was in serving as a culinary bat signal both for chefs outside the city to move there and for local chefs to step up their game. Cathy Whims bought Genoa in 1991, freshening up the old special-occasion joint. That same year, hotelier Bill Kimpton opened the Hotel Vintage Plaza downtown, hiring Dave Machado to run the kitchen at Pazzo, where his butternut squash cappelletti with toasted hazelnut and sage butter became legendary. The years 1994 and 1995, however, stood out. Greg Higgins opened Higgins. Cory Schreiber, whose family had been involved in Oregon's oyster trade since the 1860s, came back to the city from the East Coast and opened Wildwood. Boulot moved up to Portland from San Francisco and took over the Heathman. And Vitaly Paley, a Soviet Union–born, ex-Juilliard concert pianist turned chef, moved to the Rose City from New York (spending some time cooking at Pazzo) and then opened Paley's Place with his wife, Kimberly.

DURING RUCKER'S FIRST INTERVIEW at Paley's Place, Vitaly Paley was opening a giant container of marrow bones. Rucker was blown away by the restaurant, tucked into an adorable house at Northwest Twenty-First and Northrup, and liked the menu full of snails, marrow, and other foods that weren't typical for the time, but seeing Paley working his way into those bones created another Pavlovian trigger in Rucker. He had to work there. Paley suggested he come back and stage (a French word for unpaid internship), and asked about his experience at a grill station. Rucker had no real experience at a serious grill station, and certainly not one doing triple the nightly covers of Southern Exposure Bistro, but he wasn't about to let the truth get in the way. So he exaggerated, didn't embarrass himself, and got hired full-time. Still barely twenty-three, Rucker felt he was in way over his head, and he was constantly terrified. Each day for the first month, after leaving the restaurant, he was convinced Paley and the other cooks were going to recognize that he didn't know fuck all and that they'd call him on his shit. But that wasn't really Paley's bag.

Head chefs have different styles, like university professors. Some are intensely research-oriented—those who care about the work and the work itself above all, and see the people around them as a means to finishing that work. These folks get labeled "brilliant but mercurial," rising quickly and burning out just as fast, or cycling through different restaurants. Other chefs fall more into the teaching professor category—they take the time to show younger cooks how to do things, and view the kitchen as a place to train—where mistakes are inevitable, not just excuses to scream casual obscenities and toss hot pans against the wall. This doesn't mean these chefs are soft, or even less likely to swear. It just means that though they might still throw you in the deep end, at least they'll show you how to swim.

Vitaly Paley worked the chefs in his kitchen hard, and if you were a numbskull, he was going to ride you even harder. But he knew talent, and recognized that though Rucker was a numbskull, he also had the drive, passion, and skills to do more, and so he gave him enough rope to either succeed or hang himself in the process. Paley liked to create and make new things in his kitchens, and he recognized Rucker as a kindred spirit. Rucker remembered working on a steak and kidney pie with Paley, proud of the fact that Paley was mildly impressed he could make an acceptable puff pastry rather than ask the pastry chef. This was a rare opportunity—the man with the awards and his name on the door taking the time to cook with a twenty-three-year-old, not out of necessity, but because he wanted to.

About six months into Rucker's time at Paley's, a new cook named Jason Barwikowski joined the line. A Michigander who was an avid mountain bike racer and sport climber, Barwikowski had been working in Jackson Hole, Wyoming, for the past seven years. Rucker's and Barwikowski's cooking styles were completely different. Jason was a technician, completely competent and highly skilled. But he also could lose confidence and get rattled quickly if things started to go off script. Rucker was different. Rucker, Barwikowski said, was never flustered. He was almost weirdly calm at all times. Even as everything was going to shit around him, even as you fucked up the sauce he needed right that minute, he seldom yelled. You could see, even when he was so damn young, that he was the guy you wanted to fly the plane if the pilot died.

For the next eighteen months, things went smoothly. Rucker was no longer always in the weeds, and he'd gained the respect of Paley and the other cooks in the kitchen. Things settled into a routine. The staff would get slammed, get through it, and then go unwind at Wimpy's six blocks down on

Hoyt and Northwest Twenty-First to drink. Or Joe's Cellar to drink, play pool, and eat popcorn. Or go back to Rucker's house, because he'd brought the pool table up from Santa Cruz and his house was just too damn perfect for house parties.

But it was at someone else's house party where Rucker ran into Tommy Habetz. Habetz had come to Portland in the nineties as a Habitat for Humanity volunteer, then started cooking in New York. When he came back in 2002, he tried to get on at Paley's, but there was no room, so Paley had passed his résumé over to Cathy Whims at Genoa, and he cooked there for a year before meeting a young guy named Michael Hebb. Michael and his girlfriend, Naomi Pomeroy, were creating all sorts of buzz around Portland with these semi-illegal underground dinners they'd been throwing under the banner of a catering company called Ripe. Ripe, and these fateful introductions, would end up permanently altering Portland's culinary world.

BEFORE MICHAEL HEBB BECAME the most controversial person in the history of Portland's restaurant scene, he was its savior. The youngest son of a big Oregon developer, Hebb—with his blond hair and well-manicured scrabble—looked like an actor who finally got his big break in a serious drama after being mostly pigeonholed into surfer roles. He studied architecture in school in the mid-nineties, but always worked in restaurants, including at Paley's Place and as a busboy and valet at Zefiro.

Hebb first met Corvallis-born Naomi Pomeroy, a striking young brunette and Meryl Streep–esque Lewis & Clark grad, after she'd gone on a few dates with his older brother. But said brother lived in New Mexico, and it wasn't long until the younger Hebb and Pomeroy became an item, ensuring later family vacations would be awkward.

Hebb liked to throw potluck dinner parties, but when he started dating Pomeroy (who, as a hobby, studied cooking all over the world, from Southeast Asia to India), her cooking skills fit with his front-of-the-house acumen like a completed jigsaw puzzle. Maybe, he thought, they could turn that into a catering business. Problem was, they didn't have any clients, and they weren't sure how to get them. Then one day, while at a store getting fabric for their house, they came across a very Portland ad for "Portland's Alternative Bridal Show." Interested to find out if they had a caterer, Hebb called the organizers and, lo and behold, they'd just lost said caterer and were scrambling. Hebb assured them that his hot, up-and-coming, extremely popular catering company could take the event on. To his surprise, the organizers agreed, and so, without a location, or a name, or really any long-term plan in place, what would soon be called Ripe was born.

The bridal expo gave them access and exposure to weddings, which they started to book, but they needed more clients. Because he still worked at Zefiro, Hebb knew Tracy Savage, a successful art dealer in town, and asked if she'd be okay with them sending a letter to each person on her rather large art-world-connected mailing list, promoting the catering business and healthy cooking classes. She said yes, and this led to jobs catering gallery openings and an in with Portland's burgeoning art scene. The food Pomeroy was making was trendy nineties, mostly pan-Asian—lots of green curries, peanut sauces, and sushi with duck in it—but it was delicious and cool and hip, especially by catering standards. Instead of the normal catering uniform of white shirts and black pants, Ripe let its workers wear whatever they wanted as long as it was all-black, exposing tat sleeves and making them seem sleek, cool, and different.

Hebb, ever the master marketer, began sending restaurants and prospective clients, as well as other rival catering companies, a beautiful package featuring four seasons of menus on gorgeous paper stock, using a woodblock print stolen right out of the Chez Panisse cookbook. They would meet clients at coffee shops and Hebb would allude to the beautiful, off-site catering space they were cooking in, even though it was actually just the basement in their house, retrofitted for a second stove. Soon Ripe was catering prestigious events all over PDX. They did everything from city hall events for mayor Vera

Katz, to the opening exhibit unveiling Kenny Scharf's totem-like sculptures after the Lovejoy Bridge was eliminated to make room for the Pearl District, to the wedding of the Dandy Warhols' Peter Holmström at his parents' house. Hebb and Pomeroy were twenty-two years old.

The catering was popular, but in 2000, Hebb and Pomeroy had a daughter and realized they needed to do even more. During the slow spring season, they decided to throw a dinner party. They invited eight friends and had each bring a friend. It was BYOB, but to help cover food costs, they charged five dollars. At the end of the night, they'd lost money, but that wasn't the point. The dinner, from the conversation to the music, to the food, to the energy in the room, was unlike anything else. Immediately, they agreed they should do more dinners and turn it into a regular thing, naming it Suppers at Ripe.

For a certain crowd in post-Y2K Portland, these impromptu supper clubs became the coolest thing they'd ever seen. Artists and downtown gallery owners and baristas and chefs and cobblers would mix with poets and advertising executives and set designers and Hebb's neighbors and *Food & Wine*'s Kate Krader. There were themes. For instance, when Gore Vidal came to a dinner, Pomeroy read an excerpt from *The City and the Pillar,* and tried to create a menu around it. Gore Vidal loved it. Or maybe he didn't. Gore Vidal was hard to read.

It was all a little self-serious, but the thing was, people fucking ate this shit up. Hebb and Pomeroy started an email list to alert people when and how they could get into a new dinner, and the list soon grew to more than twelve thousand people, a good number of whom didn't even live in Portland.

Quickly, Pomeroy realized she couldn't be the only one cooking, so they began recruiting other cooks, both for the catering events and dinners. Their recruitment strategy was simple: when they had an event, they would just grab cooks from Zefiro and offer them more money than they'd make in a restaurant on that same night. They'd pay well, give them autonomy, and try and make it fun. Word spread quickly among chefs.

By 2002, with this spotlight suddenly thrust upon them, Hebb and Pomeroy could no longer cook everything in their house, especially with an infant. They desperately needed to find an off-site catering space. On North Interstate Avenue, in an industrial section of the Eliot neighborhood close to where Page meets Albina, they found a building. The landlord wanted a coffee shop in the space, so they agreed to do coffee and pastries there in the morning and, in exchange, were given permission to build out upstairs as a kitchen and use it to host their dinners. They liked that the space had a cool backstory and history, and that the name seemed regal and a little haunting. The Gotham Building.

IN 2003, A SAUSALITO, CALIFORNIA, restaurateur who'd spent five million dollars building out his restaurant tried to recruit their best chef, Morgan Brownlow. Hebb and Pomeroy were crestfallen. They thought Brownlow was the most talented chef working in Portland, a true kitchen ninja. Yes, his personality was abrasive and he was mercurial, but they couldn't let him leave. So when Brownlow told them about the offer, Hebb countered. "If we build you your own restaurant, would you stay?"

At first, Pomeroy was dumbfounded. Hebb and Pomeroy had said that they'd never open a restaurant. That restaurants were stupid and archaic and limiting in the type of experience you could deliver for your diner. Fuck restaurants. They said that all the time. In fact, Hebb had been talking for years about his magnum opus, a book called *Kill the Restaurant*. How do you write *Kill the Restaurant* when you're opening a restaurant?

But if keeping Brownlow in Portland meant giving him a restaurant, they'd figure out how to do it. After getting rejected for a loan by the banks, they recruited investors from some of the fancier people at the dinners, found another space in southeast industrial Portland on Water Street, and, in February 2004, opened Clarklewis, with Brownlow in the kitchen and Hebb running the front of the house.

Eating in Clarklewis was uncomfortable. There was an open kitchen with a wood-fired hearth, and they hadn't figured out the ventilation system, so it was smoky as hell. So damn smoky that diners used to send the restaurant their dry cleaning bills. There was piercing hip-hop or Talking Heads playing on high volume at all times. The servers acted as if they didn't really give a shit about the customers, and that might've been true. And it was pitch-black. Like slip-and-fall-injury dark. It was so damn dark they put MagLite flashlights on the table for people to read the menus (many of which were stolen).

But with its big, roll-up garage windows, concrete columns jutting with railroad spikes holding bottles of wine, and metal fabricated wall with reclaimed glass sculptures from glassblowing masters at Esque, it was inarguably cool as hell. And the ever-changing, rustic Italian–leaning menu, influenced by former Chez Panisse and Oliveto chef Paul Bertolli's style, with its fresh pastas, wood-fired meats, and whole-animal butchery, became a sensation. The *Oregonian* named Clarklewis Restaurant of the Year barely three months after it opened. The national press started to swoon, though some more perceptive industry folks suspected things weren't adding up. One local chef recalls going to dinner there with former Carafe Bistro's chef Pascal Sauton. After the meal, the chef was blown away and told the veteran French chef as much. Sauton sipped his wine, gave him a little smirk, and said, "You can do incredible things when your food costs are fifty percent." (A normal restaurant's food costs usually range from 20 to 30 percent).

Meanwhile, back in the Gotham Building, Pomeroy and Tommy Habetz (who'd come aboard after meeting Hebb) continued to do the catering and dinners, now called Family Supper, but they were getting restless. Now that the No-Restaurant-Omertà had been broken, it didn't seem unreasonable to do another one. This venture would have a heavy pasta presence, but it would also be inspired by the things going on in London with Fergus Henderson. He was blowing everyone's mind with his nose-to-tail cooking at St. John, seeding the gastropub movement that was just starting to take hold in America.

They'd call it Gotham Building Tavern, to evoke that idea of a casual meeting place. But they needed more talent.

That is how Habetz found himself at a legendary early-aughts Portland Christmas party, where the hosts would dress up like Santas and you would sit on their laps and they would give you presents in the form of bottles of liquor, joints, whip-its, and other intoxicants. Rucker, resplendent in a used 1970s baby-blue leisure suit, and Habetz started to talk about the restaurant and Rucker potentially coming on as a sous chef. When Rucker heard "sous chef," his ears perked up. The cool kids of Portland's cooking scene at the time were telling him to come aboard *and* that he'd get a promotion? He was in, and recommended his buddy Jason Barwikowski, and soon enough both made plans to leave Paley's Place.

As Barwikowski remembers it, Paley was relatively ambivalent about his exit, but pissed Rucker was leaving. Paley recalls thinking that he and Rucker were going to do glorious things together, but also recognizing that someone with his talent wouldn't stay a line cook for long. Rucker remembers Paley, who is an emotional guy, yelling at him that he was "finished in this town." Rucker couldn't blame him. He was twenty-three, and selfish, and hadn't even considered what it might be like to lose two of your best line cooks on the same day. But, alas, he gave his notice and left.

Even more so than with Clarklewis, investors clamored to be involved with Gotham Building Tavern, falling over each other like crabs in a barrel to latch on. It is hard, at this point, to overstate the hype. The coolest underground supper club, a favorite of the art, politics, and local celebrity scene, launches one restaurant that immediately becomes the critical darling of local and national food critics, and then decides to do a second restaurant, and for that not only will Pomeroy, the founder of the group, and Habetz, its most accomplished, NYC-experienced chef, be co-running the kitchen, but they would be bringing in two of the best young chefs from Paley's Place as sous chefs and recruiting a Chez Panisse alum, Troy MacLarty (who Tommy had met at a wedding), to take over the Family Dinner suppers upstairs. On paper, it was a veritable Murderers' Row of cooking talent, and they'd be working for a man in Michael Hebb who appeared to be some sort of renegade visionary, the culinary emperor of Portland's dining scene, an oracle who wouldn't just propel Portland out of the shadow of Seattle, but make New York and San Francisco sit up and take notice too. His confidence was addicting, his way of talking, the way he simultaneously made you feel important and cool but also insecure, since you weren't quite sure that it added up, because everyone else seemed to get it—why would you be the only one to suggest this all didn't make sense?

Rucker didn't realize when he put in his notice at Paley's that restaurants rarely open on time. For the first month, he found himself not in Gotham's kitchen, but sanding and staining the hivelike art installation structures designed by Hebb and the sculptor James M. Harrison with a bunch of Burning Man types, trying to get the place ready for action. When they did finally open the doors, in April 2005, the hype was louder than the hip-hop at Clarklewis.

IN PRACTICE, POMEROY AND HABETZ being "co-chefs" at Gotham made little sense. Though both hyper-skilled in flavors and balance, Pomeroy was essentially self-taught, had never really worked in a kitchen, and had never done the dance on the line. She was obsessed with the farm-to-table movement, with the Chez Panisse side of things. She had very specific ideas about sourcing and dressing salads. Rucker remembers ordering the wrong greens and getting absolutely chewed out. You didn't fuck with Pomeroy's salads. She was also a natural manager, well organized, and had a high motor. Even when she partied, she'd be in the next day, ready to bring it.

Habetz had an unassailable fine-dining background, having worked in some of the best kitchens in America, and his abilities as a big-time kitchen chef in the moment were never in doubt. Rather than Chez Panisse, his interests lay in Europe and England, in making pasta and the entire nose-to-tail movement. He was also relatively chill, but not as organized or interested in the slog from an operations perspective. And he was not someone who bounced back well after a big night out, and—for nearly the entire Gotham staff—every night was a big night out.

It would start with a few beers during prep upstairs. And it would continue during service. Rucker was at the sauté station, cooking pastas and expediting. The seafood pasta called for Pernod, and Rucker would fill up a ramekin, alternating between sips for himself and the pasta (thus earning the nickname "Pernodchio"). And then there were the drugs. Cocaine was everywhere, with most of both the back and front of the house resembling a 1980s Wall Street trading desk, tweaked out and bug-eyed, speaking at two hundred words a minute, ideas bubbling over like overfilled pots. In many ways, cocaine was the perfect drug for Gotham. It was expensive and gave you a hollow confidence. And two months in, the cracks started to show.

About this time, Barwikowski broke his back in a freak accident, and Hebb and Pomeroy's relationship, under the combined duress of parenthood, businesses, and partying, finally fractured as well. During this initial separation, Hebb banned Pomeroy from the kitchen. Rucker, a twenty-four-year-old who spent the majority of his time both on and off work getting drunk, didn't really notice the relationship dynamics, but did notice more responsibilities in the kitchen. But soon after she was gone, the couple made a go of it again, and she was back. Habetz, meanwhile, was working through his own issues from too much partying. The work environment, if one were to take a survey, would likely have been described as "not great."

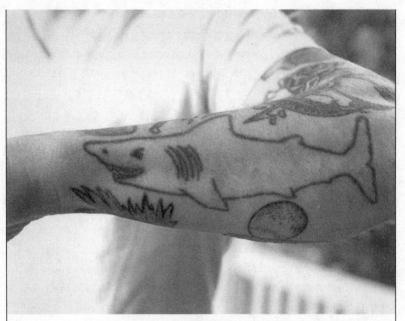

Gabriel Rucker's "poorly drawn shark" tattoo

Gabriel Rucker's First Tattoo, as told by Jason Barwikowski

Gabe saved my life. Legitimately saved my life. I would've definitely drowned. We went to the Washougal River over in Washington, and we were having a really great day. It was cool where we were swimming; there was a little natural water slide and small rocks to jump off into small pools. We were having fun, but then we were like, "Let's have some more fun!" So we talked to some guys and they told us about a real big rock up the road about half a mile. So we went up there and we walked up and it was, honest to God, the police told me later, it was like a sixty-five-foot drop. We watched this kid jump off. If the kid hadn't been doing it, I'm a hundred percent sure we wouldn't have done it. We went there and I remember we looked at it and then we started to walk back and I heard Gabe run and I didn't even see it, but he jumped. I was like, "Dang!" And he's like, "Watch out, man, it's big!" So I jumped. Now a month earlier I was in the hospital for five days with some kind of bacterial infection or virus and I was really sick. I never knew what it was, but I ended up losing a lot of weight. And I didn't even think about it. Living in Wyoming for seven winters, snowboarding and biking, I never got hurt. I'd jumped off a lot of cliffs. But being sick, I guess I didn't have the leg strength to push out far enough. Last thing I remember is a bunch of people go "ohhh!" like I could hear that happen because they could see I was going to hit rocks.

When I came to, Gabe was fireman-cradling me, bringing me back to the riverbank. I would have drowned because I was definitely a hundred percent unconscious. Facedown. Dead man's float. Crazily, ten minutes after it happened a state trooper pulled up to the spot because a woman had fallen off the same rock face hiking. Got close to the edge and lost her footing and fell to her death. And so the police came . . . and it's, like, eleven miles up this bad dirt road. He called radio dispatch and the ambulance showed up an hour later. While we waited, Gabe did an amazing job keeping me calm. I kept going in and out of consciousness, but he kept putting water on my head because we were in the sun on the edge of a river. I used to draw this crappy shark on the blue tape in the kitchens we'd worked at together. We called it, literally, "Poorly Drawn Shark." And Gabe sat there and kept me together, telling me, "If we make it through this, I'm going to get Poorly Drawn Shark as a tattoo." And sure enough, when they eventually helicoptered me to Portland and I survived, Gabe got the shark tattoo. It was his first.

On top of the kitchen getting in its own way, Gotham had another problem: as the new restaurant allure started to fade, people became less interested in traveling to the industrial part of Eliot. The restaurant was no longer packed each night. They tried different things to cultivate excitement: bringing in "writer-in-residence" Matthew Stadler, putting HP sauce on every table and transitioning the menu to full British "gastropub," getting rid of reservations, putting servers in street clothes to make it less formal, making it steak-centric, putting a burger on the dinner menu, cutting the price of breakfast, doubling the size of the breakfast menu, creating a happy hour, dumbing down the wine list, adding malt liquor and jug wine and cheap well drinks, hosting DJs for after-hours, anything. But instead of resurrecting the restaurant, all of this flailing just smelled of desperation. Andy Ricker remembers walking in, watching the "dude in the cage write some bullshit poems" as they butchered whole spring lambs with absolute creative freedom, and thinking the entire enterprise was doomed. It was the *Reality Bites*–era version of the tuxedo-clad band continuing to play as the *Titanic* sank.

On April 27, 2006, the bottom fell out. Hebb told Pomeroy he couldn't pay the ninety-five people Ripe employed, and on top of that, he was leaving the country. Pomeroy told the major investors and senior management, and the decision was made to immediately shut Gotham Building Tavern and all its associated businesses down. When Gotham's employees went to work that day, they found the doors locked and a note taped up: "Michael left."

The next day was Gabriel Rucker's twenty-fifth birthday. All the staff came in to collect their stuff, and that night they had a party. Rucker brought his turntables. It was supposed to be a fun gathering, a quality send-off, but the abruptness of the closing and the fact that it was becoming clear people were not going to get paid darkened everyone's mood. What had started as a party turned into a mass scavenging. Chef John Gorham from Toro Bravo said it reminded him of that scene from *Apocalypse Now* under the bridges. Delirious, half-naked dancing. Everything being taken off the shelves. Cocaine, which was consumed somewhat conspicuously while the restaurant was open, turned it into a *Scarface* scene. By the end of the night, as Rucker spun tunes, expensive, half-drunk wine bottles littered the floor. The hives, the art project that took so much time and capital, were one of the only things left standing.

Meanwhile, Clarklewis would survive for a time, initially with Brownlow still as chef and major investor David Howitt as sole owner, though eventually he would sell Clarklewis. The man who bought it understood a few things about having a hot restaurant in Portland. His name was Bruce Carey. In 1990, he had opened a place called Zefiro.

THE CLOSING OF GOTHAM BUILDING TAVERN changed the face of dining in Portland. It had a chilling effect on the restaurant scene. The twenty-two investors who got burned on Gotham and Clarklewis were among the most well-heeled and passionate food people in the city, and that sort of dog-bites-hand experience soured them on committing any more money to other projects. Up-and-coming chefs who had no part in the Gotham implosion found themselves taking collateral damage. Investors simply ghosted.

In some ways, this was the moment when Portland's food scene grew up, when it became real, with a steelier edge and a more pragmatic worldview. Portland's true food identity wasn't going to be built on the back of a bullshit shell game, or some high-minded sophistry, or some baroque Xerox of a New York City or London gastropub. It would have to happen on their terms. And with as little money as possible.

Other Gotham players had found work quickly after the meltdown. Barwikowski joined up with Gorham's squad at Simpatica. Pomeroy, now divorced and bankrupt, found herself in the general manager role at Clarklewis, forced mostly to sit in an office and attempt to figure out who was owed what while everyone outside the office glowered at her. Habetz got a job in Northwest Portland as chef at Meriwether's. MacLarty at Lovely Hula Hands. But Gabriel Rucker needed a job. Eventually, he found a gig at Cathy Whims's Nostrana slinging pizzas. Nostrana, which had just opened the year before, was one of a few new places around town quietly reenergizing a scene seemingly tapped out from all of the Gotham drama.

Meanwhile, former Genoa chef John Taboada opened Navarre, a hyperlocal little restaurant serving basically whatever was given to him by nearby farmers. Ricker, the former Zefiro line cook turned successful commercial painter, finished painting the Jupiter Hotel's Doug Fir bar and opened a tiny little restaurant he'd built piece by piece out of a house on Division, serving spicy Thai bar food in the style he'd been eating on long trips to Thailand during slow painting seasons. He called it Pok Pok. John Gorham took the success he'd been having with the Spanish Simpatica dinners and turned it into Toro Bravo. Micah Camden, who would go on to open Blue Star donuts and become one of Portland's most prolific restaurateurs, opened his first restaurant, a Japanese pub called Yakuza, with Dayna McErlean. Ken Fork-ish, a baker who years earlier had opened one of Portland's first serious, French-style bakeries, opened Ken's Artisan Pizza, putting his transcendent skills with bread to yet another use. And then there was Colleen's Bistro.

Colleen French was a twenty-nine-year-old chef, a true believer in the Slow Food movement. Her place, co-owned by Paul Brady, was an ode to Slow Food's ethos taken to the extreme. Everything made from scratch, every-thing made-to-order. The food, especially the brunches, was universally be-loved. But the labor-intensive, hyper-expensive dishes resulted in half-hour waits for coffee, ninety minutes for waffles. It was literally slow food. Despite its critical acclaim, Colleen's was losing money each month. Lots of money. Perhaps inevitably, Brady and French split ways.

Looking for a new chef, Brady heard about Rucker and reached out. Brady didn't even ask Rucker to cook for him. The truth was, he thought the place was folding and was just trying to recoup a little bit of his money before he scrapped it. He was hiring a twenty-five-year-old who'd never helmed a res-taurant to run his kitchen because, frankly, veteran chefs weren't interested in an experimental situation that might fall apart in a couple of months. You don't put in the old guy to throw a seventy-yard Hail Mary. You put in the kid and pray.

Rucker liked Brady, and thought it might be fun to see what he could do. He'd never really wanted to do a French restaurant, but he walked into Col-leen's and saw the floral wallpaper and the vintage chandeliers and the cop-per hood and he felt like there was a certain type of food that the room asked for, and it was at least vaguely French. He knew that sounded like hippie Cali-fornia crap, but he couldn't explain it any other way. You cook for the space you're given, and Gabriel Rucker was given a French restaurant.

Before they reopened, Tommy Habetz would sometimes come into the kitchen and cook with Rucker. One day, Rucker started firing off potential names for the space. Bad names. Basically just objects Rucker had seen around town, like "Bridges" and "Lanterns." Habetz, after telling him his ideas were dumb, glanced down and noticed the pigeon tattoo on Rucker's arm. "I think you've got a pretty good restaurant name on your arm," he said.

After Poorly Drawn Shark, the pigeon tattoo was Rucker's second, and he'd gotten it as sort of a shout-out to the small-bird-eating, cream-chugging antihero Benjy from his Silverado days, and also because, in a French kitchen, the pigeon is considered the pledge, the plebeian, the sucker, the person who scrubs the toilets and cleans up the messes. And the more he thought about it, the more he realized that when you have your own little place, you are the pigeon. Or, to frenchify it, Le Pigeon.

Le Pigeon's first day of existence was June 1, 2006, an uneventful Thursday. Brunch, the one successful aspect of Colleen's, remained busy, but at the beginning, dinners were a ghost town. It was bleak. Brady was putting coupons in the yellow pages. Rucker remembers cooking an entire dinner service

An early Le Pigeon brunch menu, Fall 2006

himself for maybe twenty covers, including his parents and girlfriend, and still having time to shut the place down and go bowling by nine thirty p.m. But slowly things started to click.

Rucker's time working pastry in Santa Cruz; deveining foie, building a risotto base, and celebrating little birds in Napa; the complicated sauces and butter-basting techniques from Paley's; the nose-to-tail cooking at Gotham— you could see each of those elements play out on Rucker's early menus. If you knew the history, it read like an origin story, from the foie gras au torchon with peach butter and warm challah, to the veal sweetbreads with pickled strawberries and braised leeks, to the fennel and cipollini onion risotto, to the half-grilled pigeon with Bordelaise sauce.

A few weeks in, he managed to pull in a sous chef, Erik Van Kley, who'd been over at Nostrana and also Gotham beforehand, alongside another Gotham vet named Su-Lien Pino. On Tuesdays, they would do light prep and go back and forth planning a menu. Everything was exciting and nothing seemed to matter—it was going to come crashing down anyway, so they might as well cook cool shit. They started to think about what they could do with pig's tails and lamb's tongue and some of the other things no one seemed to be eating. Creative, weird dishes just spilled out. To call it French would be technically accurate yet also absurd. It was more like French food cooked by a fast-food-obsessed punk-rock gourmand who spent a summer at Fergus Henderson's St. John in London. Beef cheek bourguignonne. Duck nuggets with sun-dried plum mustard dipping sauce. Trotter potato cakes with sauce gribiche. Warm beef tongue and potato salad with honey-glazed onions. Pig tail soup.

Rucker took foods that sat in the edgy corner of most people's palates and pushed them off a ledge. His obsession with foie and comfort with pastry made him want to attempt a foie gras profiterole. At first, he made a regular profiterole shell, foie ice cream, and a cognac anglaise sauce. Van Kley tasted it and recommended caramel and sea salt. Their new German pastry chef gave Rucker a better recipe for the ice cream. Then Rucker learned about tapioca maltodextrin's amazing ability to turn fats into powders, so they created foie powdered sugar. And foie gras butter for both the caramel and pastry. And suddenly they had a foie gras profiterole in which every element featured foie. It was batshit crazy and over-the-top and a little bit silly, but the technique was impeccable. Thanks to dishes like the foie profiterole, which became one of Le Pigeon's signatures, after a few months you stopped being able to easily recognize Rucker's influences and things started to feel just … new. By riffing on his previous riffs, the menu started to distance itself from anything else going on in Portland.

Word of the victual wizardry going down in Southeast Portland spread through PDX like a tawdry rumor. First came other chefs, to eat and drink and try to figure out what the hell Rucker was up to. Then the local writers. A few months in, *The Oregonian*'s legendary king-making food critic Karen Brooks, wondering what had become of this former Gotham sous chef, came by and gave the food an A-. Then, in *Portland Monthly*'s August 2006 issue, Camas Davis said, "25-year-old chef Gabriel Rucker has gracefully elevated the humble fowl's image to new heights, in more ways than one." Then, in the November issue, only four months after the restaurant's open, *Portland Monthly* named Rucker 2006 Chef of the Year. Brady could stop putting discount coupons in the yellow pages.

Meanwhile, the hype surrounding Le Pigeon morphed from local buzz into a national fever pitch. In *Bon Appétit*'s February 2007 issue, Andrew Knowlton called Rucker a "bold young chef" and mentioned his apricot-bacon cornbread with maple ice cream and warm bacon bits and his "predilection for organ meats." He was named one of the best new chefs in America in the July 2007 issue of *Food & Wine*. And then, on September 26, 2007, Eric Asimov of *The New York Times* wrote a story titled "In Portland, a Golden Age of Dining and Drinking."

The article became the forerunner in the "Hot New Food Town" genre, mentioning "a cadre of farmers committed to growing environmentally responsible produce" to give to chefs in "funky neighborhoods," and "affordable real estate" for chefs and other like-minded creatives who are "going at it in sort of an indie-rock way." Asimov quoted first-iteration chefs from the Zefiro era like Paley, Machado, and even the French chef who recognized something wasn't right at Clarklewis, Pascal Sauton. But he spent most of his time on Pok Pok chef Andy Ricker and Rucker, comparing them to the young chefs who flocked to "the East Village and Brooklyn in the 1990s." Ricker's Pok Pok was a "ramshackle Thai takeout shack," which had "won acclaim for dishes like juicy game hens roasted over charcoal and stuffed with lemon grass, garlic, pepper and cilantro." Rucker's Le Pigeon was a "kind of new-wave bistro" and "an informal, slightly manic spot with seasonally changing, nonconformist dishes like braised pork belly with creamed corn and butter-poached prawns, sweetbreads with pickled watermelon, and just about anything that can possibly involve tongue."

The *Times* cosign fully solidified it. The New York Food Mafia was now telling its national audience, the people who cared about food, who still seemed unperturbed in this pre–social media era to label themselves as "foodies," who might spend hours on Chowhound debating the various merits of different slow cookers, that Portland was the new New. This represented a change, a torch passing, as the Bay Area and New York had long dominated America's national food culture conversation. Until now, Portland had been a place with no food identity, a place where chicken and jojos seemed to be the only touchstone, a place that felt insecure even in comparison to Seattle. It meant that other young cooks who'd been toiling in San Francisco and New York City could see people their age running restaurants in Portland, tattooed twenty-six-year-olds like Rucker winning national awards and riding around on fixie bikes and drinking PBRs with the guys who foraged their chanterelles. They could see people like Ricker building an entire uncompromising Thai restaurant by hand out of a house for less than the cost of a decent commercial range hood.

The parallels to Brooklyn would be inevitable. But unlike Brooklyn, where that bohemian Manhattan-adjacent spirit was born out of a creative people who could no longer afford the Lower East Side, the things happening in

Portland represented a move not just to a cheaper neighborhood but to a completely new city. In the short term, this would lead to a sort of mass creative immigration to Portland. But in the long term, Portland would become the prototype for second- and third-tier American cities that were just now realizing that the way forward in appealing to this postcollege generation, who were getting married later and sticking around cities longer, was to create the narrative of a rebirth, a creative renaissance in your city, especially through food and drink. The Portlandization of America was near.

IN THE NATIONAL SPOTLIGHT, unwitting choices Rucker had made out of necessity or random chance became templates to be studied and copied. The mismatched chairs, the Goodwill plates and silverware, the lack of tablecloths. Even the tattoos. Rucker's casual and unconscious interest in marrying high and low concepts helped popularize what would become the signature for the Culinary Revolution: casual fine dining. It meant scratch-kitchen-level food made by hand using local ingredients, but without white tablecloths and fancy service. It meant gambling that diners would care more about what was on their plate than how you were delivering it to them.

By 2007, at the age of twenty-six, Rucker was a nationally recognized chef, but it wasn't clear he was really paying attention. There was a Wild West, fiesta-like atmosphere in Le Pigeon in those days, and it wasn't just the barbecued eel toast and the lamb tongue. Rucker's drinking, which had only increased during the drug-intensive Gotham days, was not yet tall enough to ride the issues roller coaster, but stayed in the theme park. On the line, he'd drink Miller High Lifes in coffee steamers, and tequila in water bottles, and Chilly Billies (essentially blueberry vodka and ice) in whatever vessel you handed him. Toward the end of the night he'd offer guests Marlboro cigarettes or American Spirits with the filters torn off with their cognac, and smoke a couple himself on the line. He turned the Clap Your Hands Say Yeah up loud. He wore a Stumptown Coffee Roasters shirt instead of a chef's coat and rocked a hat featuring a rat peeing on it, with the word "Piss" emblazoned along the front.

He and the other cooks and most of the staff would finish most nights at the B-Side down the street, or Rontoms if they wanted to hang with the skinny-jeans crowd and needed drugs. Whatever they were doing, Rucker refused to go home after a shift. Nothing depressed him more than waking up, going to work, then coming home and sleeping. The party would continue.

How the New York Food Mafia Discovered Portland: Theory #1—The Conference

In 1998, the International Association of Culinary Professionals (IACP) held their twentieth annual conference in Portland. April is extremely hit-or-miss in Oregon, and more often than not, it is a grizzly scene of misting sideways rain and gray sky and a general sort of malaise really only good for penning imitation Carver stories about metalworkers. But this week in 1998 was beautiful. Magnificent even. And the chefs in Portland put on a show. There were Dundee Hills wine tours. And fishing in Astoria and Newport. And a showcase of the farm-filled glory so close to the city, thanks to the urban growth boundary. Cory Schreiber took over his family's restaurant and did one hundred years of Oregon cuisine. It was an epic culinary showcase. Also, people got quite drunk.

Because the New York Food Mafia likes a good free press trip, and the IACP is something to cover, the NYFM happened to be there during this glorious week when the weather gods smiled upon Portland and all of the chefs put on a show and there were wines to be sipped and oysters to be slurped, and the NYFM came away from that trip with this idea of Portland as, if not a culinary capital, at least a contender. The seed was planted. It would just take a few more years for it to grow.

How the New York Food Mafia Discovered Portland: Theory #2—The Sideways Conspiracy

Of course, there is a conspiracy, friends. A conspiracy whispered only in the shadows, the damp residue of a rumor, the faint outlines of an idea that most people claim to be silly but that clings to at least the appearance of plausibility. And there's also the fact that such a butterfly effect could be achieved from two Paul Giamatti sentences in the 2004 film *Sideways*.

Famously, Giamatti's character—a wine snob—tells Thomas Haden Church's character, "If anyone orders merlot, I'm leaving. I am *not* drinking any fucking merlot!" Those lines became the signature calling card of the movie, an independent, Oscar-winning critical darling that came out of nowhere to gross $72 million domestically. Merlot sales, which were already trending down, continued to fall, but more importantly, pinot noir became the new belle of America's wine ball, rocketing up 16 percent in domestic sales in the months after *Sideways* was released. And no place in America was better poised to reap the benefits of America's newfound love than Oregon's Willamette Valley. As loving Oregon pinots becomes a generally accepted behavior among the class of people who feel they should have an opinion on wine, the New York Food Mafia began to spend more time in Oregon to tell this delightful trend story. And as the story goes, it was during these trips to Oregon to taste and talk about pinot at the International Pinot Noir Celebration and on other, smaller excursions that the NYFM discovered Portland's fertile culinary scene, and started writing about it too. Portland might've had the proper machinery in place, but it took two sentences from Paul Giamatti to get it running. Or so goes the conspiracy.

CHAPTER 2

TV Dad, Tom Colicchio, New York City, New York

In 1977, twenty-nine years before his son's television show started making hundreds of chefs famous and hundreds of thousands of people want to be chefs, Thomas Colicchio, a former barber turned Union County Jail correctional officer, found a book in the jail library he thought his son, Tom, might like. Tom liked to cook.

When he was thirteen, Tom had worked in the snack shack at the Gran Centurions Swim Club. He'd originally been hired to work the cash register and scoop ice cream, but by the end of the first week he was on the grill, making a name for himself by cooking the best damn grilled cheese sandwiches in Clark, New Jersey. He loved it: making $275 a week under the table, spending all day shirtless in flip-flops cranking out grill food, smoking weed with his boss on the drive from his hometown of Elizabeth, using a *knife*.

So when Thomas stumbled upon *La Technique* by Jacques Pépin sitting among plumbing instructionals and Louis L'Amour novels, he took it for Tom. As much as Tom liked to cook, he hated following recipes. They didn't interest him. They were boring. But here was this French guy making the case that recipes didn't matter as much as learning a few crucial techniques—for cooking green vegetables, making stocks, a few mother sauces, etc. The techniques were transferrable. If you knew how to roast a veal, you could roast a rabbit. When Tom read that, it was a revelation.

In the Colicchio family, cooking was not considered some sort of fuckup fallback gig. Thomas's time as a barber taught him to respect a craft. Tom's mother had worked in a photo store, then had run a school cafeteria, but she'd also cooked for the family every night. They did fine, but Tom wasn't growing up in tony suburbs like Saddle River, or Chatham, or Alpine, where the moms didn't work and the kids wore double popped collars and drove foreign cars in high school. He slept in a bedroom with his two brothers until he moved out of the house. The only time they went out to dinner was on Fridays after his dad's softball game, and then always to Spirito's, a red-sauce joint in Elizabeth with decent pizza but great veal cutlet. If it was a big night, and the family was feeling flush, they might throw in an Italian salad and substitute the imported provolone. They were a working-class Italian-American Jersey family.

Thomas Colicchio wasn't a guy who spent a lot of time having long talks with his kids, but he was more present than most. He loved music and played it all the time around the house and on the eight-track in his car—old stuff like Elvis and Frank Sinatra, but newer, cooler stuff too, like Jimi Hendrix and Janis Joplin and Simon & Garfunkel. He loved politics—he was president of his correctional officers union—and he helped out on local campaigns.

When Tom was sixteen, his dad sat him down. "Tom, you like to cook. Why not do it for a living?" He'd brought home some brochures for cooking schools. And he knew a guy in the refrigeration business who had a hookup at a seafood place in town called Evelyn's, and he managed to get Tom a job working in the front of the house during high school.

In 1980, when he graduated from Elizabeth High School, Tom started working in the kitchen. Evelyn's was popular—it would do about a thousand covers on a Saturday night—and Tom held down every job in that place, working the line, in the bakery, in prep. Just like at the snack shack in Clark, he loved the atmosphere, the energy, the frenetic pace, the excuse to hang around twentysomething waitresses at seventeen.

He kept cooking. Next, he was knocking out veal parms for a red-sauce Italian joint in North Jersey, then taking the night chef gig at a Hilton in Secaucus, where he honed his creativity and experimented, creating two to three specials a week, always thinking technique first. Eventually he got to 40 Main Street in Millburn, the most serious restaurant in Jersey, a New American joint with a menu that changed every day and a three-star review from *The New York Times*. Tom liked the collaboration there, sitting down and talking over the menu with the cooks, who would at least consider his suggestions.

His experience at 40 Main Street helped get him a gig at Quilted Giraffe, an American take on fine French country dining. Giraffe was one of the most celebrated New York restaurants of the eighties, a four-star exalted museum piece of that high-flying decade, a bastion of moneyed New York power with its fifty-dollar "beggar's purses" crepes filled with beluga caviar and topped with gold leaf—and the audacity to start closing on the weekends to keep out the bridge-and-tunnel riffraff. Despite the high-profile kitchen competition, Tom's star shone brighter. He was made sous chef within four months. Culinary school, which had originally been his goal, seemed pointless. He was going to pay money to a school, get out, and then what? Try and get a lower position at a four-star New York restaurant?

Quilted Giraffe gave him focus. He realized that, as good as he was, in order to stand out he needed style, and that wasn't going to happen for an early-twenties kid in New York. So he went back to Jersey, to 40 Main Street, and took over as co-head chef. He spent eight months there figuring out his style and then bounced around between New York City, France, and Virginia before taking a job with a chef named Dennis Foy at his new fancy restaurant, the Mondrian, at 7 East Fifty-Ninth Street in New York. The plan was to go to France again—Tom had worked out a deal to stage for six months at two different top French restaurants, but then he heard from his dad. A two-pack-a-day smoker, his father had been diagnosed with late-stage lung cancer. The doctors said he didn't have much time, so Tom put his France plans on hold and started cooking with Foy. A few months later Thomas Colicchio was dead. He was fifty-two.

Heartbroken, Tom went back to work at the Mondrian but wasn't into it. He didn't like Foy's needlessly hard-ass style. So he finally left and headed to France to work for Michel Bras. But two months later, the owner of the Mondrian called and asked him to take over the kitchen from Foy. He did. A few months after that, at the age of twenty-six, Tom got a three-star review from the *Times*. He had a style and a name. He was on the map.

THERE WAS ONLY ONE PROBLEM: the Mondrian was a financial disaster. The original lease had been signed in 1986, a year before the market crashed, and here they were a few years later paying $28,000 a month in rent, on top of nearly $3 million in renovation costs. When Tom took over, he tried to renegotiate the lease, but the landlord wasn't having it. All the critical success, the fact that famous NYC chefs like Daniel Boulud and Jonathan Waxman and Gérard Pangaud were coming to see what Tom was doing, was moot. The Mondrian was a dead restaurant cooking.

In 1991, Tom got named one of the best new chefs in America by *Food & Wine*. Out at the event in Aspen, he ran into Union Square Cafe owner Danny Meyer.

"I'm going to call you when we get home," Tom said.

"Cool," said Meyer.

Tom told him about the Mondrian's imminent closing, and suggested they open a spot together. Meyer declined, saying he didn't want two restaurants, but called Tom back a week later and said he was interested. A mutual friend had told Meyer, "If Sandy Koufax wants to play for your team, you'd say yes, right?" Meyer thought, at this point, Sandy Koufax was too old to play for anyone's team, but he understood his point. The two men went on a trip to Italy together, got along, and figured out a restaurant.

In 1994, they opened Gramercy Tavern, a high-concept play on the idea of a tavern with food that was all Tom—French technique and Italian influences with a little American Jersey sensibility. Tom's style was starting to come into its own: clean, clear ideas, bold flavors, eclectic harmonies. He liked to build his food vertically, something a lot of people related to his brief time with Alfred Portale at Gotham Bar and Grill, and at Gramercy, his eggplant napoleon—a vertical stack of fried eggplant disks on top of each other, held together by more eggplant and green rosemary oil—became legendary. In 1996, *New York Times* restaurant critic Ruth Reichl gave Gramercy three stars, saying, "Mr. Colicchio's cooking has lost the tentative quality of the early days; he is now cooking with extraordinary confidence." Four years later, Tom won the James Beard Award for Best Chef in New York City.

Tom wanted more. He opened another restaurant, his own, in 2001. The restaurant, Craft, had a nearly sacrilegious simplicity: What if we serve dishes family-style? What if we just roast a piece of fish with fresh herbs and olive oil? What if we just serve fresh sugar snap peas when they're in season in a bowl? Can we get away with that? What happens when we remove the garnishes and the sauces and we let the food speak for itself?

It was a confident chef's restaurant, radical in its simplicity. And it worked. The return to unfussy, straightforward food predated that trend by half a decade at least. The Spartan design aesthetic—the Chilewich place mats, the Edison bulbs, the naked wooden tables—did as well.

Tom got married, wedding a filmmaker named Lori Silverbush, who he met when she'd waited tables at Gramercy Tavern to pay bills while she made her films. They left for their wedding in Martha's Vineyard on September 10, 2001, and considered postponing it after the attacks the next day, but friends from New York used the occasion as a way to push aside their sadness.

By 2006, Tom was restless. The Craft empire was taking off—in 2002, Craftbar had nearly single-handedly brought bar dining back en vogue, and then there was 'Wichcraft and *good god there were so many ways to put* craft *on things*—but he felt a certain complacency with Gramercy Tavern. He loved it. It was successful and had turned into an iconic New York restaurant, but with both Tom's and Danny's restaurants doing so well, it felt weird to share Gramercy.

Originally, Tom thought he might buy Meyer out. But in the end, he thought it would be too hard to keep the restaurant at the same caliber with so much on his plate, so he sold his shares to Meyer. It was said to be "amicable" and maybe it was—Meyer and Tom both had reputations for being nice, reasonable guys—but Tom still had to feel something. Gramercy was his baby, the first thing he'd ever done, and Craft was just around the corner. He had to walk past Gramercy every day.

On one of those days, Tom got a call. It was a producer named Shauna Minoprio. She wanted to create a food competition show in conjunction with *Food & Wine* magazine, but it was going to be more serious than other cooking shows. They needed a head judge, a serious chef with a name. By now, Tom was a name, a regular mention by Florence Fabricant and Amanda Hesser and Warren St. John and Eric Asimov and Julia Moskin and Sam Sifton and William Grimes and Frank Bruni and Michael Ruhlman and Adam Platt and Alan Richman and John Mariani and Andrew Knowlton and Caroline Bates and Jonathan Gold and Pete Wells and Ed Levine and Dana Cowin and Ben Leventhal and Josh Ozersky and Adams Sachs and Adam Rapoport.

Tom said no; he didn't want to do TV. Most of those shows were jokes, embarrassments to the industry. She kept calling him back. The fourth time, he said maybe, but there would be some rules. One, the competitions would have to be real. If it said thirty minutes on the timer for some quick cooking thing, it would be thirty fucking minutes. And two, he would have control over who wins and who loses, not some producer who just wants to keep the misogynist guy with boy-band hair because he's spiking the ratings. She agreed. This show would be different, she said. Yes, she was going to throw them all in the same house and put them on camera for sixteen hours a day. The contestants wouldn't have TV or phones, and they wouldn't go in public on their own. But when they came into the kitchen, they would cook and Tom would judge their food and the people who failed would go home. They would call it *Top Chef.*

They shot the first season in San Francisco. The original contestants were a motley crew—some of them, like Tiffani Faison and Harold Dieterle and Lee Anne Wong, were legit chefs with actual chops. Others had more eclectic backgrounds. There was a health food guru nutritionist named Andrea and a culinary school student/model named Candice, and Lisa, a self-taught cook with no professional background, and a prickish Vegas sommelier with late-nineties hair and overconfidence that bordered on magical thinking, and a profane Long Island caterer-to-the-stars named Cynthia, who called Beyoncé "a doll."

The *Top Chef* pilot premiered right after the *Project Runway* finale, on March 8, 2006. The host of the first season, Katie Lee Joel—at the time best known for being Billy Joel's much younger wife—spoke the first words in the history of the show: "What does it take to make it as a chef?" Tom was shown in B-roll in the kitchen, and he was introduced as "head judge and culinary giant." His catchphrase—"I've been cooking for about twenty-five years, received three stars at the age of twenty-six, recipient of five James Beard Awards. I think it qualifies me to be a judge here"—was in retrospect a little too glib and arrogant, especially for the role he'd end up playing.

The first season was not great television. There were awkward diagonal camera angles during the Judges' Table and incredibly clunky brand placement from KC Masterpiece and Toyota and, incredibly, AOL. Though *Food & Wine* writer Gail Simmons was perfectly competent, concise, and TV-ready, Katie Lee Joel appeared almost physically sickened by the camera (she would famously be replaced in the second season by Padma Lakshmi). The

non-media-trained guest judge chefs alternated between being nonsensi-
cally compassionate and mean.

And yet, there was that reality show raw energy that only came from
spending sixteen hours a day being filmed while also deprived of the normal
items one might use to balance out anxiety. Naturally, each chef on the show
started to magnify their own particular character traits, often turning into
feral caricatures of their real selves. And in that way, *Top Chef* fulfilled all
effective reality show stereotypes.

And yet, each show was built around two challenges—a Quickfire Challenge and then a longer, more drawn-out Elimination Challenge—which
smartly provided the viewer with two things most reality shows can't: process and payoff. The process of watching the chefs take on these challenges
and figure out their strategies to attack them; the process of picking out the
ingredients and planning; the process of actually executing the dish. And
then the payoff in the sense of the finished dish, but also in the sense of getting to hear a verdict and judgment handed down by Tom, Gail Simmons, and
the other judges. Merit sat side by side with spectacle.

As the show blew up, becoming a smash hit with domestic spin-offs like
Top Chef Masters and international spin-offs in dozens of countries, Tom
became a kingmaker in the food world. *Top Chef* winners went from getting
a hundred grand and a Kenmore Elite Kitchen provided by Sears, to winning James Beard Awards, writing *New York Times* bestselling cookbooks,
hosting their own shows, and becoming Big Names themselves. Chefs were
some of the first actually accessible reality stars; instead of the rare possibility of getting the chance to do kamikaze shots with them during a college town
club appearance and living with the whole "famous for being famous" mantle
first bestowed on *The Real World*, *Road Rules*, *The Bachelor*, and *Kardashians*,
you could actually visit their restaurants and eat their food. Couple *Top Chef's*
success with the explosion of Anthony Bourdain's *No Reservations* (then in its
second season), and what you were witnessing was celebrity chefdom 2.0.

Unlike the 1.0 class of cooking demo pros, like celebrity New Orleans chef Emeril and Bobby Flay, the new contestants were out from behind the stove, either showcasing the entire spectrum of their personalities on these shows or sitting in exotic places, eating squeamish foods and making droll comments.

These shows helped propel an entirely new generation of people into the restaurant industry and contributed to the soaring number of culinary school applicants. The Career Education Corp., which operated Le Cordon Bleu's US locations, saw enrollment increase nearly 50 percent from 2008 to 2011. The newfound glamour and fame surrounding the profession attracted an entirely new type of student, interested in both the romance of physical work and the idea of making a Big Name. This, of course, would soon be the generation of the Personal Brand, where building a Big Name was your ticket to whatever ephemeral, far-reaching goal you claimed to want, even if that was ironically just acquiring a Big Name.

Tom, meanwhile, went from being a name in the food world to being a Big Name, period. He became one of the rare television celebrity chefs whose actual cooking chops couldn't be assailed. Outside of the strange vertical facial hair under his lip favored by nineties pop-ska bands, Tom did nothing to sully his reputation in the industry, still the only place he cared about having a reputation. On screen, he was earnest and serious, with a wry sense of humor. He dispensed advice and commented firmly and didn't pander. The things you knew about his cooking—the clear ideas, the maturity, and the techniques—also translated into his attitude. He was the guy who could tell the dickish Irish chef Ken that he was being rude in disrespecting chef Hubert Keller at his own restaurant. He was the one to tell Tiffani Faison her attitude was crappy when her attitude was crappy. He, as the kids say, gave zero fucks.

But the chefs on the show idolized him. Thomas Colicchio's son was the one they wanted to please. As the show went on ten and then fifteen seasons, as he won an Emmy in addition to Beard Awards, as he executive-produced his wife's documentary on hunger, as he testified before Congress on school lunches and assailed the billions of dollars cut from food stamp programs, as he created a legislative scorecard for food issues, as he became one of the most politically active, knowledgeable, and famous chefs in the country, Thomas Colicchio's son's word was the only word that really mattered.

CHAPTER 3

Anjan and Emily Mitra, San Francisco, California, Part 1

It started with flavors. When Anjan Jayanta Mitra was a child, his mother, Sujata, used to make bites of food for him and his older sister, Piya. Sujata had an uncanny, nearly magical ability to balance spices and textures. She would add poppy seeds and potato for starch, and green beans for crunch, add lentils with cilantro and mustard seed, throw in some raw onion for pungency, or green chile for spice, and then squeeze just a bit of lime for some acid, and show him how to mash the potatoes with his fingers, show him the control he could have if Anjan just learned what she showed him.

Anjan grew up on Juhu Beach in North Bombay. Both of his parents were Bengali Hindus, whose people came from the region of Bengal in the east of India, by Bangladesh. The family first had Piya, and then four years later, on October 16, 1966, Anjan was born while his father, Jayanta Kumar, a pilot in the Indian Air Force, was stationed near New Delhi. After his father got out of the air force and joined Air India, they moved to Bombay (it was and will always remain Bombay and not Mumbai to Anjan).

North Bombay in the early seventies was hardly developed—Anjan remembers seeing an old farmer in a loincloth pulling a cart in the burning sun directly across from their house in Juhu. Because of its proximity to the studios and the beach, the neighborhood was crawling with Bollywood actors.

In the evenings, everyone went to Juhu Beach. It was too hot during the day—the only people you saw there at that time were either tourists or fishermen—but at night the street stalls were alive with activity. Anjan ate his first dosa—the papery, thin, crepelike South Indian staple—on the beach when he was five, standing with his mom at the counter as he watched the man in front of the hot tava expertly drizzle the batter in a circular motion and fill it with a potato masala.

He could feel the anticipation of waiting for the man to put the masala dosa directly onto his plate, next to the sambar and the chutney, then tasting the hot, spiced potatoes and the crisped edges of the dosa mixing with the cold, refreshing sweetness from the coconut chutney and the spices of the sambar. Again, the textures sold it. But dosa was just one of the seemingly infinite kinds of glorious street food you could try right there. *Pani puri, bhel puri, dahi papdi chaat,* sugarcane juice, corn grilled on charcoal with spices, *vada pav, pav bhaji, ragda pattice, sev puri,* Bombay sandwiches, *malai kulfi, falooda, frankies, romali roti, dahi kachori.*

Growing up in Bombay meant a culinary mélange. Surrounded by Muslims, Shiite Muslims, Parsis, Sikhs, and South Indians, you couldn't help but gain exposure to each of their distinct styles of cuisine. At home, his mother cooked Bengali food—fish or prawns with a mustard sauce or coconut, a vegetable, a lentil, roti, all the different components at the table—but because she'd spent part of her life with Punjabi cooks, she'd also grown to love the food of the North, and she introduced kebabs and *pakhoura* samosas as well. With his dad as a pilot, plane travel was either heavily discounted or free. Jayanta Kumar loved Asian foods of all sorts, and so they'd go off to Thailand or the Philippines and try every spicy dish they could find, Anjan and his father and cousins locked in a battle of wills, watching each other profusely sweat from the spice, wondering when someone would bow out.

As he got older, attending the Bombay International School from fifth standard (essentially, grade) through eighth, Jamnabai Narsee School for ninth and tenth, and Mithibai College for the first and second years of junior college, India began to seem isolated to Anjan. At the time, under Indira Gandhi, the country had socialist leanings; there was just one bank, and one airline, and both were state-run. Pakistan was much more strategically important to America during the Cold War. India felt hegemonic, and after traveling around with his father to Hong Kong and London and other parts of the world, he yearned to get out.

So Anjan applied to college outside of the country. One school in America was building out its international program and trying to attract students, offering full scholarships through a grant in their international studies program. When Anjan was offered the scholarship he couldn't believe his luck. He envisioned himself in America, absorbing the culture in a truly cosmopolitan city, finally feeling what it was like to be in the pulsing, beating heart of commerce, entertainment, and industry. But then he got to Indiana University in Pennsylvania.

Unfortunately, in 1986 Indiana County, Pennsylvania, was not the pulsing, beating heart of damn near anything. An hour east of Pittsburgh, the entire area was still reeling from the aftermath of steel and coal mine closures. It was hardly the ideal initial American experience for a worldly twenty-year-old Indian. The IUP cafeteria, shockingly not a bastion of Bocuse disciples, offered up little in its affinity for steaming buffet trays filled with beef Stroganoff.

Desperately homesick, Anjan and the nine or so other Indian, Pakistani, and Bangladeshi kids on campus would get together at a friend's off-campus apartment and cook, making chicken and lamb curries, convincing the wealthier kids' parents to send spices from home. He couldn't understand the way Americans ate just one thing with a bland flavor, that you wouldn't think to start from the most mild and work up to the spiciest, that you might order an entrée and only get a steak and potato and that would be the meal, that there would be no rice or bread or vegetables or chutneys or spices to tweak, that you couldn't change the textures, that, using a knife and fork, you don't feel your way through a meal like you can when you use your hand, that you can't drop in spices or take out cloves or cardamom pods along the way. American food was incredibly, almost shockingly bland, and so he and most of his Indian friends developed the habit of dousing every single thing they ate with astonishing amounts of Tabasco in the vain hopes of paddle-shocking some flavor into the cuisine.

By sophomore year, things improved. Anjan had started dating a German graduate student who was three years older than him. After she graduated, she moved to New York City, and so he began to visit and understand that eighties Indiana County, Pennsylvania, was not the barometer by which all American cities should be judged. On one trip, they went to a fine Italian restaurant on the Upper East Side. When the dishes came, Anjan asked for Tabasco. The waiter, an Italian immigrant, was horrified. "No, no, please. Try it first," he told him. "Have a bite."

To Anjan's surprise, the pasta was delicious. It was so basic and yet so flavorful, and he didn't even miss the heat. He'd been in America for four years, but this was the first moment he'd even begun to consider that foods outside of his comfort zone could actually be delicious. Most Asian cuisines made sense to him—Vietnamese, Thai, Chinese, etc.—because their spice profiles paralleled those in Indian food and he had grown up traveling to eat them, but American and European palates confused him.

Awakened and invigorated by his Italian restaurant experience, he continued to branch out and was delighted by more foods, like the sausages and breads and eggs in Germany, the intricacies and varieties of pizzas, and the stinky blue cheese on a steakhouse hamburger.

But then, on yet another trip to New York, Anjan discovered what he thought was the answer to all his culinary woes: on Sixth Street in the East Village, between First and Second Avenues, a line of fifteen to twenty restaurants with names like Gandhi, Raj Mahal, and Passage to India. His girlfriend told him it was called Curry Row. As they walked into one of the restaurants, Anjan was overjoyed: Finally, I'm home, he thought. Taking a seat, he noticed that most of the men working at the place were actually Bangladeshi, but that didn't bother him. And yes, well, the menu was basically just North Indian dishes and a few things he'd never heard of, but he expected that, so he ordered samosas and a butter chicken dish, and when it came it was...nearly unrecognizable. There was no spice in the dishes, and there was so much cream. He was hoping at least one of the dishes would remind him of home, but none of them did.

Anjan looked at his girlfriend. What the hell was going on?

THE STORY OF WHAT THE HELL was going on with Indian food in America starts in the late nineteenth century. The first South Asians to come to the United States in any sort of numbers were sailors and textile merchants (mostly from Bengal), who came in the 1880s and '90s during a craze by upper-class Americans for "exotic" Indian items, originally spurred by the same sort of British fervor after Queen Victoria had been named Empress of India. Thanks to the Chinese Exclusion Act of 1882, which forbade Chinese immigrant laborers from emigrating to the United States, animosity toward all peoples of Asian descent was high, and so most of the South Asians that chose to stay ended up assimilating, according to historian Vivek Bald, into other immigrant communities of color, such as Harlem in New York City. This sort of assimilation became even more crucial after the Immigration Act of 1917 (also known as the Asiatic Barred Zone Act), which banned immigration from the entire Asia-Pacific Zone, passed in the House and Senate overriding president Woodrow Wilson's veto. And though it's believed many of the first Indian restaurants were in these communities (many of the originals were unnamed, though places like Eshad Ali's Bombay India Restaurant and Ameer's on 127th Street later became famous African-American gathering places), the first actual Indian celebrity chef showed up in New York City in 1899. His name was J. Ranji Smile.

Smile was born in the Karachi region of India, and first began cooking in that city before moving to England to work in hotel restaurants like the Savoy and the Cecil. England had a long tradition of Indian restaurants (the first was believed to be Dean Mahomed Hindoostane Coffee House, opened in 1809) that only increased after 1858, when the British Empire officially claimed India as a colony. Historian Sarah Lohman details how many British soldiers and government officials would send Indian recipes back to their families, "in part to satisfy their families' curiosity about their exotic lives abroad." As they came back, sometimes with Indian servants and cooks, the popularity of curries skyrocketed, and "as early as the mid-eighteenth century, curries could be ordered at local coffeehouses."

By the 1890s, Smile had acquired a reputation big enough that Louis Sherry, a New York City restaurateur with an eponymous restaurant across from the legendary Delmonico's on Forty-Fourth and Fifth Avenue, brought him to New York. His arrival was covered in the New York papers, and once he'd begun cooking at Sherry's, they breathlessly covered him again. A famous story with the incredible headline "A Chef from India, Women Go Wild over Him" was first published in the *New York Letter* but, according to Lohman, "made the rounds, Associated Press style, in newspapers across the country." His menu, featuring items like Kalooh Sherry, Murghi Rain, Curry of Chicken Madras, and Indian Bhagi Topur, would become a template for imitators.

For the next twenty years, Smile miraculously managed to stay in the news, often as he traveled around the country setting up cooking engagements and demonstrations (mostly for ladies' groups). He pawned himself off as a prince when convenient, got into and then broke off engagements with respectable women all over the country (after traveling to America with an English wife, whom he later claimed passed away), eventually married and divorced a Broadway star, and basically preempted celebrity chef culture by about a hundred years. His luck ran out, however, in 1917 with the passage of the aforementioned Asiatic Barred Zone Act and his inability to gain citizenship. He stuck around America for another decade or so, before eventually returning by ship to England, alone, allegedly to return to the Cecil. Lohman points out that no record of his whereabouts exists following this journey but one imagines Smile opening the world's first Pickup Artist academy somewhere around Southampton.

Though Smile was the first famous Indian chef in America, he never had his own restaurant. Technically, former US consul to Calcutta Charles Huffnagle had a private museum in his New Hope, Pennsylvania, home starting in 1847, and as Vijay Prashad notes in *The Karma of Brown Folk*, tourists were allowed in on Tuesdays to "eat crystallized Calcutta sugar and to sip Mocha coffee and rare Assam teas." But a private Pennsylvania home serving imported sugar cubes on a weekday could hardly be called a restaurant, even by 1847 standards, and so the mantle of first Indian restaurant in America falls to the Ceylon India Inn, opened by Times Square on Forty-Ninth Street in 1913 by former Sri Lankan circus performer K. Yaman Kira. This was followed in 1918 by the arrival of the Taj Mahal Hindu Restaurant on Forty-Second.

From there, a combination of America's isolationist and nativist tendencies kept things static. In George Ross's 1934 guide *Tips on Tables*, out of 365 restaurants, he only names one Indian restaurant, the Rajah, on West Forty-Eighth. Prohibition and the Great Depression had fundamentally shaped the restaurant industry, then World War II happened, and in 1947, British India was split into Pakistan and India, with repeated conflicts in the disputed Kashmir region raising tensions for decades and eventually escalating into all-out war in 1965. That same year America passed the Immigration and Nationality Act, which replaced the quota system based around national origin with a system based on professions and family ties.

The Indians who were granted permission to immigrate to America during this time were what Sanjoy Chakravorty, Devesh Kapur, and Nirvikar Singh, in *The Other One Percent: Indians in America*, referred to as "early movers," and their ranks were made up primarily of scientists, doctors, and engineers, professions that had little overlap with the culinary arts. But because of the conflicts between Bengalis and Muslims in East Pakistan, which eventually led to the Bangladesh Liberation War of 1971, hundreds of thousands of Bengalis were displaced as well, mostly into India, but also throughout Great Britain and America. These Bangladeshi people tended to be poorer than the other early-moving Indian immigrants, and so they found themselves in service and labor jobs.

In 1968, an East Pakistan immigrant and University of Michigan grad named Manir Ahmed and his five brothers found an old Japanese restaurant for rent on East Sixth Street, and they took the space, using it more or less as a clubhouse where they cooked food and hung out. But the East Village in 1968 was filled with curious hippies who kept wandering in thinking it was a restaurant, or at least an unfettered place to potentially do drugs. Eventually, the brothers saw the food side of this as a business opportunity and opened Shah Bag. Though all the brothers were Bangladeshi, they marketed the restaurant as Indian because, as one other Curry Row restaurant owner told *The New York Times*, "nobody knew what Bangladesh was!" The menu that came out of that restaurant was an eclectic mix of British curry house hits like chicken tikka masala (a dish originally invented in England or Scotland), *saag paneer*, *rogan josh*, and korma alongside a variety of curries and naan, always naan. Spice content was low, cream content high. Curried chicken cost $1.25. Buffets were a must.

Either way, the hippies loved it, so the brothers started opening more and more restaurants—inexplicably all along the same block—and soon other Bangladeshi immigrants also joined, most coming from a tea-growing region close to the Himalayas called Sylhet. By the time young Anjan arrived at East Sixth Street in the late 1980s, Curry Row had become the biggest, most well-known "Little India" in America, despite the fact that it was almost entirely run by Bangladeshis from a very small region at the foot of a very big mountain.

THOUGH ANJAN DIDN'T LOVE THE BASTARDIZED, watered-down, Americanized Indian spin-offs he was eating, it certainly beat the foods back at

IUP. Luckily, he didn't have much more time there, because in 1991, he graduated with a double major in economics and computer science and moved out to Palo Alto, California.

Working for a small tech company, he got a small apartment off University Avenue in Palo Alto, and moved in with his then-girlfriend in Menlo Park. But after they broke up, he suddenly wondered what he was doing living in this suburban environment in his early twenties. He moved to San Francisco, working with Sun Microsystems and Netscape, a single guy with a good job and years to go before the original tech bubble burst.

At the time, a burgeoning house music scene was developing in Berlin, London, and New York City, and San Francisco had its own version. After getting connected to original promoters in the SF house scene, Martel and Naviel, Anjan became a regular at clubs with house DJs. Like giant Russian nesting dolls, these clubs were actually filled with smaller and smaller VIP clubs within clubs, and Anjan was in a VIP room within a VIP room at a Saturday-night party called Release at 1015 Folsom when he made eye contact with a tall, beautiful brunette girl with hazel eyes across the dance floor. Within seconds, he'd made his way across the room.

Emily Gilels was from suburban Syracuse, New York, the daughter of a second-generation Jewish Polish mother and a first-generation Russian father. Even in the seventies in upstate New York, her family had progressive ideas about food. Her mother was basically a vegetarian (though she, perplexingly, also ate bacon), and both her parents loved to talk about food and restaurants. When she was twelve, she watched her mother cut up raw chicken on a cutting board, thought about the flesh and blood, and decided right there she wasn't going to eat meat. Of course, her mother didn't push her, and other than one regrettable taco salad her freshman year in college, Emily never ate meat again.

She graduated from the University of Michigan in 1994, and six days later drove from Syracuse to settle in San Francisco, getting a little studio apartment on Fillmore. She worked all sorts of jobs—writing book reviews for the

Sierra Club's magazine, working at a café and a health food store—but it was a grind, so she ended up finding a steady paycheck in the glamorous world of vision insurance, which gave her enough money to go out with her friends, which is how Emily Gilels ended up in Release's VIP room on her friend's twenty-fifth birthday at three a.m.

She didn't know what to make of Anjan—he was startlingly handsome, even while wearing a blue bandanna, and he was a fantastic dancer. After regrouping with her friends, she reconnected with him and ended up staying out with Anjan until seven in the morning; then, writing on a matchbook, she embarrassingly gave him all her numbers—her home phone, her cell phone, even her fax number. But luckily, he didn't play it cool either, and by the time she'd gotten back from breakfast with friends, he'd already left a message on her home phone asking if he could see her again.

Their first real date was a few days later at the Indian restaurant Rasoi. Much to her relief, Anjan did all the ordering, and she was blown away by the breadth of flavorful vegetarian options in Indian cuisine. She became obsessed, which was perfectly fine with Anjan, who was happy to take her all over the Bay Area, out to Vik's in Berkeley, and to Indian enclaves in Fremont, Newark, and Sunnyvale, showing her Indian grocery stores and little shops selling *uttapam*. It was on one of these trips Emily experienced her first dosa.

At a table with Anjan's aunts, she sat frozen, suddenly feeling very self-conscious as this giant crepe filled with spiced potatoes lay in front of her. Using her side-eye, she intently watched the aunts as each attacked the snack in a different way, one of them breaking through the middle with her fingers, the other nibbling on the end. As she attempted to get a handle on her own dosa, it broke and her face turned bright red, but she pushed through and became obsessed.

"Why didn't you tell me about these things?" she asked Anjan as they drove back. "You've never mentioned it!"

"Oh yeah," he said, "I grew up with those. Everyone remembers their first dosa."

"Well," she said, "we're going to get more next week."

It was 1998, and both their careers were taking off. With Anjan's encouragement, Emily got a job at Talk City, an early chat room company. She became director of sales, and then, in 2000, she jumped over to director of sales at Broadcast.com, the company Mark Cuban famously sold to Yahoo! just before everything cratered. That same year on New Year's Eve, on a rooftop in Bombay, Anjan asked Emily to marry him. As they planned the weddings, Emily quit her job, realizing she wanted to own her own business. Almost immediately she started working on a business plan. At first it was for a yoga studio, but she quickly realized that she had no idea how that would make even a little money. Her next idea was a café—she loved restaurants, but she wanted kids and was worried a full-service spot would pull her away—and she envisioned an organic diner of sorts, and even came up with a name: Brekkie.

Over the next few months, she started going to cafés and restaurants and studying them. She found the ones she admired, especially ones with female chefs or owners, and would go up and blindly introduce herself, tell them she wanted to open a place, and ask if they had a little time to talk to her about it. Almost without exception, these women, total strangers, would take the time to offer her advice.

One night after service, a couple who owned a local Italian restaurant took her down to their office. Closing the door, they slid the profit and loss statement across the desk. Once she looked through it, the wife started to talk in a low voice. "Just so you know," she said, "it's a really hard business. It's really hard for us as a couple, we work more hours than we ever have before, and at the end of the day, we're probably making half of what we used to make in other jobs." That year they'd made around eighty thousand dollars.

"I want you to go into this with your eyes open," she continued. "So many people don't; they think they're going to spend their nights going table to table and having a glass of wine and talking to friends. It isn't that. Or it is that, but maybe for twenty minutes a night. The other twelve hours are work. So if you're going to do this, you have to really want it."

Leaving that night, Emily felt relief—finally someone was giving her real numbers. She'd been frustrated because she felt like people were being vaguely encouraging or discouraging without providing hard data or even real truths. Getting those, she steeled her reserves. She still wanted to do this.

And anyway, she thought, it's not like Anjan and I would be working together.

They had two weddings—one in Big Sur, California, and another in India, a five-hundred-person affair considered extremely small and modern by the standards of a typical Indian wedding. Emily loved being an Indian bride, despite the fact that there were important ceremonial things going on she didn't know about until they were actually happening. To her. During her own wedding.

"Oh, yeah," Anjan would say out of the side of his mouth. "Forgot to mention."

The day after the wedding, they sat around a big table at the JW Marriott in Bombay, watching folks going to the dosa station, and somewhat absent-mindedly Emily told Anjan, "You know, someone should open a cool South Indian place, a dosa spot."

They stared at their young, hip friends, who likely wondered why the newly married couple were intently looking at them. "Like a place we'd go on the weekend with friends?" Anjan said. "Is there already a place like that?"

They paused, racking their brains, but neither could think of one.

Emily: "Am I crazy, or is this a great idea?"

Anjan: "Look, if you go home and write this business plan and it makes sense, I'll quit my job and come be your partner."

Emily: "Wait, really?"

They shook on it, then immediately went quiet. If someone else made a cool South Indian restaurant that incorporated seasonality in the food, they'd be crushed. Suddenly it became a race against an unknown competitor.

IN THE TIME AFTER THE GLORY CURRY ROW DAYS, Indian food in America, on the whole, only marginally improved. As far back as 1977, *New York Times* restaurant critic Mimi Sheraton had declared in a review that New York had a "rapidly growing roster of expensive and elegant Indian restaurants, apparently one of the 'in' ethnic trends of the moment," citing Raga and its "lavish and equally luxurious appurtenances of the Eastern maharajahs" as well as its "tandoori chicken" and "ground lamb seekh kebob" as worthy of praise. Sheraton declared her love of the cuisine again in a 1979 review of Bombay Palace, noting, "It is easy to understand the ever-increasing popularity of Indian food, given its savory counterpoints of spices, its decorative presentation, and its contrasting crisp and silken textures."

On the West Coast, Paul Bhalla's Cuisine of India in Los Angeles was, as Sameen Rushdie described in *Indian Cookery,* "groundbreaking," and led him to start a small chain of restaurants throughout Southern California and Las Vegas. On the East Coast, by the mid-eighties, the Indian restaurant of the moment was Dawat, which opened in 1986 to much fanfare because actress and celebrity cookbook author Madhur Jaffrey had consulted on the menu. Two years later in Memphis, Raji Jallepalli, a microbiologist who, along with her husband, had first come to America as a medical student, quit the medical field after an Alice Waters–esque epiphanic trip to France and opened Restaurant Raji, a French-Indian fusion restaurant that became nationally influential.

She was just one person mentioned in Florence Fabricant's 1998 *New York Times* piece with a very long title, "American Palates Awaken to the Bold

Tastes of India: As the Latest Fusion Star, Creative Indian Cuisine Vies with Its Asian Rivals." The story also contains the first *Times* mention of Indian chef Floyd Cardoz, who, Fabricant pointed out, would be chef at a new restaurant called Tabla, which "will be about as Indian as you can get without serving rogan josh," and is "a departure from the clichés and cheap buffet lunches of the budget places on East Sixth Street, or even from the tandoor Taj Mahals of midtown."

Cardoz's restaurant, which got three stars from *Times* critic Ruth Reichl in 1999, crowned him as the celebrity Indian chef in America, though the cuisine, featuring dishes like mustard fettuccine with veal, was more in the fusion camp than strict Indian. In 2001, Avtar Walia's Tamarind opened in the Flatiron (hiring Raji Jallepalli as executive chef, until she sadly passed away from cancer at fifty-two). This was followed by two Indian restaurants, Amma and Dévi, from Suvir Saran, a chef who also taught a popular Indian cooking class, at New York University and, of course, Jean-Georges Vongerichten's 2004 ode to all of South Asia, Spice Market.

Outside of New York, Indika, Anita Jaisinghani's 2001 Houston stunner, electrified the scene there with its crab samosas and tandoori duck, served out of a little white house in the Montrose neighborhood. Other spots, like K. N. Vinod's Indique in Washington, DC (2002), and Vik Kapoor's Tamarind Bay in Cambridge, Massachusetts (2004), made smaller waves while trying to push the conversation forward, but for the most part, Indian restaurants aiming to be hip and current felt the need to go fusion, to combine French dishes with Indian spices, or incorporate the entire roster of Asian foods.

As soon as she and Anjan got home, Emily wrote the new business plan. Now they just needed an actual space and a chef. Oh, and another thing: Emily was pregnant. Again, the doubt crept in. "Maybe you shouldn't do this now," friends said. But Emily knew that if she stopped the project, she'd never be able to restart. It just wouldn't happen. Finally, her sister gave her the moderating advice she needed: have your baby, make sure she's healthy, and, if she feels like a good kid, an easy kid, then open the restaurant.

On July 29, 2004, Eila Simone Mitra was born. She was a sweet, healthy baby, easy to sleep-train, and generally easygoing. This was the blessing Emily needed. They decided to move forward with their plans.

In order to get a place, they needed a small business loan. In order to get a small business loan, they needed to convince the people at Wells Fargo that giving lots of money to first-time restaurant owners to open a full-service South Indian restaurant in the Mission actually made logical sense. And somehow, after warning Emily that her business posed the highest risk and made the least amount of sense, they approved the loan. Banking!

With the loan in hand, they were finally freed up to try and find a space to actually put the restaurant. They ended up at 995 Valencia in SF's Mission District. It was small, maybe sixty seats, with ten at the bar. It had been a not-very-good Italian restaurant called Spiazzino and many other short-lived restaurants before that. And just the process of buying Spiazzino, which involved getting into a bidding war with another South Indian restaurant, drained half their resources. But the Mission, especially in the mid-aughts, was exciting. The national press had finally noticed the superiority of the Mission burrito shops. Chef Sam Mogannam had taken over his family's grocery business, Bi-Rite Market, and turned it into a specialty food store, with an ice cream and baked goods shop, Bi-Rite Creamery, across the street. Chad Robertson and Elisabeth Pruiett's Tartine Bakery, which opened in 2002, was winning national awards for its pastry. Craig Stoll had opened his Italian restaurant Delfina in 1998, and the more casual Pizzeria Delfina next door in 2005. Cameron and Phil West's Range, which combined ambitious cocktails and modern cooking, opened the same year. If they were going to have a shot, they felt like this neighborhood was the place. But they had to find a chef. It turned out this was going to be complicated.

FOR MANY YEARS, as India looked to get out from under the shadow of its colonization by Great Britain, there was an incredible focus on organically developing an internal infrastructure, which meant that engineering and both the medical and computer sciences became the most important job tracks for the sons of families of any sort of means. Because labor was cheap, these families, even if they were middle class, usually had their own cooks, and in an attempt to exert some sort of control over a precarious situation and keep jobs within families, most of these cooks didn't write down their recipes. On top of that, actual culinary programs really only existed within hoteling schools, and these programs were designed around the needs of the tourist, which meant the "professionally trained" chefs were learning safe, watered-down dishes aimed primarily at pleasing the palates of people from outside of India. And on top of *that*, the majority of young Indian folks actually getting a chance to come to America were coming on the H-1B visa program, granted to specialized employees with unique skills (often in engineering, computer science, or medical science), often with jobs already guaranteed.

All that meant that in 2005, it was very hard for Anjan to find a young native Indian chef in America who possessed both the innate understanding of the cuisine and a progressive sensibility about expanding and adapting that food to Northern California. They tried out four chefs, often going to their current restaurants and having them cook, but each time something didn't feel right. Anjan and Emily even considered trying to cook themselves, for about four total hours, before dismissing that idea as absurd. In fact, the whole thing seemed somewhat absurd and frustrating. Then they met Senthil Kumar. Only twenty-six, Kumar was from South India, and had been in America for four years, stuck working in unambitious restaurants.

Emily and Anjan came into the tiny Indian restaurant on Castro Street in Mountain View around three p.m. The restaurant was slightly shabby and stereotypical, the exact type of place that bothered Anjan. He readied himself to be disappointed. Ten minutes in, Kumar brought out sambar, a deceptively complex vegetable stew. For Anjan, it was the most critical and telling dish any Indian chef could make, because it involved a delicate dance between thirty-five different ingredients. Anjan had a highly trained palate, a strange ability to decipher exact ingredients in a dish and break them down in a listlike fashion, and after one taste of Kumar's sambar, he was sold. "This is our guy," he said to Emily. Everything about it was perfect. They made their offer later that night, and suddenly they had the chef and the space. Now all they had to do was build and open a restaurant.

They hadn't wanted to use a designer. For one, they couldn't afford it, but also they were so particular about the details that it seemed pointless to try and bring in another vision. Instead they had their architect lay out the structure of the restaurant, and they filled in the blanks. The first thing was coming up with a name. All previous dosa restaurants they'd found used the name as part of something bigger: Dosa Palace, Dosa Kingdom, Dosa Universe, etc. But Emily thought they should just simplify and call it DOSA. Two syllables, easy to say, boom. They went online and found some guy who had a website and paid him to design their first logo. They asked the guy to put the *o* in the shape of the dosa, and once that was done, they put a sign in the window featuring the logo and reading, "DOSA, coming soon."

The response just to this simple sign was incredible. As they worked on the space, finding warm food colors like red and orange and figuring out exactly how a ten-seat bar would work, people would stop in just to ask when they were opening. It wasn't just Indians either. White folks who'd traveled to India for work, the kids of hippies whose parents lived in West Marin, or those who'd had an around-the-world college experience and spoke about their India experiences in a semi-annoying, dreamlike reverie—they all came through, checking on the status. As the timeline crept up, the stress built.

Hedging against the very likely possibility that the restaurant could be a massive failure and cost them $250,000, Anjan made an agreement that he would keep his day job for the first six months while working evenings in the restaurant and then evaluate where they were. If it was financially possible (and the restaurant still existed), he would then quit his job and work full-time. In the meantime, it would be Emily's project.

She kept plodding forward, terrified but unable to stop this machine they'd put in motion. They now had a staff, and a chef, and a restaurant on the cusp of opening. It was so scary that Emily was sure her body was releasing hormones just to protect her from the trauma. The night before they opened, they were down in their garage with a moving truck's lights illuminating the scene as they varnished the chairs they'd need the next night, the fumes making them dizzy and nauseous as Eila mercifully slept upstairs.

On December 5, 2005, at five thirty p.m., DOSA on Valencia opened to the public. Anjan and Kumar had worked together on a simplified menu—they obviously would have dosas and *uttapam* and curries, but the curries had to be just right. Anjan's focus was on making sure everything tasted super fresh and not drowned in oil—each dish needed to distinguish itself from the average curries—and so they introduced a prawn curry with coconut and a spicy, peppery Tamil lamb curry from Chettinad. Because the food was so vegetable-forward, they didn't even think to include salads in the original menu. At the bar, they were serving soju cocktails, beer, and selections from an impressive wine list, put together by a Michael Mina sommelier named Mark Bright, who gave Anjan a crash course in wines.

They'd hoped to maybe get thirty to forty guests the first night, just enough to start testing out the staff and putting the kitchen through its paces. It did not happen like that. The first night, they did a hundred covers, a truly astonishing number considering they'd basically just swung their doors open. One of these guests was the San Francisco editor of the incredibly influential women's culture/food e-newsletter *DailyCandy*, and the following day, news of DOSA's opening led off the newsletter's email. From the third day onward, the sixty-seat restaurant was doing more than two hundred covers every single night.

Emily was excited but completely overwhelmed. As a first-time mom trying to also be a first-time entrepreneur, she'd hoped for some sort of ramp-up, a time where she could learn on the job and have some runway to change, but it wasn't happening like that at all. After the first night, when she returned home at one a.m., she passed out in bed. When she woke up a few hours later, she started hysterically crying. Anjan woke up in a panic. Emily was not a crier. She told him she couldn't do it again; she couldn't go back. Anjan listened silently and then gently told her to go back to sleep and see how she felt in the morning.

The next morning, Emily still felt panic, but there was nothing to be done. No matter what, they were going to open the doors at five thirty p.m., she told herself. She would have to figure it out. There were still so many things they didn't know. The first night, after Anjan had left to be with Eila, the waitstaff came over and asked how they were going to cash out. "Wait," said Emily. "What the fuck is cashing out?"

They figured it out. Anjan was a master with Excel, and eventually came up with his own customized, amazing cashing-out system, complete with assumptions and tip pool information. They prided themselves on knowing mistakes would be made, identifying them quickly, and trying to never do them again. For the first three weeks, Emily acted as bookkeeper, and she couldn't figure out why every day people would come to her office asking for checks.

"Um," they'd say, "you need to pay us?"

"Now?" Emily would say. "Already?"

By the third week, with 150 bills due, she broke down and hired an actual bookkeeper.

They figured out other stuff too, like how to get their waitstaff to make novices feel comfortable ordering and to gently explain, or suggest, a way to eat the dosa. Emily was adamant that she wanted none of the awkwardness she'd faced when first eating dosa with Anjan's aunts. It was also an uphill battle to get some people to understand they weren't going to be serving the stereotypical British-style North Indian/Bangladeshi cuisine they'd been conditioned to accept as Indian food. At least a couple of times a day, people would walk in, not look at a menu, and say, "I'll have the chicken tikka masala, and the butter chicken, and the naan," and Anjan, Emily, and their staff

An early DOSA on Valencia menu, 2006

had to be like, "Well, first of all, we have none of those things," and then slowly guide them to dishes actually on the menu they might like.

Anjan worked with Senthil and the other South Indian line cooks, bringing them down to the SF Farmers Market early to show the bounty of fresh produce available. Most of the cooks were incredibly talented at cooking nuanced South Indian cuisine, but they'd also been working in places where a menu would be created and then not change for two years. The idea of incorporating seasonality and changing the menu according to the vegetables available was anathema to what they were used to, but they took to it. And after enough customers—in very San Francisco fashion—inquired about the lack of salads, they even added a salad.

One Friday in the middle of February 2006, Emily got a call at DOSA from *San Francisco Chronicle* restaurant critic Michael Bauer. In San Francisco at the time, there was a sense of energy and excitement around several new restaurants, from Nopa and farmerbrown to Coi, Terzo, and Front Porch. Bauer, who'd been reviewing restaurants at the *Chronicle* for twenty years by that point, was incredibly powerful and his opinion carried massive sway in the small city, heavily influencing which new restaurants succeeded and failed. He'd apparently dined at DOSA three times in the previous months, but Emily hadn't seen him there and, to be honest, didn't even think to look.

Bauer had a few specific questions about ingredients, so Emily frantically called over Kumar and they sat with the phone on speaker as Bauer asked him about the makeup of the masala dosa and whether he tasted kaffir lime in another dish. At the end, he thanked them for their time and told them the review would be coming out Sunday.

Sunday morning, Anjan hurried to get the paper. The review, titled "Fire and Spice: DOSA Offers a Contemporary, Hip Taste of South Indian Cuisine," came out on February 19, 2006, and—for the most part—was glowing, saying that "the newly opened DOSA in San Francisco's Mission District has done what no other San Francisco establishment has been able to do—make Indian food trendy." It went on to highlight the calamari, "with a spicy sauce made with ginger, garlic, cashew paste, tomatoes, chile, coriander, cumin, cilantro and coconut milk," as "one of the best calamari dishes I've had in recent memory," and mention the crowds, "packed around the bar waiting to experience the magic of what DOSA has to offer."

The impact of said good review was immediate. Despite having no reservations, in the first three months they were getting around two hundred covers a night, but the Tuesday after the Bauer review came out, a line started to form outside the door around four p.m. By opening time, that line had stretched out past the health food store next door and turned the corner down Twenty-First Street. Many of the people waiting in line were holding the newspaper review under their arms. DOSA went from being popular to an undisputed sensation. Much to the delighted surprise of the Wells Fargo small business crew, they paid back their entire loan in six months. They felt like they were flying.

But the Bauer article also brought up a subject Anjan had been quietly struggling with since before they opened: "DOSA represents an important step in mainstreaming and authenticating an important regional cuisine. Yet, several snobs on various Web sites lambasted this place soon after it opened in December, saying the food wasn't 'authentic' and the owner was from—big gasp—Bombay (now Mumbai) rather than South India. One blogger even trashed the place without trying the food."

In the story, Bauer dismisses this notion as "lame," saying, "A chef or owner doesn't have to be from a particular culture to appreciate it; often an outsider may have more respect for the indigenous cuisine than a native. Was Paul Bertolli raised in Italy? Is Thomas Keller French? It's what's on the plate that counts, and the Mitras have created a restaurant that is contemporary and respects the traditions of South Indian food."

Nothing infuriated Anjan more than this authenticity argument, that he somehow shouldn't be doing South Indian food because he was from Bombay. He was fiercely protective of making sure they respected traditions, and nothing brought him truer joy than seeing a huge group of fifteen Indians of all ages piling into the restaurant. Most of the quarrels he found himself in were with first-generation Americans, twenty- or thirtysomethings who'd been born in the States to South Indian parents and didn't have historical context to understand that four million South Indians lived in Bombay, that there were entire neighborhoods in the city that were exclusively South Indian, that the beauty of a cosmopolitan city like Bombay was the diversity of cuisines you'd experience. How do you explain to someone, without looking defensive, in a Yelp response or a blog comment or a passing conversation, that your best friend and first girlfriend were South Indian, and that you'd grown up eating in their homes and attending their festivals? Plus, his chefs and line cooks were all South Indian!

Actual Indians would rarely bring up this sort of argument—if they were from India, they would get it—but Anjan felt the need to respond to these sorts of things. (Over the next few years, he would respond, either publicly or privately, to more than three thousand Yelp reviews.) The blogger Bauer had referenced had been an Indian-American woman from Stockton, California, whose parents were from South India, and the blog writer who had trashed DOSA without actually eating there also called out Emily as a hippie American chick. Anjan and Emily were both outraged at this random character assassination, and Anjan responded to her blog post in the comments as politely as he could, but he also knew a mic drop opportunity when he saw one: "Oh and by the way, I'm actually from Bombay, not Stockton, CA."

If the writer hadn't called her a hippie, Emily would have reminded him that engaging in these sorts of arguments is futile, but he never thought that. "This is about my identity," he said, "and I have to respond to an attack on my identity." But beyond that, it hurt him. Why are my own people being so critical? he wondered. Shouldn't they be celebrating the fact that we want to bring the conversation forward, that we're trying to do something different and special, something that they can be proud of? What is the point in tearing us down? These types of things kept Anjan up at night.

Despite the external battles, they continued doing well. And just as promised, six months to the day, Anjan quit his job, and as soon as he got home from work and changed clothes, he went to DOSA and got behind the host stand. When Emily saw him come in, she gave him a kiss, went home, and went directly to bed. She hadn't gotten a full night's sleep in a year.

CHAPTER 4

King of Trucks, Roy Choi, Los Angeles, California

The story of the Great Food Truck Insurrection really begins with Emeril. Well, technically it begins in Seoul, South Korea, in 1970, with Choi being born, his cleft lip split wide open as he came out, so that when they finally stitched it back together, it left him with a lightning-shaped scar on his upper lip. His parents—mom from Pyung-An Do in the North, dad from Chollanam-do in the South—had met in America and moved back to South Korea, but found it wasn't as they'd remembered, so they made their move back to America permanent in 1972, settling in Los Angeles. Once back, the Chois were scrappy and quick to hit the reset button on their job prospects if they weren't working out. His father, who'd been in the military in Korea and been sent to study diplomacy and international relations at the University of Pennsylvania, nonetheless took what he could get in America, first running a Koreatown liquor store, then selling hippie jewelry door-to-door alongside Choi's mother. Choi's mom was a talented cook—her kimchi and *panchan* were famous—and she'd sometimes sell snacks in parking lots and bowling alleys. Eventually, her talents led the way, and the Chois opened a Korean restaurant called Silver Garden in Anaheim.

When the restaurant went under, they started selling jewelry again, but this time it was expensive pieces on consignment. They would borrow the jewels and hide them on Roy as they walked around downtown LA, rationalizing that robbers wouldn't expect a twelve-year-old to be loaded down with hundreds of thousands of dollars of diamonds. Within three years, Choi's parents went from scraping by to "actually, waiter, we'll have the bottled sparkling water" rich. They bought a Cadillac Fleetwood Brougham and a half-million-dollar house in 1983 money, a fancy house that used to belong to a fancy professional athlete in a fancy place called Villa Park in Orange County, two square miles of rich, white, professional dads practicing their golf swings on manicured lawns. Choi was one of three Asians in a middle school full of Chads and Justins living in seven-thousand-square-foot homes with six-car garages. He played the class clown and survived into high school, where the mix of kids from Orange and Anaheim balanced out the excess wealth and whiteness. Once there, Choi took up with the Grove Street Mob, a crew of multicultural kids sort of like Captain Planet's Planeteers, except instead of controlling elements of nature with special rings, they all wore heavily starched jeans and got into fights.

At home, Choi was still Good Roy, living in a mansion in a wealthy enclave, even if he stubbornly refused to take an allowance, instead earning his money at a toy store or washing dishes at Leatherby's or busing tables at Cask 'n' Cleaver. But with his friends in Grove Street, Choi morphed into Bad Roy, getting into fights, taking drugs, and storing shotguns under the seats of cars. By his senior year, he'd purchased and tricked out a 1987 Chevy Blazer, earning him a spot in a Latin car club called the Street City Minis. This was Cool Car Roy. Choi's world was weird and fractured and multiethnic, filled with fights, petty crime, custom car shows, and a doting, successful family with a beautiful home. Choi was living two, maybe even three, lives, and it was hard to tell which was the real one.

After high school, Choi went to California State University, Fullerton, and majored in philosophy. But then, as Choi tells it, his life turned into a series of dramatic montage scenes from *Rounders*, *Casino*, and the scarier parts of *Goodfellas*. He spent a summer in Korea, met a girl, ate around Seoul with the girl, lost the girl, and ended up in New York at a YMCA smoking crack for a week after a con man swindled him out of his last $120 by pretending he was an adjunct professor who was going to bring Choi to an expensive lecture. He went home, started to get his shit together enough to go back to college, and then became a gambling addict for the next few years, playing Asian Pan 9 and Pai Gow games at the Bicycle Club Casino in Bell Gardens. At first, Choi was a damn good gambler, winning $34,000 on one hand, eating pho, drinking milkshakes, and getting massages while bluffing Telly Savalas; blowing his winnings at Koreatown nightclubs while hanging out with people named John John Boy and Davy Baby and Marty Party; watching a guy win $150,000 at the casino, only to hear a few hours later he was murdered in the parking lot with an ax. You know, that sort of thing.

Eventually Choi's luck ran out, but he couldn't stop chasing it, and soon he was pawning everything he had, selling his clothes and shoes, stealing from his parents and his sister, taking anything he could. Finally, his parents intervened and brought him to their house to detox, and he started getting his shit together. He began working as a mutual funds broker at First Investors, initially on some *Boiler Room* shit, but soon he began doing well, even making six figures. But then the cycle shifted: Choi reconnected with an old friend, the old friend loved to drink, they went out, one night turned into a week turned into a month turned into six months, and it all bottomed out when an ex-girlfriend's new boyfriend and his friends beat Choi senseless and stuck guns to his head in the karaoke room of a Koreatown nightclub. Choi was asked if he wanted to live or die. Choi didn't answer, and was allegedly brave or drunk or stupid enough to stagger to his feet, flick them off, walk out of the room without getting shot, and wake up the next morning in the passenger seat of his own car. Peak Bad Roy.

And that's how we get back to Emeril. As most origin stories do, this one has turned into myth, with different iterations and angles and locations, but it goes something like this: Choi, hungover on the couch a few weeks later, was coming in and out of consciousness. In the background of his haze, he could hear a man seasoning the ever-loving shit out of meats and yelling phrases more commonly associated with the storyboarded sound effects from Adam West's *Batman*. It was *Essence of Emeril*. The Fall River/NOLA man/bear hybrid was revving up the crowd with his discussion of beef bourguignonne. As Choi came in and out of this world, Emeril stepped into his dreams and gave him a pep talk while possibly letting him smell basil.

Emeril, more than the ax murder, or the pawning of his shoes, or the guns to his head, was the tipping point for Choi. He was going to be a chef.

IN SIX MONTHS CHOI WAS BACK, living with his parents, working at First Investors, and enrolled in a local culinary school. His parents offered to pay for serious school, so Choi applied and got into the Culinary Institute of America (CIA) in Hyde Park, New York. In the winter of 1996, he entered the school, and though most kids were much younger than him, Choi took to the geeky side of things, learned the techniques, and even got an externship with Eric Ripert at Le Bernardin. When he graduated from CIA, he got married and took a job as a junior sous chef at La Casa del Zorro in Borrego Springs, California, making Kit Fox salads for snowbird retirement folks and German tourists. That job led to another in South Lake Tahoe, running the food program for the Embassy Suites.

Choi kept moving up over the next six years, eventually overseeing the culinary decisions at ten of their properties before making his way back to Los Angeles to become chef de cuisine at the Beverly Hilton. From there, he was recruited by the Cheesecake Factory founder David Overton to help chef Mohan Ismail (an influential Singaporean chef who'd worked at Tabla and Spice Market) open RockSugar, their Asian concept. Everything went fine in the test kitchen, but when the actual restaurant opened, Choi was constantly in the weeds. He couldn't handle the huge menu, and found himself breaking down on the line, forgetting how to do things and what he'd ordered and what he needed to tell the line cooks. Ismail fired him. Choi went to his car and threw up, and then, for three days, pretended to his wife that he wasn't fired, getting dressed in the morning as if he were going to work and then just driving around the city, numb.

Choi had a family, a young daughter. He couldn't fuck around. He needed a job. But it was 2008. No one was hiring. The economy was on the brink, and he was either overqualified or underqualified or overconfident or underconfident. He couldn't even get a full gig, even an entry-level one. Things were becoming dire. He was thirty-eight years old, and if he'd been treading water before, now he was starting to drown.

The call that saved him came from the place that almost killed him: Koreatown. His buddy Mark Manguera, a Philippines-born, Cali-raised fellow chef from the Beverly Hilton, had been drunk eating Mexican food with his sister when he'd had an epiphany: Why the hell wasn't anyone putting Korean barbecue on tacos? Mexicans had been living in Koreatown for decades, and their cuisines were like cousins. Didn't that make sense?

At first, for Choi, it didn't. He and Manguera weren't really that close at the Beverly Hilton, and the entire thing seemed so basic. But the more Choi thought about it, the more he realized this was a puzzle he wanted to put together. And anyway, he didn't have shit going on anywhere else.

Manguera and Choi started to experiment in Manguera's tiny Koreatown kitchen. What they came up with—stuffing Korean barbecued short ribs garnished with *salsa roja* and cilantro-onion-lime relish into homemade, griddled corn tortillas—seemed simple, but the flavors were deceptively nuanced. This, more than anything else, was something all the Roys—Good Roy and Bad Roy and Car Roy—could contribute to. Learning Korean flavors from his parents' restaurant. Going to huge cookouts with his Latino car club homies. Breaking into Tastee Freez to cook chimichangas with the Grove Street Mob. It was all in there.

It was also November 2008. Businesses were melting, and banks were barely allowing people to take money out of ATMs. Small business loans did not exist. There was no way Choi and Manguera could get a brick-and-mortar

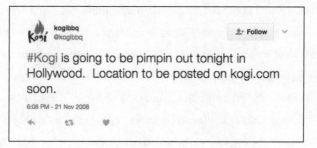

The first ever tweet by Roy Choi's Kogi taco truck, which helped to revolutionize social media use in the restaurant industry

space, so instead they rented a Grumman catering truck from the eighties and decided they'd sell the tacos out of the truck for two dollars apiece.

Around Thanksgiving, the Kogi BBQ Taco Truck hit the streets with Choi cooking, Manguera in the front of the truck, and Manguera's wife, Caroline, as the financial brain. Sales were okay. People liked the tacos, but it was hard to build a word-of-mouth audience when they were constantly setting up shop in different locations. Sometimes they'd have to give away free taco samples just to get things going. But then, through the grace of God and VC money, Twitter exploded. The nascent social media company had launched two years earlier, but it took off in 2008, going from 1.6 million total tweets posted in 2007 to 400 million the following year. Choi started tweeting to let followers know his location in real time, and the combination of his addictive and affordable fusion street food and the in-the-know feeling of discovering the truck's latest stop created a cultural food phenomenon. In an early 2009 review in *LA Weekly*, food critic Jonathan Gold detailed the scene: "Followers keep track of Kogi's whereabouts on a frequently updated Twitter feed—twitter.com/kogibbq—and the sudden materialization of hundreds of people is like what used to be called a flash mob—but with much better food. The frequent tweets make you feel connected to Kogi, as if you were friends with the owners instead of just another hungry mouth, even if your only contact with them has been a quick fist bump when you picked up your tacos."

The juxtaposition of his CIA degree, his résumé that could name-check Le Bernardin and the Beverly Hilton, and his heavily tatted, flat-brimmed, swagger-heavy persona quickly made Choi and the Kogi truck the face of the burgeoning food truck movement. With no hope of securing loans or getting new jobs, more and more professionally trained chefs took to the streets, joining the ranks of progenitors like Choi in LA, and Nong's Khao Man Gai owner Narumol Poonsukwattana in Portland, creating, all around the country, an explosion of intensely creative, singularly focused, cheap, delicious foods. But few had prepped their entire lives to be able to capture the high and the low like Choi. His talk of Pépin's *La Technique* came as easy as Grove Street anecdotes about stashing weapons in cars. Choi had grown up poor *and* rich, and that dual identity captured the essence of the food truck revolution more succinctly than any other narrative.

CHAPTER 5

André Prince Jeffries, North Nashville, Tennessee, Part 1

André Ella Prince Jeffries wasn't entirely sure how to pronounce her own name. There was a chance it was French. Her daddy, Bruce Prince, had fought in World War II, and came back talking about the French Riviera as if it was the greatest place on earth, and he had been the one to name her, so maybe it was French. Her parents had usually said "An-ray," without the *d*, but her teachers and friends had always called her "André," and so, for Jeffries, it became a choice: Which way should I say it in my own head? She settled on keeping the *d*.

She was a born-and-bred Nashvillian. For the first two years of her life she lived right off Jefferson on Phillips Street in her grandmother Ella's house, but when she was two her parents moved onto Marina Street in East Nashville. It was a small house, or at least that's how it felt to Jeffries, living there with an older brother and younger sister, and she used to ask her parents why they didn't just get a bigger one, considering they had good jobs. Her mother, Wilhelmina, was a first-grade teacher at Ford Greene, and her father was a supervisor at the main post office in downtown Nashville.

Wilhelmina was adventurous and inquisitive and spontaneous; she was fascinated by acrobats and could do flips and stand on her hands, but more than that, she wanted the kids to see there was an entire world outside of

Nashville. Because she had the summers off as a teacher, she would take all three of them on road trips. Jeffries was twelve when she took her first trip out of Nashville—her mom and her brother and another friend who had a license all piled into their 1959 Edsel and headed down to Dallas for a church retreat. Her father, however, wouldn't go along.

Bruce Prince was a quiet man. He didn't brag about his important job at the post office, and Jeffries didn't even realize her father was anything more than a postman until much later in life, when people came into her restaurant and told her, "Your daddy was my boss." He doted on his daughter André, though, and would always get her favorite strawberry ice cream from the corner store around the way from their house, especially if she'd just gotten a spanking from her mother.

As much as his wife loved to travel and explore, Prince didn't like to leave the neighborhood, let alone drive through six states to see the coast, so he'd stay around Nashville while the rest of the family went on these trips. He was also a night owl, always working the third shift at the post office, and Jeffries never once saw him working during the day. Her mother was independent and acted as if she didn't care that he wasn't there, but there was something amiss in the absence. Prince didn't move around with a ton of friends, but Jeffries suspects that was probably intentional, as he was a womanizer; if he'd kept about with a bunch of friends, that part of the story might've gotten out.

But, in fact, womanizing may have been the whole reason the Prince family had a business. Her father's uncle, Thornton Prince, owned a pig farm up off Nolensville Road. His other uncle was also in the post office business, and the funeral home business too, but back in segregated Nashville, if you wanted to make a living, you had multiple jobs both on and off the books to make things work and keep a little money in your pocket. The origin story of Thornton's second job, however, was famous.

The fame didn't necessarily clear up the factual accuracy of the story. There are several iterations, all of which shift according to who is telling the story. The main takeaway was this: Thornton was handsome. Often pictured in his white cowboy hat as an older man, he still gave off the vibe of an aesthetically engaging Hollywood actor playing a pig farm–owning serial philanderer who used to go on famous, night-long benders. But as the story goes, after one of these famous benders, his steady girl (or not—it's never been made clear) was tired of his cheating ways, and so she decided to make him a special breakfast of fried chicken. This, however, was not going to be any old fried chicken, friends. Oh no, she had a diabolical plan, and that plan was to spice the ever-living shit out of the chicken and break handsome Hollywood Thornton in half like a Kit Kat. In some tellings, this fed-up, heroic woman went out to the garden and collected a bunch of cayenne peppers she'd grown; in others, she just happened to have cayenne pepper and mustard seed around the house. Either way, she had a lot of hot spices, and she packed the chicken with them and then served it to Thornton. But much to her chagrin, Thornton liked the chicken. Actually, he loved it. So much so that after she left him, he dedicated all his spare time to trying to, *CSI* style, re-create the recipe in his own kitchen. Or . . . she just showed him how she cooked it, and repeated the recipe for his family and friends.

Whatever it was, Thornton realized there was a money-making opportunity in this fiery revenge chicken, and so, in the late 1930s, he decided to open an after-hours place where he could sell it at dinnertime on weekdays after he stopped working on the farm, and late into the night on the weekends. He started looking around for a space on Jefferson Street. Jefferson was the road that took you through Fisk University, a renowned African-American college housed in what was once an old Union Army camp. The street was the main thoroughfare in the African-American business community, and Thornton wanted to stay close. Finally, he found a space at Twenty-Eighth and Jefferson Street in Hadley Park, and opened his hot chicken destination. He decided he'd call it the BBQ Chicken Shack.

Before she owned it, Jeffries went to her great-uncle's hot chicken restaurant just twice. By the time she saw it, it had moved from its original location on Jefferson near the Missionary Baptist Church to a space downtown close to the famous Ryman Auditorium, home of the Grand Ole Opry. The area—known as Hell's Half Acre, thanks to its nineteenth-century reputation for lawlessness—was another African-American neighborhood, but its proximity to the famous performance venue meant they also occasionally drew in white folks, especially the musicians who were frequently performing in the area and kept strange hours. Country singer George Morgan was the BBQ Chicken Shack's most famous customer, and he became an evangelist for the food, often getting others to go eat it with him after performances.

Jeffries remembers her father taking her to the restaurant and showing her a small room painted green through a back door behind the kitchen. "This," he told her, "is where the white people eat." The Shack's popularity with white people during segregation had brought about an interesting issue. Though, of course, there was no law preventing whites from eating in primarily African-American establishments, the stigma of being seen was too much for some, and so Thornton got around this by inverting the segregated model, installing a "Whites Only" room through a back door.

Though she rarely went in, she had chicken every Sunday morning, as her father—after a night out—would invariably bring back a greasy bag and leave it on the stove for her mother to add to the Sunday-morning breakfast before church. As soon as they were awake, Jeffries and her siblings would race downstairs and fight over who got to have the choicest parts, but other than that weekly ritual, she paid no mind to the Shack for the better part of her childhood and teens.

She had better things to do. She'd gone to Ford Greene Elementary (where her mother had taught) across the street from her house, Washington Junior High, and then Pearl High School. Founded in 1897 and reconstructed in 1937, for a long time Pearl was considered the best, most modern African-American high school across the South, and Jeffries loved it. She was a beautiful, outgoing girl, and had no trouble socializing, so she sung in the choir and joined a high school sorority that performed at halftime for football games.

She first met Kermit Jeffries when she was in tenth grade. Three years older than her and from Birmingham, Alabama, Kermit was a friend of her older brother's at Tennessee State and pretty quickly developed a crush on her, but she wasn't allowed to date until she was sixteen. When she finally hit that age, Kermit was waiting to take her out, and dating was, as she puts it, "the bomb." There were Friday-night dances, and trips to the movie theater. On their first official date, Kermit took her to a little restaurant on Jefferson called the Mecca House, which was housed in the Dixon Building, alongside a barbershop, beauty parlor, and real estate office. The Mecca House was popular with college students over at Fisk and Meharry Medical College, and so it felt especially cool for a girl from Pearl High to be seen there with a handsome college gentleman. Plus, Jeffries had never been out to dinner before, so eating delicious pork chops, surrounded by older college kids and a cute date in a restaurant without her parents around, felt just about perfect. But there was a catch: as soon as her brother found out Kermit had eyes for her, he dropped their friendship like a hot cake. Even to this day, if Martin Prince sees Kermit Jeffries, the most Kermit's going to get out of him is "hello."

In 1964, Jeffries graduated from Pearl and started at Tennessee State. She was a biology major; she loved plants and animals, and had plans to be a pediatrician so she could take care of kids, and she was determined that would be her path in life. But she was also seriously dating Kermit. She loved that he was a romantic; he would always send her flowers, and leave notes, and he was the type of gentleman who would open the door for you and stay put until you got inside. As their relationship progressed and she fell more in love, she got pregnant.

Dreams played an important part in Jeffries's life. They would come up again and again in special ways, but the first of those important dreams happened while she was pregnant with her first child. Back then, they weren't testing for whether it was a boy or girl, but one night she had the most vivid dream, woke up, and told Kermit, "We're having a girl, and we're going to name her Yeae." She had never even heard of anyone with that name, but five months later, Yeae Jeffries was born.

Jeffries returned home for a time but eventually decided to go back to Tennessee State to try to finish her degree. And then she got pregnant again. This time, the name didn't come from a dream, but instead a Nina Simone concert. When her second daughter was born three years after Yeae, she named her Semone.

For a time, she and Kermit tried to make things work. They'd gotten married, and for the first three years she didn't have a job and stayed home with the girls. But as real life set in, the romanticism of their early years faded. Nearly every weekend, Kermit would come back from his job and go play cards. Even after segregation, public social activities were limited for African Americans, so most of the events revolved around either someone's home or the church. For Kermit and his friends, that meant card games. He'd go to someone's house on Friday night, play cards until the wee hours, come back Saturday to get something to eat, chill for a bit, then change clothes and go back. The card games wouldn't end until Sunday morning. To this day, Jeffries hates card games.

Eventually, Jeffries and Kermit divorced. Much like Jeffries as a child, their youngest daughter, Semone, was a daddy's girl, and the split devastated her. At four, she stopped learning altogether, refusing to read or interact in class at all, and they were forced to take her to a therapist. Jeffries moved her to a Seventh-day Adventist school, F. H. Jenkins, and they began to work with her closely and she started learning again, but it took a lot out of everyone.

By now, Jeffries was twenty-four, divorced, and jobless. She'd moved back in with her parents in the inner Nashville suburb of Bellevue, but she knew she needed work to support the kids and help pay the bills, so she started working at the north branch of the YMCA on Jefferson, and from there she went to the tax assessor's office downtown at the courthouse. For many years, Jeffries just got on with it. She took care of her two daughters, and worked for the tax assessor appraising property; she went on occasional dates but spent the majority of her social currency at the Gay-Lee Christian Church. And then, in 1979, she found out her mother had been diagnosed with an advanced form of breast cancer. The world stopped again.

MEANWHILE, THE BBQ CHICKEN SHACK had stalled out. After Hell's Half Acre was destroyed during an infamous urban redevelopment project, the Shack moved and then moved again, to Seventeenth and Charlotte, once they realized the initial location was too far out of town to attract any business. In the 1970s, mischievous ladies' man Thornton passed away, and his brother, Will Prince, took over the business, and he too was forced to move the restaurant, this time to Clarksville Highway and Twenty-Eighth. When Will passed away, his wife Maude's cousin and his wife came in to run it for a time. Their names were Bolton and Francis Polk.

The duration of time during which Polk and his wife, along with two twin cooks, ran the BBQ Chicken Shack is unclear, and the circumstances are fuzzy. Reports of Polk's role change with the story, as some identified him as a fry cook, or the actual cook, or sometimes a disgruntled business partner of Thornton's. Whatever it was, Maude Prince's cousin Bolton Polk was running the chicken shack for a time before Jeffries's mother got cancer. And very soon after her diagnosis, Jeffries's mother made sure the BBQ Chicken Shack went to her daughter.

Jeffries had dreamed about this moment too. In the late seventies, she was returning from visiting her brother in California, and he was accompanying her on the drive back to Nashville. They had a system: she would drive a hundred miles while he slept and then he'd do a hundred while she slept, and they kept switching off until they were done. At one point, she'd woken up with a vivid memory: she had a restaurant full of people and there were more people waiting outside. And after she did her hundred miles, right around Memphis, she went back to sleep and the dream picked up right where it had left off: she started dreaming of this business again, this restaurant of hers, and how it was always full of people.

She thought this was crazy because she wasn't a cook. At all. In fact, the only time she'd ever even been shown how to cook was when she was twelve and she was playing in the front yard with her friends and her mom yelled out her nickname, "Oranges!" and told her to come inside; her mom then showed her how to cut up a chicken, to split it down the middle and cut it into either fours or eights. But after that, her mother had never pursued teaching her more things in the kitchen, and Jeffries hadn't wanted to learn. But now here she was, with this restaurant.

At first, she was reluctant, because a) she didn't know what the hell she was doing, and b) she wasn't crazy about taking on two jobs. But her mother was adamant about it, especially as she got closer to death. When Wilhelmina finally succumbed to the cancer, the family took a few days and buried her on a Saturday. The next week, despite being distraught about her mother's passing, André Prince Jeffries had reopened the BBQ Chicken Shack under a new name, one she thought would honor the family that started it and, finally, accurately describe the kind of food they were selling: Prince's Hot Chicken Shack.

THE FIRST DAY WAS A DISASTER.

As she'd predicted, Jeffries didn't know what she was doing. She couldn't figure out how to cook the chicken and take care of orders and handle the hundreds of other little jobs a restaurant requires, so basically whoever walked in the door that day became a part-time employee. Thankfully, her sister had sent down a local boy named Michael, who'd just turned sixteen. Jeffries would soon hire him as her first cook.

Slowly, she started to piece it all together. For that first year, every day during the week she would get off her job at the tax assessor's office and head over to the Shack, open it up around six p.m., work until midnight, close it down, go home, and start the process all over again. And on the weekends, she stayed true to her great-uncle's original vision and stayed open until four a.m. The work burned her out, but she loved it—she'd always quietly wanted to have her own place, and she enjoyed the energy of the crowds. There was something particular about Americans—all you needed to do was look at them and they would tell you their entire history. She liked having the old heads coming in and telling her stories about working with her daddy or the trouble her great-uncle would get into; the drunks acting like fools at two a.m. after leaving clubs like Saturdays, making a big deal out of getting just the right meal, then falling asleep before they'd even finished eating their food; the couples eating the chicken as an aphrodisiac and then going off to their cars to blow off some steam. All of it was more entertaining than evaluating property for governmental tax purposes. So in 1981 she resigned from the tax assessor's office. She would make the Shack her full-time job.

The first thing she did was add lunch. Initially, this was strange for folks; it had always been a late-night place, and the idea of going in there with your kids seemed a bit off-putting, like having a family picnic in a fraternity basement during daylight hours. But that damn chicken brought them in.

Jeffries knew as long as they followed the family recipe, the chicken would be absurdly, almost aggravatingly good. She'd always loved it herself, especially the little flat part of the wing, that little bone in the middle. The batter was thin and crispy, the chicken incredibly moist, and the color looked like someone had taken normal fried chicken and twisted the red saturation knob all the way to the left. But the secret, of course, was the heat from the oil-based cayenne paste that covered the chicken. The heat came for you later, as if its clock was set to a different time zone. It was, as Jeffries called it, twenty-four-hour chicken. The pain was patient. It waited out your initial preparation, your readying of a glass of milk or some ranch dressing. It laughed as you ate the white bread it came sitting on. It let you think you got the best of it, that you'd conquered it. The heat played possum. And then it came seeking vengeance.

This too was Jeffries's idea. When her great-uncles owned the place, they only made the chicken one way, which she guessed to be her "mild" version, and that was still plenty spicy. But now that she had lunch, she'd heard folks with kids talking about how they wanted the kids to try it but it was too spicy for them. And then, of course, she'd heard other folks bragging about how they needed more heat. So she thought, Why don't we offer different levels of heat, from no spice all the way up to extra hot? Customize the experience? So around 1982 she made that happen.

Almost immediately, she noticed an uptick in business. Now the folks who brought their kids in for lunch could get them chicken with no spice at all if they felt like it, and guys who thought they were tough and could handle it could come get the hot or extra hot and hurt themselves. The chicken became a conversation piece—you could bring a date in and order hot and they could talk about it, give their opinions, and suffer together. In truth, Jeffries found that many, many more women ordered the extra hot than men. Guys would come in and order it once on a bet, get hurt, and never get it again. But the women would come back to it. Jeffries thought this made sense: women are fiery and have the rage in them and know the pain of childbirth, and if they could stand that, a little spicy chicken wouldn't hurt them. And speaking of childbirth, she'd seen plenty of pregnant women come in over the years, trying to stir the hornet's nest and get things moving with the chicken. It was a conversation piece and an aphrodisiac and a labor initiator. Her chicken was versatile.

She would never reveal the recipe. Later, as the years went by and the interviews piled up, folks would always try to get her to reveal little tidbits about it, sometimes with educated guesses, sometimes with lighthearted bullying, sometimes with almost rude interrogation techniques. Things would occasionally get out: that it was cooked in a cast-iron skillet (well, originally, before they got so popular they had to switch to deep fryers to speed up the process), that she used vegetable oil and not lard, that the chicken was marinated in . . . something. But most of the time, Jeffries would flash her golden smile, say "Lord have mercy!" and change the subject.

ONE DAY IN 1985, Jeffries was at her restaurant when there was a knock at the kitchen door. When she went to see who it was, she found a young boy standing there, asking if she had any work available. The boy's name was Mario Hambrick. He'd grown up in one of the more dangerous public housing units in the city, but from his youth, Hambrick just acted older.

Jeffries wasn't quite sure what to make of this child coming in asking for work, but she decided to make him a deal. She would pay him ten dollars a day to help out for a couple of hours after school. Excitedly, he agreed. She figured he might show up a couple more times and then lose interest, like a normal child. The next day, Hambrick was there, to wash windows and take out the trash and sweep and do anything else Jeffries asked. And then he was back the next day. And the next day. He never missed a single day of work.

She started giving him more challenging jobs, having him flour the chicken or even start to cook a little bit, and he took it all in stride. He never complained. And at the end of the day when she peeled off ten dollars and handed it to him, he would slip it in his pocket and then deliver it to his mother. She knew that in the Bible it said a child would lead, but she didn't think it would happen like this. Hambrick quickly became like a son to Jeffries and a sibling to her daughters.

As her daughters got older, Jeffries began to worry more about the time the restaurant was taking away from raising them. She had them come to the restaurant after school, and the two girls would often hang out in the front so she could keep an eye on them as they played the radio in their navy Chevette and ran across the street to the McDonald's to flirt with the guy at the register.

After graduating from high school, Yeae went off to Tennessee State.

While there, she majored in business, and the rest of the family assumed that she would come back and help Jeffries out with the Shack. But then she met a man and fell in love and moved to Tuscaloosa, Alabama, and got married and suddenly that idea was out the window. Semone, meanwhile, had gone off to Nashville Tech. Her true dream was to be a neonatal nurse in the air force, a flight nurse, but when she tried to go enlist, her mother wouldn't sign the papers, so she ended up at Tech and did well until she met a football player named Tim over at Tennessee State while visiting her friend's church. The story was eerily similar to Jeffries's own with Kermit.

And just like Jeffries, after a couple of years dating, Semone got pregnant and had a daughter, and though she and Tim tried to make that relationship work for a few years, eventually they parted ways, and Semone ended up back with Jeffries, bouncing around between school and jobs at Kroger, Anderson-Little, and other places around town, before she finally came back to work at her mom's restaurant. She didn't do so happily. She had hated the place. From her perspective, it had taken everything—her mom, her childhood—and now it was going to take her too. But she wasn't naive. She knew it paid the bills for the family, and so she went back, twenty-three years old, with a two-year-old daughter, doing every bottom job at her mother's restaurant, determined that it would only be a temporary thing until she figured out the rest of her life.

Jeffries had wanted to stay in her space and kept offering to buy the property, but the landlord didn't seem interested, constantly moving the price up and playing games until finally Jeffries got fed up and decided to move on. One day, as her father drove to the Sam's Club up off Dickerson Pike, he saw a "For Rent" sign on Ewing Drive, and made some inquiries. Once he knew it was available and they could afford the financing, he called Jeffries and told her Prince's Hot Chicken Shack had a new home. The next week, in the summer of 1989, they moved over to 123 Ewing Drive.

For thirty years, the Prince family had a monopoly on the hot chicken business in Nashville, but this changed in the late seventies when Bolton

Polk, Maude Prince's cousin who'd run the BBQ Chicken Shack before it went to Jeffries, opened his own business, which he called Columbo's Chicken Shack.

When Jeffries took over and revitalized her family's spot in 1980, the Nashville hot chicken scene suddenly had its own Cold War rivalry, complete with a defector backstory. And this is about the time Bill Purcell came into the picture.

Purcell was born in Philadelphia and grew up in suburban Pennsylvania, and he attended Hamilton College in upstate New York before moving to Nashville to go to Vanderbilt University School of Law. After graduating in 1979, he first worked as a lawyer at West Tennessee Legal Services for a couple of years, then spent four years in the Metropolitan Nashville Public Defender's Office, before getting elected to the Tennessee House of Representatives. While working in downtown Nashville, he discovered Columbo's and became addicted, eating there nearly every week until, in the late nineties, Nashville made a huge push to get an NFL team. As part of that, they started construction on a football stadium that would house said team (originally called Adelphia Coliseum), and Columbo's, sitting in the construction zone, was forced to close. Purcell was distraught, but had heard from other folks about Prince's Hot Chicken Shack, and so he journeyed out to Jeffries's joint and was blown away by the quality and the heat. He quickly befriended Jeffries and became a regular.

Meanwhile, by the mid-nineties Bolton Polk had fallen ill. Knowing he wouldn't be able to open another chicken shack before he passed, Polk confided his own hot chicken recipe to his nephew Leroy Bolton Matthews, who, alongside his wife, Dollye Ingram, opened up Bolton's Spicy Chicken and Fish in a small concrete building on Main Street in East Nashville in 1997.

Outside of the grumblings around origin, the Prince's and Columbo's/Bolton's rivalry didn't much matter from a financial perspective. Each restaurant had its own territory—Prince's up in North Nashville, and Bolton's in East Nashville—and for the next ten years, the food more or less remained a specialty confined to Nashville's African-American communities, occasionally receiving a shout-out from musicians, such as Yo La Tengo on their seventh album, *Electr-O-Pura*, which was recorded in Nashville and featured "Flying Lesson (Hot Chicken #1)" and "Don't Say a Word (Hot Chicken #2)."

Of course, there were a few places that tried to get involved in the hot chicken game during this time. Winner of Name Best Capturing the Zeitgeist of the First Dot-Com Bubble and most famous example was Hotchickens .com, a restaurant opened in 2001 and owned by country music hot chicken evangelist George Morgan's daughter (and country singer in her own right) Lorrie Morgan, along with her then-husband, fellow country singer Sammy Kershaw. As the story goes, Kershaw and Morgan offered a Prince's cook named Billy five thousand dollars to leave and cook for them, and they initially were incredibly popular, but a variety of factors (including Billy leaving) and the breakup of the Kershaw-Morgan marriage ended the business in just under five years, and Kershaw eventually filed for bankruptcy thanks to business debts related to the venture.

Other spots came and went as well. There was Boo's Spicy Hot Chicken on Donelson Pike, which closed in 2004. There was Wilma Kaye's in the early 2000s, but the proprietor, Wilma Kaye Hinshaw, was a Louisiana native, and so the spicy chicken fingers didn't quite fall into the same category.

But Bill Purcell's passion for hot chicken was impressive to the point of devotion. Before he left the Tennessee House of Representatives in 1996, he even proclaimed that Prince's Hot Chicken, "in recognition of extraordinary interest in governmental processes and for culinary excellence," should be named "The Best Restaurant in Tennessee," an extraordinary gesture (and most excellent public relations boon). On top of that, while in office, he'd worked to have the area around Prince's fall in his district so he could be said to represent their interests.

After leaving the House, Purcell spent the next few years back at Vanderbilt as director of the Child and Family Policy Center, before running and winning the race for mayor in Nashville in 1999. In 2003, he thrashed all comers, winning reelection with nearly 85 percent of the vote. At the end of that term, he had meetings discussing what to do for the city's two hundredth birthday party. Eventually, they came up with Celebrate Nashville, a nine-month-long party aimed at highlighting "the many things that make Nashville unique." It would start on the day Nashville was incorporated as a city (October 1) and end on the Fourth of July. He and his staff batted around ideas for a while, but they kept coming back to hot chicken.

As the one true hot chicken believer, Purcell had been the food's biggest public supporter for years, but here he realized, as a popular mayor in his last term, he actually had the capacity to truly do something to celebrate the food. After all, he thought, what other food is actually indigenous to Music City?

Excited by his seeming epiphany, Purcell reached out to Jeffries and said he had an idea he wanted to run past her: What did she think about being part of a little hot chicken festival in East Park on July 4?

CHAPTER 6

Freret Street, New Orleans, Louisiana, 2008, Part 1

They told Neal Bodenheimer and Matt Kohnke they were stupid. They said Freret Street was never the same after Bill Long Jr. got killed in '85 during a botched robbery attempt by a local teenage boy. Bill Long's Bakery had been serving challah and French bread and sandwiches at 4500 Freret since the 1930s, but after Long was killed the family closed it down. Coupled with the Canal Villere grocery store closing the year before, and the Barreca family turning their longtime restaurant Frank's Steakhouse into a catering business, the threads that seemed to hold the street together unraveled. There were no more walking businesses. By 1991, Nash Barreca had even closed the catering side of the business. The Barreca family, who'd been there since the 1930s and owned most of the block, were blamed then for letting it languish into a blighted landscape. Even the Krewe of Freret stopped building floats for Carnival and disbanded. About the only place anyone went anymore was Celestine Dunbar's Creole Cooking for all-you-can-eat red beans and rice, and the white high schoolers from Newman and Sacred Heart and college professors and administrators from Tulane and Loyola mostly only went during lunch.

Residents black and white alike started to view Freret as daytime-only, and the shops that came in or survived—nail salons and Dennis' Barber Shop and Bean's Formal Wear and the discount seafood market and the auto shops—mostly all shut down by the evening. Federal money that had come in for the Neighborhood Commercial Revitalization Program in 1978, which had helped build the drugstore and the veterinarian's office, dried up. The drugstore closed. There was a Domino's Pizza, but it was surrounded by bulletproof glass and survived on delivery or quick takeout. The nonprofit Neighborhood Housing Services, headquartered at Freret and Valence, did what it could, creating a community garden and a street festival and trying to restore blighted homes, but after commissioning a study of the neighborhood by the University of New Orleans, the nonprofit was faced with an uphill battle to change, as Coleman Warner put it in his 2001 *Louisiana History* journal article, the "public perception of lawlessness in Freret."

Then came Katrina. Hurricane Katrina decimated nearly all of Freret, with water rising four or five feet into most of the properties on the street. The veterinarian's office shut down. Dunbar's was forced to close and move onto Loyola's campus. At this point, the only real night-time business on the block was a bastion of underage drinking called Friar Tuck's (although Tulane students frequented it, in New Orleans parlance it was considered a "high school bar").

And it was at this point, in April 2008, that Bodenheimer and Kohnke decided to purchase an old electrician shop in an even older firehouse across from Bean's at 4905 Freret.

Both Kohnke and Bodenheimer were from New Orleans, but Bodenheimer was living in New York at the time of Katrina. He came back within a year, pulled by the same sort of indescribable, magnetic energy that brought so many New Orleanians back to the city after the storm. Bodenheimer had been actively trying to open a bar in New York, and when he told Kohnke about his idea, Kohnke, a builder, partnered with him. "I've got just the place," he said. Both their families, from their parents to their siblings to their cousins, told them Freret Street was a bad idea. It was unsafe. It was dead. No one wanted to compete with Bean's Formal Wear.

But Kohnke could see it. All the infrastructure was there. People used the street to get uptown and downtown. It had been a Jane Jacobs–approved walking neighborhood before.

"It's going to be amazing," he told Bodenheimer.

"At least we can afford it," Bodenheimer told him.

The idea was to have a stand-alone destination cocktail bar. They wanted to call it Apothecary, but it was illegal in Louisiana to have that name if you weren't a pharmacy. Another name was put forth, evocative of that idea of taking your medicine.

They would call it Cure.

CHAPTER 7

Phil Ward, New York City, New York, Part 1

In the seventies and eighties and into the nineties, most cocktails sucked. It wasn't that you couldn't get a good cocktail anywhere—there were still steakhouses and the occasional old-school bar where they stirred their martinis and could make a functional old-fashioned—but they weren't cool. There was a logic to this: most of the people going out during these decades had been kids during the sixties, when all besuited working adult males apparently drank three to four martinis at lunch, slept on the couch in their office until it was time to take the train home, had another couple cocktails during a dinner primarily made up of meats captured in gelatin, and then passed out in their undershirts while their wives secretly fantasized about trysts with socially liberal Republican politicians.

But then America had its cultural revolution, and suddenly everything classic was old. As cities declined and became daytime work centers for white-flight suburb dwellers, architecturally interesting downtowns were blown up and replaced with parking lots. Music became generationally divided and fractured. As the younger generations started having casual sex and protesting America's nascent foray into secret wars, they looked at the old people starting these wars and judging their music, and thought their archaic drinking rituals were something to be ridiculed, not replicated.

As the sixties morphed into the seventies, the "fern" bar movement gained traction. Fern bars were essentially bars where women felt comfortable drinking, ostensibly because having ferns, couches, lamps, and other home-decor items made it feel more like someone's apartment party, which was allegedly the only place you'd find morally appropriate single women in that era. So places like the original T.G.I. Friday's in New York City and Henry Africa's and Perry's on Union Street in San Francisco became sensations, both for the single women of that time and the men who wanted to meet them. The cocktails at these places were sweet and sugary, under the asinine assumption that women didn't have the palate for balanced drinks.

This style of bar proliferated around the country as disco took hold, and the "disco drinks" of that era essentially borrowed the fern bar template and shoved it into a more audacious jumpsuit. Thick blended or shaken drinks using coconut cream, Baileys Original Irish Cream, or really any other cream-based liqueur became popular. As did neon tiki knockoffs using melon liqueur or blue curaçao. Cocktails made with sour mix and/or orange juice concentrate provided sugary bursts of energy while you did the Funky Chicken or the Bump. As the seventies turned into the eighties, and everyone started purchasing Memphis Milano blocky couches in loud, clashing colors and Patrick Nagel prints of 2-D glamazon women who all kind of looked like Demi Moore, bars cared less and less about the actual cocktails themselves, and more and more about the Tom Cruise in *Cocktail* glamour and pageantry and the Michael J. Fox in *Family Ties* hip, young, Republican, "greed is good" ethos. Also using drugs.

My God, the drugs. Cocaine was the lead actor, and everything about its effects—the irrational confidence, the brashness, the energy, and the bloody noses—seemed exactly in line with the country's exuberance. But quaaludes, snorted heroin, and plain old marijuana all found themselves in the mix too, effectively drowning out the importance of alcohol and pushing it into a supporting role, the public face of a night mostly spent consuming illicit substances in private.

Vodka skyrocketed in popularity mostly because its tastelessness enabled it to act as a willing dance partner in nearly any concoction. At first, Stolichnaya became the vodka of choice, as drinking something Russian and imported gave it almost an air of danger; but after the Soviet Union shot down Korean Air Flight 007 en route from New York City to Seoul via Alaska on September 1, 1983, killing all 269 passengers and crew aboard, Russian goods were boycotted en masse. Into the void stepped Absolut, a Swedish vodka company that had been gaining some traction due to its staggeringly popular ad campaign, first created by the agency TBWA in 1980, with the iconic "Absolut Perfection" tagline. The combination of the campaign and the Russia boycott cemented Absolut's place as the brand of choice during vodka's moment, and helped spawn an era of Absolut martinis, cranberries, and infusions.

Peach schnapps, however, was right there too, sloshing clumsily at vodka's heels. DeKuyper's Original Peachtree Schnapps sold two million cases in 1986, only its second year of sales. Other brands quickly got into the game as well, and by 1988, there were more than forty peach schnapps on the market, helping to fuel a late-eighties full-on peach-flavoring fetish, followed closely by kiwi. These were dark days, friends.

But into this cocaine-fueled, peach-fetishizing, flair-bartending hellscape stepped legendary restaurateur Joe Baum, who calmly decided to alter the course of cocktail history.

BY THE EIGHTIES, Baum had done pretty much everything you could do in the New York restaurant world. In 1954 he got his first chance in the New York area, turning what seemed like an impossible task—managing a fancy restaurant in Newark Airport—into a financially successful business. Working for blandly threatening, mafia-sounding Restaurant Associates, he opened several incredibly popular and influential restaurants in the late fifties, including Four Seasons, Forum of the Twelve Caesars, and La Fonda del Sol. In the seventies, he created all twenty-two World Trade Center restaurants, including Windows on the World, and consulted on restaurants all over the country, from Montreal to Kansas City. But it was his 1986 eclectic French restaurant Aurora, and the person he picked to run the bar, that helped put the cocktail renaissance's wheels in motion.

Like most longtime bartenders, Dale DeGroff was actually an actor. In the seventies, while not getting acting gigs in New York, he worked at one of Baum's spots, Charley O's, as a waiter and service bartender, making Irish coffees for senator Daniel Patrick Moynihan. After Charley O's, he spent years bartending at the Hotel Bel-Air. In 1985, he moved back to New York City to run the bar at Aurora for Baum, who demanded a classic cocktail bar with none of the bullshit shortcuts popular at the time: no juice concentrates or sour mix, no soda guns, nothing.

Baum, who spoke in a sort of mumbling, cryptic code, told DeGroff to check out *How to Mix Drinks: Or, The Bon Vivant's Companion* by Jerry Thomas, a bible of cocktails first published in 1862. After scrounging around, he finally located an old copy of the book and was captivated by the drink recipes. His classic cocktail list for Aurora was well received, especially the Ritz, which was topped with champagne and a flaming orange peel, a flashy move DeGroff had first seen at Chasen's in Los Angeles. For a while, Aurora was one of the hottest restaurants in New York, but then, on Black Monday, October 19, 1987, the Dow fell 508 points and everything the eighties stood for seemed to fall apart. Aurora had to let more than half its staff go, and the entire place, which closed quietly a couple of years later, was never the Place to Be Seen again.

But soon Baum moved on, and was working on the twenty-five-million-dollar Rainbow Room renovation in Rockefeller Center. The Room, sixty-five floors up, had originally opened in 1934 and been the glamorous event space for the boldly named philanthropy set of that era, but had since fallen off and was badly in need of a revitalization. Baum wanted to re-create the 1930s glamour, almost literally, with women in pillbox hats selling cigars and cigarettes and a bar program that, as much as possible, authentically captured the post-Prohibition spirit. DeGroff went to work researching era-appropriate drinks for the Promenade Bar in the Rainbow Room and created a sixteen-cocktail list, filled with classics most of the world had forgotten, like the original Hemingway Daiquiri, the Pisco Sour (a sly nod to Baum's fifties Latin-American joint Fonda del Sol), and the Ramos Gin Fizz. He also created a few of his own, including the Gin Thing, a simple shaken drink with simple syrup, lemon, and angostura bitters, which was eventually rechristened the Fitzgerald to better fit with the 1930s vibe.

As at Aurora, they followed Baum's rules regarding fresh juices and soda guns, but DeGroff, having fully caught the cocktail geek bug, took it further, sourcing hard-to-find liquors and bitters and making "tribute" drinks most people in America hadn't seen in decades, being careful to offer up a works cited list with their origin stories, as with the Mary Pickford (Hotel Nacional de Cuba, Havana, c. 1920). He also actively banned "disco drinks" and kept a list of the worst offenders, as if the drinks themselves were folks he'd previously banned from the bar.

Visiting DeGroff's bar at the Rainbow Room became a must for nearly everyone in New York even remotely interested in drinking, but especially for the newly identified "yuppie" class, who were better traveled and wealthier than their parents, and thus more concerned with knowing and talking about food, especially in a place packed every night with eighties celebrities. Cher. De Niro. Liz Taylor. Tina Turner. Rich people who'd been at Julian Schnabel and Jacqueline Beaurang's wedding. DeGroff, a natural charmer and storyteller, could play all the Tom Cruise *Cocktail* flair bartender notes and, on top of that, could free-pour incredibly well-balanced drinks. As former *New York Times* restaurant critic and eighties *Esquire* cocktail columnist William Grimes put it, the Rainbow Room was DeGroff's own little "Wurlitzer organ, cranking out the fabulous sounds of cocktail music no one else was playing." As word got out, industry folk started showing up just to watch him work. Trend watchers braced for a cottage industry of DeGroff copycats and

Rainbow Room knockoffs through the end of the eighties and into the nineties.

It never came.

BUT THERE WERE GLIMMERS of classic cocktail culture. At the beginning of the decade there was the Odeon, which Keith McNally opened in 1980, a brasserie whose deco-style bar served perfectly competent classics (and famously no Long Island Iced Teas) to a celebrity-laden clientele of artists, actors, and people who ingested drugs in a British phone booth with Jay McInerney. If you were old or funded by a Condé Nast expense account, the small nook of the Blue Bar in the Algonquin Hotel would serve you fitting classics under Al Hirschfeld drawings.

During the nineties, *Sex and the City*'s band of hip thirtysomethings, gossiping about sexual escapades while hanging out in clubs that had replaced couches with beds, helped usher in the rise of the Cosmopolitan (ironically invented by bartender Toby Cecchini as a staff drink at the Long-Island-Iced-Tea-banning Odeon). In 1996, the surprise indie hit *Swingers* brought about a short-lived interest in 1940s culture, including old-school cocktail joints and cocktails, but people soon tired of wearing suspenders and learning to swing dance to the Cherry Poppin' Daddies. At the turn of the millennium, vodka was still king, spawning an out-of-control arms race of vodka martini riffs that went to dark corners, bottoming out with the rise of the Appletini. During this somewhat shameful time period, a few bartenders and places separated themselves from the pack with a focus on quality and technique, like Fred McKibbin's Grace, Michael Waterhouse's Dylan Prime, Keith McNally's ode to Russian vodka, Pravda (DeGroff trained the bartenders), Toby Cecchini's eclectic bar Passerby, and Del Pedro and Toby Maloney's Grange Hall. And then there was Angel's Share.

A second-floor bar located in the back of an East Village Japanese restaurant, Angel's Share was opened in 1994 by the seemingly anonymous, behind-the-scenes owner who wanted to quantum-leap the exact Tokyo cocktail bar experience into New York. While American bartending had turned into some sort of vaudevillian juggling show/poetry slam, for decades Japanese bartending focused almost exclusively on what we now think of as "craft."

Everything about Angel's Share went against not only everything popular in American bar culture at the time but also general business marketing practices. The bar itself was an almost-impossible-to-find hushed cocktail seminary in the back of a nondescript restaurant. There was zero advertising. There were rules. It was not entirely welcoming. Unlike Rainbow Room, Angel's Share had a distaste for notoriety, which, combined with its practice of exclusively hiring Japanese bartenders (many of whom spoke limited English), made it feel like a one-off. But because the world is backward and makes little logical sense, the very fact that it was unapproachable made it exactly the perfect muse for a Manhattan Communist with a Trotsky haircut who wanted to open a bar.

Sasha Petraske liked old things. Jazz. Two-toned shoes. Marxist theories. Sasha Petraske also liked order and rules. He'd spent three years in the army, and there are certain things about a life organized to the extreme that are soothing to a peripatetic mind. After wandering the world both in and out of service, Petraske returned to New York and worked in the East Village wine and beer bar Von, but spent many nights in Angel's Share, astonished by the atmosphere and unassailable technical savvy of the bartenders. Petraske longed to open a bar of his own, and eventually got a tiny space on Eldridge in the Lower East Side, renovating it using every single dime he had, plus whatever money he could beg and borrow from friends. On New Year's Eve, 1999, the day before Y2K, he opened the little bar, which he'd named Milk & Honey.

If Rainbow Room brought back classic post-Prohibition cocktails and made them with the fresh, quality juices and care of the pre-Prohibition era (when high-quality bartending was a profession and before drinkers' palates were ruined by bathtub gin), and Angel's Share showcased the art of the process and craft of building a drink in an unmarked, unpublicized, rule-based environment designed to sanctify cocktails, Milk & Honey was the crossroads of those two ideas and the place where American cocktail culture would exist, especially once Petraske's own eclectic, vintage-feeling tastes for retro suits, old music, and inclusion of a Byzantine reservation-only system were factored into the equation. It would become the most influential cocktail bar in the world.

Julie Reiner was an outlier. After growing up mostly in Hawaii, Reiner spent time working in bars in San Francisco before moving out to New York in 1998 to take a bar manager gig at a place called C3. At the bar she became known for her creative booze infusions, which led to media coverage, which led to sour grapes from the C3 chef, which led to her unemployment.

A friend linked her up with wealthy socialites, and they offered to go in on a bar with her, but only if she'd put up her own money. She borrowed and scraped together sixty thousand dollars, and she and her partner and girlfriend from San Francisco, Susan Fedroff, opened Flatiron Lounge in May 2003. Flatiron was not a precious, tiny cocktail nook. Reiner's vision was that the drinks needed to be solid and balanced and correct, but they also needed to be done quickly and in volume. There would be art, but there would also be commerce, and they needed to hire competent people who could get things done right, and fast. So they put an open call on Craigslist. And that's when Phil Ward showed up.

Ward grew up in Pittsburgh, in the Mount Washington neighborhood, aka Coal Hill, aka Where You Can Take Old Wooden Cable Car to the Top with All the Goddamn Tourists. After high school, Ward had spent a year in community college, and another one at Indiana University of Pennsylvania, and then a few more years back in Pittsburgh working server and bartender jobs, until, by 2002, he had saved up enough money to travel in Europe and Africa for four months. Though he felt ambivalent about Europe, Ward found glory in Tunisia, checking out Roman ruins in El Djem, riding camels, popping into random little dusty towns, and finding their little one-room drinking clubs, where he could sit with a beer and boiled beans and watch life go by. Then with his last remaining funds he flew to New York City because it was nine hundred dollars cheaper than Pittsburgh. He loved that you could explore New York without a car, but he needed a job, so he scoured Craigslist and found one waiting tables at Michael White's Fiamma Osteria during Restaurant Week. It was horrible. The only thing that made it less horrible was that after Restaurant Week, they fired him. Every day after that, he checked Craigslist, and a few days into his early retirement, something interesting came up. A new drinking spot had an open barback call. It was called the Flatiron Lounge. Though Julie Reiner mistook the lanky Ward, whose mullet at the time was nearing full strength, for a homeless person, Susan Fedroff recognized something beyond his Tennessee top hat hairstyle and hired him as a barback.

Working under Reiner was a revelation. She was whip-smart and empathetic, but immediately called you on your shit. At the time, Ward was in the volume-alcohol-consumption phase of his life, always looking to maximize his booze intake for the cheapest possible price, ordering terrible disco-era drinks that had been outlawed at the Odeon since 1980. But watching Reiner work, Ward could tell this was no Southside Pittsburgh Yinzer bar where Kamikazes and Irish Car Bombs reigned. Reiner's fluency and speed and technique impressed him, but anyone can learn to pour things quickly. It was only when he tasted the quality of the drinks that he realized Reiner was playing chess while he'd been throwing rocks at stop signs.

The cocktails weren't overly sweet or sour or stiff or watered down. They were balanced, which was a term Ward hadn't really associated with cocktails before. Recognizing his eagerness, Reiner gave him newer books like DeGroff's *The Craft of the Cocktail*, cocktail historian David Wondrich's *Esquire Drinks*, Gary Regan's *The Joy of Mixology*, and Ted Haigh's *Vintage Spirits and Forgotten Cocktails*. And older books like Charles Henry Baker's *The Gentleman's Companion* and Jerry Thomas's *How to Mix Drinks*. Ward, whose general modus operandi is not liking things, liked these books. He liked the fact that cocktail books existed in the first place. He liked looking through DeGroff's recipes and thinking about how to build drinks. But even more so, he liked reading Baker's stories about different drinks' origins, because his pompous style meant you got some history, plus a breakdown of who Baker was with at the time, and weird recipe clues like "three squeezes of lemon" and "a pony of vermouth."

Ward quickly went from a competent worker to the best barback at Flatiron, essentially implanting himself in Reiner's brain, becoming a *Minority Report*–style precog who could see ahead of time exactly the ingredients she'd need to make future drinks. And Flatiron was making a ton of drinks. The bar was hugely successful, regularly doing over ten thousand dollars in sales a night. But Ward's competency was tempered by his refusal to conform to hygiene and style norms, and Reiner kept shying away from making him an actual bartender. His first shot came by accident, when a new hire for the downstairs bar bailed on a Sunday shift. Ward worked the shift, and everything went smoothly, so Ward began to lobby Reiner on Tuesdays when they worked together for more opportunities behind the bar. Finally, possibly because he succumbed to peer pressure and got a normal person's haircut, Reiner let him work in "the Hole," the downstairs bar. This was his chance. Phil Ward was officially a serious cocktail bartender.

ANOTHER BARTENDER who would become instrumental to Ward's development was Audrey Saunders. Saunders came from the DeGroff school, basically volunteering for free at cocktail events DeGroff worked for years before he asked her in 1999 to join Blackbird, his next project after the Rainbow Room. Despite DeGroff's magic, Blackbird failed within a year, and Saunders found herself bouncing around to places like Beacon, Tonic, and Bemelmans bar in the Carlyle Hotel. During this time, she began to move on from just refining classics to inventing drinks (her signature, the Gin-Gin Mule, came from her time at Beacon), and the city's cocktail nerds started paying attention.

With Flatiron printing money, Reiner's business partners wanted to open another bar. She reached out to Saunders at Bemelmans and explained the project. Saunders was down to do it, but only if it could be her baby—she was tired of playing second fiddle. Reiner agreed, and after a long buildout, Pegu Club opened up in August 2005. The timing was right: not only were the public and the media starting to catch wind of the nascent rebirth of the cocktail scene, but there was finally a roster of bartenders around the city who could actually execute the types of cocktails Saunders envisioned. The only problem: most of them worked at Flatiron.

By this time, Ward was starting to come into his own. Although he was technically the head bartender at Flatiron, this was more of a glorified assistant to Reiner, who wisely unloaded most of the annoying parts of her job onto Ward. But when he wasn't crawling into a half-size space in the attic to count liquor bottle inventory, he was experimenting. As Pegu was being built, Saunders had basically set up the downstairs of Flatiron as her office, where she could experiment and make plans. She and Ward would talk cocktails, and she taught him some of her own recipes, including her famous Gin-Gin Mule.

One day, Susan Fedroff asked Ward to make her a drink. Knowing she liked whiskey, he decided to try a play on the Gin-Gin Mule template but substitute whiskey for the gin, and lemon for the lime, because lemon's flavor profile paired much more smoothly with whiskey. Fedroff tried it, and liked it, and it scrambled Ward's circuits that he could just find and replace similar elements in a drink and make a completely different but equally formidable cocktail. In Ward's mind, it was like playing with one of those Mr. Potato Head dolls from the eighties. You could change out the eyes, or the nose, or the ears, and create hundreds of different looks for the doll, but if you tried to, say, put lips where the eyes used to be, or a nose in the ear hole, most of the time it wouldn't look right. It was the same way with cocktails. You needed to identify what type of element you were replacing (base spirit, modifying spirit, citrus, sweetener, etc.) and try to put something similar in its place. If you could do that, the possibilities for new cocktails were infinite. Ward named his come-to-Jesus moment after those dolls, and within a few years, the "Mr. Potato Head" cocktail creation strategy was being used by bartenders all over the world.

Saunders expressed interest in Ward coming to Pegu as part of the original opening team. Reiner wasn't psyched—most of her best bartenders were going to Pegu, with her blessing, of course, because she was a partial owner—so Ward agreed to at least initially split time between the two spots until Reiner could find and train up some suitable replacements.

When Ward began working at Pegu Club, he couldn't get over the level of talent and creativity shown by the other bartenders. At Flatiron, Reiner was very clearly the creative motor behind the cocktail list, and while most bartenders there had great technique, they weren't spending time innovating. Partially, of course, that was because they didn't have time to, being jammed every night. But at Pegu it was just a crew of hyper-geeky cocktail nerds like Toby Maloney and Jim Meehan, who were always down to test new drinks and talk through obscure cocktail manuals and really get into the weeds. Saunders loved the weeds. This was her comfort zone. She was famous for the meticulous and particular way she tested drinks, making two dozen of one cocktail with only teensy adjustments until she was happy with it. She was a true cocktail geek, and used to spend hours in the shadowy online cocktail forum world, on message boards like eGullet, battling with other nerds about recipes and origins. And she also knew how to get press. Saunders was already a name in the New York Food Mafia world; she was *New York* magazine's 2004 pick for Best Cocktail Genius, and a reliable contact for a quotation alongside Reiner, cocktail historian and *Esquire* drinks columnist David Wondrich, and DeGroff.

By August 2005, Pegu Club's opening hype was deafening. The combination of Saunders and her all-star crew, backed by the Flatiron folk just as the cocktail scene was entering the common enthusiast's consciousness, propelled it to instant popularity. And there was a certain glory to it at the beginning, as Saunders was able to unleash her creativity among a crew of bartenders who could not only execute her vision but help expand it. With a packed house each night, and essentially the cocktail bartending team equivalent of that early-nineties Mickey Mouse Club crew featuring Timberlake, Spears, Aguilera, and *Ryan Gosling for God's sake*, Pegu Club should've been the cocktail bartender utopia. But beneath the surface, the foundation was shaky.

Partially, Saunders was stressed. The initial general manager had quit quickly, and so Saunders was basically doing that job too (she had a host named Mario deputized to do voids, but that was about it), while dealing with the bullshit that goes into running a place and trying to be the creative firepower and face of the bar. While no one seemed to dispute Saunders's creative genius, her biggest weakness seemed to be a fear of ceding any responsibility to others. This made sense because of the way Saunders had come up, fighting and scrapping for a well-deserved place at the table after years of putting in work on her own time as a second career, and now that she had it, she was determined to make it all work. But the burden of carrying all that weight on her shoulders touched others, and as Pegu Club hit its first birthday in the summer of 2006, the initial class of bartenders began to look around.

When the original head bartender, Toby Maloney, left, Ward took his place. Suddenly he was head bartender of the hottest cocktail bar in New York, and possibly the world. This should've been a moment of happiness and reflection and satisfaction and possibly even a new haircut, but Ward felt stress. He felt stress from the douche Murray Hill squad in untucked buttondowns and vanity jeans, six deep at the bar, shouting out names of drinks he wouldn't make and alcohols he didn't stock. He felt the stress of being part of an overstaffed rotation where no one made serious money the way you should if you're working at the best bar in the city. He felt the stress of working at a bar that doesn't close until four a.m., even though no one really wanted serious cocktails after two. The success and the press adulation was a double-edged sword that constantly felt like it was getting closer to his neck. So Ward did what he usually did in these moments: he went on Craigslist and started poking around for jobs.

DAVID KAPLAN, AT HIGH SCHOOL IN WYOMING, built a tiki bar with laminated menus filled with Polynesian theme drinks filled with flavored brandies. In college he built an L-shaped bar and retrofitted a dual keg out of a freezer in the Rochester house he'd bought for twenty thousand dollars. In the early 2000s he turned into a VIP host in Vegas, making sure the important people at Ghostbar and Rain got the proper water-park-esque bracelets and stepped into the right elevators. He moved to New York in 2006 and got a job at the *Vice* magazine retail store, because in 2006 a *Vice* magazine retail store actually sounded like a strong financial idea. He wanted to build his own bar in real life in New York, but he had no clue how to build a real bar in a real city, so he resorted to hanging out in real bars, literally reading *Running a Bar for Dummies*, and anything else he thought might help out.

He befriended the owner of the wine bar below him, an artist named Ravi DeRossi, and asked if he wanted to open another bar. Surprisingly, DeRossi was into it and also knew about a space a block away. He took over an old Indian restaurant's space at 433 East Sixth Street and created mood boards and a walk-through of what the bar should look like, even though he was not an architect or a general contractor or even someone who should know how to do that sort of thing. He then executed that plan with DeRossi and two other guys and no contractor, and managed to pull off a dark, cavernous hideaway, equal parts speakeasy and cave, a drinking aperture of inky

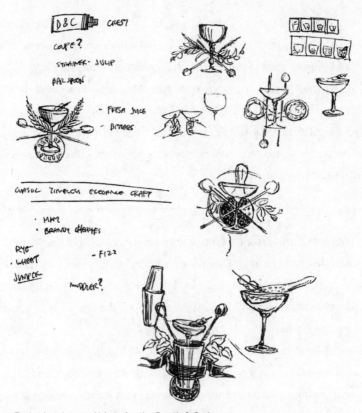

Early sketches and ideas for the Death & Co logo

blackness. The marble bar dominated the room, and felt like an altar at church. The space was so dark it verged on unsettling and sinister, like a tabernacle in a dim chapel. The layered wood ceiling's planks looked like a reconstruction of what light speed in a *Star Wars* movie would feel like in an old western theater. The unfinished concrete wall made it feel like they'd created the entire bar as a pop-up in a subway tunnel.

He envisioned a massive brass-and-cedar door with a sculpted angel handle that looked like something out of Gondor during the reign of Hyarmendacil, and the name "Death & Co," which he'd learned was both a phrase used in fake propaganda posters made by underground speakeasy bars to fool the anti-alcohol temperance movement and the title of a Dashiell Hammett short story, and that seemed about right. He took the first-ever Bar Alcohol Resource program from Dale DeGroff, David Wondrich, and several other cocktail industry dons to learn as much as possible before opening.

And when he posted an impassioned plea on Craigslist for people to work at this serious bar he'd built in the most serious real city in America, he received a cryptic response from a guy named Phil Ward, telling him, "I've been head bartender at two top cocktail bars in New York." David Kaplan was barely twenty-five years old.

WARD SAW THE DEATH & CO CRAIGSLIST AD because nothing makes a man feel more alive than going on Craigslist, checking out *new york > manhattan > jobs > food/bev/hosp*, and scrolling past job opportunities for wedding caterers, pastry assistants, and bike deliverers to find the one ad that actually mentions cocktails.

The day he went to Death & Co's open call, Ward saw the craziest fucking sunset. He was living at a place in Williamsburg with a balcony, and was sitting on it, sipping an Americano, when he saw this weird, ominous sky and felt like it was a sign of something, so he went and bought a really cool leather jacket, then met up with Kaplan. They talked for a bit and Kaplan asked him to fill out a questionnaire mostly filled with icebreaker questions like "Where do you like to go drink?" and "What's your favorite cocktail?" The one serious question Kaplan came up with was "Name as many bitters as you can." He was looking for potential bartenders to maybe know Angostura and hopefully one other. Ward wrote down sixteen, then told Kaplan he was on the clock at Pegu starting at eight p.m., and invited him to come in that night so he could make him some drinks.

After showcasing a few of his Mr. Potato Head specialties, Ward continued to meet with Kaplan, except now he was the one leading the interviews. Despite outwardly projecting cocksureness, Ward was nervous as hell, because sitting at a job at the best cocktail bar in NYC and leaving for a place no one knew about in the East Village, one run by a twenty-five-year-old first-time bar owner, seemed absolutely ludicrous. So he pressed Kaplan about ice and glassware and hours and alcohols, and this twenty-five-year-old kid seemed to have a pretty good handle on what he was doing and what he wanted to do, and Kaplan didn't want control, or maybe it was more that he knew enough to know he didn't know enough. This was not a Dale DeGroff bar or a Julie Reiner bar or a Sasha Petraske bar or an Audrey Saunders bar. The drink program at Death & Co wouldn't come from up high. If he wanted the gig, Ward, for the first time in his life, would be given all the keys to every door in the cocktail castle. Right before Thanksgiving in 2006, Phil Ward became the first head bartender of Death & Co.

Ward had about two weeks to put together the initial cocktail list. He wanted to start small, because he didn't know the other bartenders and cocktail waitresses and barbacks and what they'd be capable of, and anyway, he liked the idea of building off of a core list. His initial menu, the first cocktail list in Death & Co's history, would have seven cocktails: five originals and two seasonal specialties.

The St. Matilda was a play on La Pera, basically the first cocktail Ward got on the menu at Flatiron. The Mig Royale was based off a classic Savoy cocktail, and fulfilled Ward's desire for a champagne drink, despite having what Ward estimated to be the worst name in the history of cocktail names. The Daisy Day Martinique paid homage to the Daisy de Santiago from Charles Baker's book *Gentleman's Companion*. It took a while for Ward to figure out the measurements, as Baker would use weird language to describe quantities, but once he realized it was two parts different boozes, three-quarter citrus, half simple syrup, and half Chartreuse, this became Ward's go-to template on at least twenty drinks. Devil in a Dress was the classic epiphany drink he'd first made for Susan Fedroff at Flatiron. The Martica was a play on the Martinez, with a split base of Jamaican rum and cognac. Those last two were inspired by an Old-Fashioned and a fizz, but with Laird's Apple Jack and Vermont maple syrup because they'd just gotten the booze and loved it, and also because it was Christmas time.

Death & Co opened after Christmas, 2006, and its first few weeks were relatively tranquil. But on January 14, 2007, in the Sunday *New York Times* Styles section, a piece titled "Come to Our Club. Or Not. Whatever." roped the bar in with various other hard-to-get-into restaurants and bars across NYC, saying that they "rely on techniques, some from the speak-easy era, like obscure locations, secret (and oft-changed) reservation numbers and 'soft openings' that cater to insiders, to create the perception of exclusivity. While these are well-worn sleights of hand, a flurry of subtle arrivals suggests that small and quiet is back in vogue."

It didn't matter that Death & Co had actively tried to avoid the illusion of exclusivity with its first-come, first-serve ethos; the (Sunday!) *Times* had spoken. The next day, and basically every day after, there was a line when the bar opened.

On its face, it shouldn't have worked. There were many, many mistakes and other problems outside their control. The use of an old-timey cash register and hand-recorded books was an absolute accounting disaster. The fact that behind the bar, there was just one little hand sink, plus a little plastic tub filled up with hot water to rinse glasses, was stupid and silly and somewhat inconceivable. The dozen-beer, sixty-bottle-of-wine side of the initial menu was a complete dud. The business side of things, mostly thanks to the bartenders being given carte blanche to order whichever liquors they needed, no matter how expensive, was not healthy at all. A hellish upstairs neighbor in a Pogues cover band didn't help, as his outlandish noise complaint fictions forced the bar into a protracted legal battle, causing them to have to shut down at midnight each night and throw out a full house of paying customers and a wait list full of more of them. And yet somehow it did.

Death & Co became the greatest example of the modern cocktail movement, a mash-up of a mash-up of a mash-up, organically market-tested to perfection. There was the tranquil, romantic speakeasy vibe of Milk & Honey, without having to go through the charade of finding the unlisted number and making a reservation. There were modern, innovative cocktails like those at Pegu Club, without a crowd of bros six deep behind your chair trying to understand why they couldn't order Red Bull Vodkas. As with Employees Only, there was a food menu, so you didn't just down four old-fashioneds and fall over. There was the spirit and democratic ethos of Flatiron's "cocktails for the masses" joie de vivre, doled out in a highly controlled environment, one at a time.

Even the way they figured out new drinks to add to the menu—with a show-and-tell-style tasting, usually scheduled on the day Ward had off—was more democratic in spirit than the methods used by any other cocktail bar of that era, despite the fact that Ward played the outsize persona and, some would argue, overly weighted role of the Cocktail Electoral College.

If you had to pinpoint the most glorious, shiniest moment during the most glorious, shiniest time period for the most glorious, shiniest cocktail bar in America, it would've been sometime in that first year after Alex Day came aboard. Maybe it would be Joaquín Simó in the front, working point at the bar, charming every single person who sat up around the L, using his poetic sophistry to simply explain distillation techniques or get them to try one of his savory cocktails or another new concoction with fresh red pepper and celery juice; or Day in his place, the youngest of the group, an observant, methodical, studious, analytical kid whose side gigs at other legendary cock-tail bars, like Milk & Honey and Tailor, built him into the most well-rounded, competent bartender not yet old enough to rent a car. Miller might be back in the service part of the bar, knocking out six drinks at once in one of his colorful shirts, occasionally looking through his old handwritten journals, filled with recipe after recipe, to tell you about an obscure tiki drink he'd gotten from Murray Stenson at Zig Zag Café, or shaking a drink with such extreme violence that the entire bar would get quiet, silently watching him hurt that ice as if it had done something to his family; or Ward, in that same spot, a look of bemusement on his curmudgeonly face as he grabbed duplicate drinks and knocked them out, his hands moving from one unmarked cheater bottle to the next, then stirring two drinks at once; Jessica Gonzalez, on the floor, handling all ten tables with just one barback and a food runner, smoothly explaining flavor profiles and ingredients better than nearly any bartender in the city, suggesting cocktails other tables had just ordered so the bartenders could double up and get out of the weeds, garnishing her own drinks to help out; Frankie Rodriguez, dressed in all black at the door, taking people's names and numbers in his little book, politely explaining that though he was undoubtedly impressed that you were indeed Cameron Diaz or Mickey Rourke or a good friend of Taboo from the Black Eyed Peas, currently there was no room at the bar, but he'd be happy to take your name and number and give you a call when a spot opened up.

Ward would create more drinks. Like the Ramble, and the Rigadoon, and the Risk Pool, and the Cynartown, and the Dick Brautigan, and the Gonzalez, and the Joy Division, and the Lucino's Delight, and the Mexi-Gin Martini, and the Yeoman Warder, and the 18th Century, and the Company Buck, and the Green Mile, and the Sea B3, and the Cinder, and the Fresh Brava, and the Glandula del Mono, and the Short Rib, and the Silver Monk, and the Spicy Paloma, and the Ty Cobbler, and the Augie March, and the Saramago, and the Shattered Glasser, and the Terrible Love, and the 202 Steps, and the Double Fill-Up, and the Pete's Word, and the Scotch Lady, and the Vejk Sling, and the Manhattan Transfer, and the Scotch Dram, and the Shruff's End, and the St. Columbus Rill, and the Wicked Kiss, and the Poire Man's Cobbler, and the Sloe Scobeyville Sling, and the Lilywhacker, and the Sidewinder, and the Bitter French, and the Calva Dorsa Royale, and the Elder Fashion Royale, and the Julien Sorel, and the Seda de Naranja, and the East River Underground, and the Jersey Lightning, and the Maple Julep, and the Not Quite George Julep, and the Smoked Julep, and the Celine Fizz, and the Chinese Fizz, and the Le Gigot Flip, and the 6th Street Swizzle, and the Hyde Park Swizzle, and the

Jalisco Swizzle, and the Myra Breckinridge, and the Black Market Sling, and the Coin Toss, and the Electric Kool-Aid Acid Test, and the Little Kingdom, and the St-Germain Redux, and the Alembic, and the Cooper Union, and the Baltasar and Blimunda, and the House of Payne, and the Range Life, and the Angus Story Daiquiri, and the Arrackuiri, and the D.W.B., and the Granny's Daiquiri, and the Jovencourt Daiquiri, and the Mosquito Coast, and the Black Prince, and the Elder Fashion, and the La Conferencia, and the Arrack Punch, and the Kill-Devil Punch, and the Drunken Punch, and the Mother's Ruin Punch, and the Nuts and Sherry Punch, and the Pisco Punch. But none became more famous than the Oaxaca Old-Fashioned.

And yet, despite the fact that this is a drink that's been ordered more than any other Death & Co cocktail, that it appears on more cocktail menus around the world than any other modern cocktail, that it has forced nervous people to mispronounce "Oaxaca" aloud for more than a decade, Ward doesn't remember the first time he made it.

He thinks it was just after they'd gotten a new bottle of Los Amantes mezcal, and that he made the first one off the cuff for one of their regulars like Don Lee, mostly on a whim because no one he knew of was stirring tequila in an up drink, or using mezcal as a modifier. He's fairly certain the reception was so positive that he started making it a lot, and that Kaplan was the one who came up with the Oaxaca Old-Fashioned moniker, and he's positive they put it on the second iteration of the menu. But the origin of the drink itself is lost to time, having failed to implant itself in Ward's brain in the manner of a ridiculous fire sunset on a Williamsburg evening.

REVOLUTIONS START WHEN events big and small simultaneously and unwittingly conspire, and the craft cocktail movement was no different. In New York, Milk & Honey, Angel's Share, Flatiron, Pegu, and Death & Co were joined by Jim Meehan's PDT, Dushan Zaric's Employees Only, Petraske's West

Village spot Little Branch and his divey East Side Company Bar, Eben Freeman's short-lived but nostalgically beloved Tailor, and a host of other spots keeping the cocktail torch alight.

By that time, San Francisco, the other tentpole in the movement, was lousy with innovative drink joints: Marco Dionysos's Absinthe, Paul Harrington's Townhouse, Thad Volger's Slanted Door, Greg Lindgren's Rye, Cameron and Phil West's Range restaurant, Scott Beattie's Cyrus, Jonny Raglin's and then Neyah White's NOPA, Daniel Hyatt and Thomas Waugh's Alembic (Waugh would eventually come to New York to work at Death & Co), Martin Cate's Smuggler's Cove, Duggan McDonnell's Cantina, and Todd Smith and crew's Bourbon & Branch.

Boston had the groundbreaking B-Side Lounge in Cambridge, led by Brother Cleve and Misty Kalkofen; Green Street; Jackson Cannon's Eastern Standard; and John Gertsen's Drink, which had no back bar and no menu, and almost single-handedly began the revitalization of the Fort Point neighborhood. Seattle had legendary Murray Stenson at Zig Zag Café and Jamie Boudreau at Canon. In Northern Virginia, Todd Thrasher's PX was an island of cocktail greatness, followed quickly by Derek Brown's cocktail bar the Gibson in DC proper. Greg Best excited geeks in Atlanta with his Friday Night Flights program at Linton and Gina Hopkins's Restaurant Eugene, before Best and Hopkins collaborated to open Holeman & Finch. Houston's Bobby Heugel created a cocktail scene in Space City basically by himself, first dog-whistling the cocktail nerds by creating a shockingly good drink list at Beaver's Ice House before opening Anvil in 2009.

While writing about his various experiments on his popular eponymous cocktail website, Jeffrey Morgenthaler was messing around with fresh juices and homemade syrups and tonics at various bars in Eugene, Oregon, before moving to Portland to sling drinks at Clyde Common in 2008. A year before, Daniel Shoemaker had moved up from the Bay Area to Rose City to open Teardrop Lounge in 2007. Some of the early New York cocktail crew began planting their flags in other cities. Petraske protégé Eric Alperin went out to

Los Angeles to start the speakeasy-styled Varnish. Toby Maloney, one of Milk & Honey's original bartenders, opened the Violet Hour in Chicago, which helped train Kirk Estopinal, who—with New Orleans native Neal Bodenheimer—opened New Orleans cocktail bar Cure.

Every month, the list grew bigger. Bartenders who'd spent time in New York and San Francisco were moving elsewhere to open bars, and people were going to those bars and then opening their own. Or local bartenders might watch a YouTube clip showcasing the proper way to double-shake, read DeGroff's *The Craft of the Cocktail,* and suddenly revamp their entire bar. By the end of 2008, the craft cocktail movement had reached critical mass.

THAT VERY SAME YEAR, on the type of hot, sticky New York summer night where the festering smell of garbage slowly tightens its grip on the hairs inside your nose, Phil Ward and Ravi DeRossi stood outside DeRossi's wine bar, the Bourgeois Pig, drinking beer. DeRossi, who famously has the attention span of a twelve-year-old whose family lives inside a video game arcade, was always eager to think about the next move. After downing his beer, he asked Ward if he wanted to open another bar.

"Hell yes," Ward said. "Let's do it."

ONLY THESE DAYS, IN WILLIAMSBURG, YOU WON'T FIND STARVING ARTISTS, BUT INSTEAD CULTURAL CREATIVES WHO EAT AWFULLY WELL. | For nearly twenty-five years, Jonathan Gold, the high-low priest of the Los Angeles food scene, has been chronicling the city's carts and stands and dives and holes-in-mini-malls. | Light bulbs have been popping up behind the bar, with more cocktails developed in the last 10 years than probably any decade since Prohibition. | AVOCADOS: "POOR MAN'S BUTTER" NO MORE. | Tablecloths, Asian fusion and spherification are out (the locals aren't interested in, or rich enough to indulge in, frivolous food experiments, the thinking goes). Nose-to-tail, rustic French and Italian, and small plates are in. | *So, obviously "food blogging" is kind of a strange hobby. I get a lot of weird looks from strangers at restaurants when I photograph my food.* | On a day when the Nasdaq is down 2 percent, OpenTable is up 45 percent from its offering price of $20. | These new culinary entrepreneurs, most of them with English as their first language and little fear of police or immigration authorities, say that they are on a mission to bring better street food to New Yorkers, and ready to bring dark corners of the business to light.

2009

CHAPTER 8

Holeman & Finch, Atlanta, Georgia, January 2009, Ten p.m.

Ninety minutes before the bullhorn, the anticipation started building. They were all there. The hipsters and industry folk, with the cleaver tattoos and facial hair and tight black denim, having traveled from their apartments in Old Fourth Ward and East Atlanta and Inman Park, and mostly drinking Vieux Carré's with Fernet shot-backs or whatever experimental cocktails bartenders Greg Best and Andy Minchow threw at them. There were the Young Buckhead White Guys who went to SEC schools and Emory, clad in college golf tees, Masters visors, and Costa sunglasses attached to neoprene Croakies, talking to Young Buckhead White Ladies clad in Jack Rogers silver sandals, striped J. Crew dresses, and long fur vests from Swank, all of whom were either drinking Miller High Life or, if the bartenders could talk them into it, a whimsical take on Jack and Coke, the Southern Cola with Amaro and Mexican Coke and ice cubes made from lime juice. And there were the Old Buckhead White Folks, middle-aged males in sport coats and ladies tentatively testing out the latest weekend attire from Talbots, who, thanks to some liquid courage, crossed the demarcation zone from chef/owner Linton and Gina Hopkins's fancier Restaurant Eugene next door, eager to see what the kids were up to these days.

And what the kids were up to was eating intense, decadent yellow and brown foods, favorites of an industry crowd turned cynical and bored by chopped salads and salmon, foods like offal and sweetbreads and hog jowl and veal brains and bowls full of pig tails alongside fried catfish sticks and carbonara.

But mostly they'd come for Burger Time.

Burger Time was ten p.m., the only time outside of brunch you could get a burger at Holeman & Finch. There were twenty-four total, and if you didn't put in your order for one of those burgers by eight thirty p.m., you were likely out of luck. Tables would strategize when to sit in order to overlap with Burger Time. They might bribe their server to make sure they got one of the two dozen. Or promise to run up a bill so large while they waited that the tip would essentially count as a bribe. You knew it was Burger Time when bartender Greg Best got on a white bullhorn and screamed, "IT'S BURGER TIME!!!"

At that exact instant, chef de cuisine Adam Biderman would take twenty-four patties on two half trays and slam them on the griddle with a loud clang. At the sound of the clang, people would cheer, or walk over to the area outside the griddle to take pictures or videos, as if they were at a zoo or a particularly busy airport. Biderman would cook them two and a half minutes on one side to get 'em crispy, then flip them, and add onion and Kraft American cheese singles. They'd toast the housemade buns and hold them warm under the heat lamp. Once the double burgers were off the grill and slid onto the buns, he'd add Linton Hopkins's grandmother's bread-and-butter pickles to the meat and they'd be done.

Around 10:12 p.m., the first twelve burgers would go out. As they left the kitchen, a roar of approval would go up, and even in those nascent days of social media documentation, phones would be out and nearly everyone acted like a food paparazzi fool for that aesthetically pleasing masterpiece. As Biderman cleaned off the griddle for round two, a new crowd would gather to watch him cook the next dozen. By ten thirty p.m. all twenty-four burgers would be served and photographed and shouted about and hyped up and consumed, and the kitchen would begin cooking regular food again. Greg Best would put away his bullhorn.

The Holeman & Finch burger wasn't the first upscale burger, or the first limited-edition burger, or even the first fancy version of a fast-food burger, but it was the first to perfect the art of all three and do it in such an entertaining and aesthetically pleasing way as to create a national phenomenon. The double burger (a "burger stack," in A-town parlance) became Atlanta's signature burger style, and—rather quickly after the New York Food Mafia descended upon Atlanta to write about it—the poster burger for the Culinary Revolution, as the idea of using high-class ingredients in simple comfort foods reached a fever pitch.

Eventually, the burger's fame and the fortune and stresses associated with it would cause the original iteration of Holeman to dissolve into a divorce, resulting in co-owners Greg Best, Andy Minchow, and Regan Smith leaving for their own projects. Adam Biderman, who'd helped create the new burger concept with Linton Hopkins, had already left to help rebuild New Orleans' food scene in the wake of Hurricane Katrina, and eventually launched a beloved burger institution called the Company Burger. Linton and Gina Hopkins stayed on and launched a fast casual spin-off, H&F Burger, at Atlanta's Ponce City Market and the Atlanta Braves baseball stadium. Back at the original Holeman, they played with the menu, offering an unlimited number of burgers for a time, then switching it to twenty-four at lunch, twenty-four at dinner, etc.

Back in 2008, they'd also launched a 1,800-square-foot baking facility, H&F Bread Co., to bake their hamburger buns. After selling it off in 2016, the new owners expanded their scope. The 50,000-square-foot facility now makes twenty thousand hamburger buns a day.

CHAPTER 9

Barbecue Man, Rodney Scott, Hemingway, South Carolina

At first, it was people who'd moved out of Hemingway, either for college or the military, or for a job elsewhere. People Rodney Scott had gone to high school with. They'd come back during Thanksgiving break or on leave and bring a pound of his family's whole hog barbecue back to their roommates in Montana, or to people in their squad from Texas or California. And the next time they came back, they'd get three pounds and talk about how everyone in their dorm or platoon wanted to try this spicy pork from that South Carolina general store.

After that, it was a woman from *Southern Living* magazine in the nineties. And then South Carolina governor David Beasley, who'd bet the Scott's Bar-B-Que pork against Wisconsin cheddar in a 1997 wager based around the Carolina Panthers playing Green Bay in the NFC Championship Game. But when Charleston architect Reggie Gibson told Southern Foodways Alliance director and *New York Times* columnist John T. Edge to go try Scott's in 2009, that's when everything got complicated.

RODNEY SCOTT FIRST LOOKED UNDER a pig cooking when he was five.

Scott, an only child, was born in Philadelphia, Pennsylvania, but moved to Hemingway, South Carolina, when he was one. His parents, Roosevelt and Ella, were both originally from South Carolina, and when they got back and settled in Hemingway, they opened a general store, selling loaves of Sunbeam bread, liters of soda, and other miscellaneous items. Scott's father also fixed cars on the side, and in 1972, he started buying a whole hog on Thursdays from one of the local farmers, cooking it, and selling plates of barbecue.

Scott wasn't allowed to get close to that flame when he was little, because, well, little kids don't exactly adhere to rules around fire. His mother used to feed him pork belly because the rest was too spicy. The day he first looked under the pig, his twentysomething cousin Piccolo was tending to it, and so Scott knelt down next to him and asked him questions, and Piccolo—Scott never knew his real name—told him about crisping the skin without burning it. Scott was fascinated, and started watching every time his cousin or his father or one of his uncles cooked the hog.

His parents' time in Philly meant he was a Philadelphia 76ers fan, which meant Scott was obsessed with basketball generally and Julius Erving specifically. Scott dug his whole style of play, the way he floated through the air for several beats longer than anyone else, like he'd jumped twice, allowing him to do things with a basketball most people had never seen. And when Scott was eleven, basketball drove him to cook his first pig over the fire.

He'd wanted to go to a high school game—his favorite local team, Battery Park, was playing their chief rivals, Hemingway—and so he asked his dad. Sure, Roosevelt Scott told him, you can go if you cook that hog.

With his father instructing him, he set about completing the tasks at hand: every ten to fifteen minutes Scott would have to fire the hog, make sure there was wood in the barrel, and keep the flame going without letting the pig catch fire.

Roosevelt Scott stayed out of the way, letting his son do it his damn self, the only way he was going to learn. But secretly he told his buddy Buster to keep an eye on Rodney from afar and make sure he didn't burn the place down or catch himself on fire. Scott spent the entire process freaking out—nervously counting off the minutes until he needed to tend to the pig or the fire again. There was serious skill in figuring out that pig was done: you had to make sure there was a separation of the skin when the fat finally rendered into the meat and that the skin stopped resembling flesh and puckered back when you poked it. For twelve hours he didn't relax, wandering around that pig like it was a girl he was nervous to approach, tentative and then abruptly confident. When Scott finally thought it was all done, he flipped it over and stood nervously next to it, side-eyeing his dad as he inspected the pig.

Scott saw the skin crackling without being burnt; he saw the pucker when his father nudged at it. He knew that pig was beautiful.

"All right," Roosevelt Scott said eventually, "you can go."

WHEN HE WAS IN SEVENTH GRADE, Hemingway High merged with Battery Park, but even after that the school was small and rural, with around sixty students per class. During high school, other than one season playing baseball his junior year, Scott worked. But this wasn't work like that of a normal kid who kept an after-school job at the ice-cream parlor or Blockbuster Video.

By the late eighties, the barbecue side of the Scott family business was turning into more than a side venture. What once was strictly on Thursdays with a single hog was now three or four days a week with four or five hogs a night. They even put up a smaller white sign next to the "Scott's Variety" lettering outside, advertising "Scott's Pit Cook B.B.Q." with an illustrated sleeping pig sitting over a translucent square with a fire underneath. Inside the store, up on the wall behind the shelves, there was a poster with writing in black marker titled "Hog List," with a rundown of prices for whole large- and medium-sized hogs and how much it might cost if you wanted them to cook a hog or turkey you killed and brought in yourself. Next to that was another poster listing prices for either a full or half pound of pork barbecue, and the same for barbecued chicken.

The increased focus on cooked food meant having enough wood for the fires, which meant Scott and his dad and cousins were out cutting wood to stoke the fires Tuesdays, Wednesdays, and Thursdays. They had a hundred acres of their own wooded land, if needed, but they primarily got wood from folks around them, all of whom knew that if a tree fell on their property, they just had to let the Scotts know and they'd come chop it up and take it away, often the same day. By the time he was twelve, Scott was damn handy with a chainsaw. And when he wasn't out cutting wood, Scott was carrying hogs. And when he wasn't carrying hogs, he was flipping hogs on the fire. Rodney Scott had a grown man's job long before he was grown.

But that grown man's job got him a grown man's car. His first was a 1974 Buick Landau. It was an old-school classic, a long-ass two-door the color of a rusty pipe, with a deuce and a quarter, a hump on the truck, spoke wheels, and a Rolls-Royce grill. It had an eight-track player, but Scott got an adapter for cassette tapes; if he didn't hold the cord, it would drag, so Scott often found himself driving to school bumping Boogie Down Productions, Eric B. & Rakim, UTFO, and Biz Markie with one hand on the wheel and one holding the cord, trying to look cool as hell and not crash at the same time.

The other high school kids laughed at this ride. Pre-Internet seventeen-year-olds didn't have much appreciation for throwbacks, but Scott loved it and treated it nice, washing the car every single day. The next year, though, Scott worked his way up to purchasing a Nissan 300ZX, a *Miami Vice*–style sports car with two hundred horsepower, a five-speed stick, and a green digital dashboard straight out of *Knight Rider*. There was no need to hold an adapter because it had a system. The other high school kids stopped laughing and started asking for rides.

RODNEY SCOTT REMEMBERS the night he graduated from Hemingway High in 1989, clear as the day it happened. After the speeches and the balloons and caps being tossed in the air, he walked out of the gymnasium, electric with the pride and power only eighteen-year-olds who've recently accomplished something can feel. As his friends posed for pictures and made plans to attend crazy graduation parties, his parents pulled him aside. You've got four hours to hang out with your friends, they told him. But at midnight, you've got to work.

All the swagger and elation and excitement of the night hissed out of Scott like a popped balloon. How can you make someone work on their graduation night? he wondered. That night, the whole night, as he cooked the hogs, he radiated with anger.

The next day he pouted. But as he pouted he started to come to terms with the fact that this was his life. This was what his people did, this is how they supported themselves, and this is what he knew. Most people come out of high school and go to college to find an interest, or get a job to find a skill, but Scott already had skills. He'd been cooking hogs for seven years.

He realized that if this was going to be his life, he needed to find fun in what he did. Cooking barbecue was hard and it was long hours, but there was fun in the downtime, listening to music, reading his car magazines, whatever. Scott was determined not to toil. He might not get to go off in the woods drinking beer with his friends all night and dancing with girls, but he and his family had something, and some folks didn't have anything. Or worse, some folks had everything but stayed unhappy. That wouldn't be Scott.

He found a way to love it. To love going into the woods and picking out the right trees, same as a chef at a farmers market. To love cranking up the fourteen-horsepower log splitter and breaking down the wood. To love watching those embers fall to the bottom of the burn barrel they'd made from a torched-out oil drum crisscrossed with old truck axles to separate the wood from the embers. To love scooping those hot wood embers out of the burn barrel with a shovel and spreading them under the ham and shoulders of the pig in the pit they'd built inside an old converted garage. To love keeping that fire burning for twelve straight hours until the pig was ready to be flipped and seasoned and mopped with their homemade vinegar pepper concoction, a nectar of spicy magical secrets they kept in buckets in the pit and sold by the gallon in the store.

Soon, all those hours Scott put in by the fire started paying off.

WHEN *NEW YORK TIMES* COLUMNIST John T. Edge came to Hemingway and hung out with Scott, he was blown away. The Scott family had managed to take something hyper-traditional and find ways to update it without disemboweling its historical nature. They used discarded boxes to pad the feet of the pitmasters, similar to the way a chef would put down a gel mat. They had hot plates beneath the boning table to keep the meat warm for the Health Department. The Scotts had figured out how to keep a healthy balance of history and modernity.

On June 9, 2009, John T. Edge's story "Pig, Smoke, Pit: This Food Is Seriously Slow" appeared on the front page of *The New York Times* Food section. There was a big color photo of the ramshackle building that housed Scott's Variety, with the *o* missing from *Scott*, and watermelons sitting in shopping carts on the front porch. The story set the scene of Hemingway at three forty-five a.m., "as frogs croaked into the void and a mufflerless pickup downshifted onto Cow Head Road," with Scott giving an order to flip the pigs.

What followed was a beautiful, nearly poetic narrative of a day at the Scott's Variety store and Bar-B-Que that, to "aficionados in search of ever-elusive authenticity," must've read like pornography: a "tin-roofed and time-worn" main building; burn barrels built by "a local welder . . . from salvaged industrial piping and junked truck axles;" locals knowing to ask for "fried pig skin, still smoky from the pit, still crisp from the deep fryer."

The Scotts couldn't know it at the time, but this profile was coming during a remarkable period in the greater barbecuing world. The year before, *Texas Monthly*, as a quinquennial event, sent a team of writers and editors around the state in an ambitious and somewhat insane attempt to try every single barbecue restaurant, and set the world on fire by naming Snow's BBQ the best in Texas. This was particularly shocking because the restaurant was open only on Saturdays and was headed up by a 73-year-old pitmaster named Tootsie Tomanetz, whose day job as janitor for the Giddings school district kept her occupied the rest of the week. The improbable underdog narrative helped the story spread around the country and propel a new interest in barbecue.

The same year Edge's profile of Scott's came out in the *Times*, a thirty-one-year-old former handyman and coffee shop worker from College Station named Aaron Franklin bought a three-hundred-dollar trailer and legendary Texas barbecue scion Louie Mueller's son John's barbecue pit and launched Franklin Barbecue. Franklin had been tinkering with barbecue, throwing backyard parties for a couple of years, trading tips with another amateur barbecue obsessive, John Lewis, but when he launched his tiny operation, it immediately took off, eventually becoming the most popular and beloved barbecue operation in Texas history. Franklin hired Lewis to help him build another pit when he expanded, but eventually Lewis left—ironically, to become pitmaster at la Barbecue, Louie Mueller's granddaughter's barbecue operation. With Franklin and la Barbecue and a few other promising newcomers opening all around the same time, Austin quickly went from being considered an average barbecue town to the most sought-after barbecue destination in the state.

But as the Scott's story illustrates, it wasn't just Texas having its moment. Barbecue, one of America's oldest forms of cooking, was suddenly cool again. The new modern barbecue gods, the Franklins of the world, with their technical skills and know-how, were being celebrated, just as the old heads who'd been doing it forever were being discovered (or rediscovered) by the NYFM. The art and science of cooking barbecue, the trial and error, messing with temperatures and experimenting with different cuts of meat—these were the things that attracted food nerds, who would argue about smoke rings and bark and fire-tending techniques and dry rubs and the use of sauce on message boards all night. On top of that, regional differences gave people more reasons to get angry on the Internet, but also gave credence to the fact that you couldn't really name a king or queen of barbecue in America as much as maybe a provincial prince or princess.

Still, they tried. The Lexington Dip barbecue folks fought with the Eastern Carolina Vinegar folks, who fought with the South Carolina Gold Mustard folks, who fought with the thin-red-sauced Memphis folks, who fought with the thicker-red-sauced Kansas City folks, who fought with the no-sauce Central Texas folks, who fought with heavily sauced East Texas folks, who fought with the Cowboy-Style West Texas folks, who fought with the South Texas Barbacoa folks, who fought with the Kentucky Muttoneers, who fought with the Alabama White Saucers, who fought with the Santa Maria Tri-tippers, who fought with the Chicago Rib Tippers, who fought with whomever was working at McClard's in Arkansas.

The barbecue clans might not unite under one king, but at least now, if they were talking about it, Rodney Scott was in the conversation.

EDGE'S STORY CHANGED EVERYTHING, almost immediately. Food tourists started showing up regularly, creating lines even on weekdays before their nine thirty a.m. opening time. A racially-mixed group had always visited the Scott's restaurant, but it was usually white folks from Stuckey or Georgetown or Myrtle Beach, not Connecticut and Toronto. The bigger influx of out-of-towners meant locals were now stuck somewhere between being proud that something or someone they'd known their whole lives had been stamped with national approval, and annoyed that now it would be more of a pain in the ass to go there to get a barbecue plate and some skins.

Things began to snowball. With the burgeoning food scene in Charleston bubbling up, thanks to the likes of Sean Brock at Husk and McCrady's and Mike Lata at FIG, more and more of the NYFM were traveling down to the area to see what was happening, and part of that journey meant taking a drive out to Hemingway to have some Scott's Bar-B-Que. Soon after that,

Scott was invited to Charleston Wine + Food, and while there in 2010, they showcased a documentary about Scott's called *CUT/CHOP/COOK*, made by Joe York for the Southern Foodways Alliance, John T. Edge's organization.

Scott had no context. He'd never cooked away from home a day in his life, but all of a sudden he was meeting barbecue legends like Mike Mills from 17th Street Barbecue in southern Illinois, and serious restaurateurs like Jim 'N Nick's Community Bar-B-Q's Nick Pihakis. Whereas Scott and Mills might trade cooking technique tips, Pihakis counseled him on the business side of the operation, and eventually they became close, with Pihakis even serving as the best man in Scott's wedding.

The implicit trade-off in taming fire, in getting fire to work for you, is that it can't be tamed forever. There were always fires. From the time Scott graduated from high school in 1989, they'd had three, one in 1989, another in 1991, and another in 1993. Then nothing for twenty years.

But on the night before Thanksgiving 2013, the fire came back. Maybe it was just human error, a slippage by the folks cooking that night, someone dozing off when they shouldn't have. Maybe the hog was too fatty, and the grease burned more quickly than they were expecting. Whatever the case, the fire burned the tops of the pigs first, and then in a swirling motion began burning the walls, which caught the wood, which caught the propane tank, which started spitting fire out like a flamethrower. With everyone back home and celebrating, Thanksgiving is one of the busiest times of year for the Scott's business, so they had nineteen hogs on the fire that night. When it was done, four were left, the back shed the only other thing that survived.

Immediately, the folks he'd met in the barbecue and food communities reached out. Even folks he'd never met before. What did he need? How could they help? Soon, Scott had put together a "Rodney Scott in Exile" tour to help raise money for the rebuild, touring around Charleston, Atlanta, Nashville, Birmingham, and New Orleans.

Scott had tried to say yes as much as possible before—he'd even been to

Australia to cook for food and wine festivals out there—but being on the road constantly changed everything. He saw a lot of sites, learned how to break down his cookers efficiently, get his proteins in on time, take a nap in any position at any time during the day. He still tried to play his music and read his magazines and keep it fun. He met more and more people in the industry, and those people seemed to like what he was doing and wanted to spread the gospel of Rodney Scott's pork. The "Exile Tour" took in eighty thousand dollars to help rebuild. And for a while, things went back to normal in Hemingway. But a few years later, Scott had the urge to get out and do more. So he left.

Teaming up with Pihakis, Scott moved to Charleston and opened Rodney Scott's BBQ at 1011 King Street in 2017. A year later, he won a James Beard Award for Best Chef in the Southeast. The only other pitmaster to ever win the award was Aaron Franklin, the man who'd started his barbecue trailer in Austin the year John T. Edge came to visit Hemingway. Soon after the Beard win, Pihakis announced they were opening a second Rodney Scott's BBQ in Birmingham, Alabama, and hinted at broader expansion. *Food & Wine* put his joint in their 40 Most Important Restaurants of the Past 40 Years. Scott served as a judge on *Top Chef* and made whole hog barbecue with *Bon Appétit* and was interviewed by *Eater* editor in chief Amanda Kludt on her *Upsell* podcast.

Scott had gone from being a well-known pitmaster to just well known. But with that fame and ambition, the spotlight grew brighter and the questions got harder. *The Washington Post* profiled him, and brought up a subject that had simmered in the background ever since he'd moved to Charleston: his apparent estranged relationship with his father. The rumors coming out of Hemingway were that business had slowed since Scott moved and that this had caused tension (Scott's mother, Ella, told the reporter her husband was supportive of Rodney).

In that story, it was revealed that the current pitmaster in Hemingway was Rodney Scott's oldest son, Dominic. When asked about his dad moving to Charleston, Dominic responded, "I wasn't upset. I keep going. I know how to do basically everything he knows how to do."

Scott heard the talk coming out of Hemingway, but compared it to crabs in a barrel. He'd wanted folks back home to be proud of him, but he wasn't going to spend time worrying over it.

A half mile from Scott's Charleston restaurant, John Lewis, one of the main architects behind the Austin barbecue renaissance, opened his own Central Texas–style place, Lewis Barbecue. With both open, the barbecue folks sensed a changing of the guard. In terms of barbecue, they said, the Holy City might be the new Austin.

Rodney Scott didn't know about all that. He needed to work.

New York City Wine & Food Festival, October 9, 2009, aka "Fig-Gate"

David Chang: "I will call bullshit on San Francisco. There's only a handful of restaurants that are manipulating food. Fucking every restaurant in San Francisco is serving figs on a plate with nothing on it."

CHAPTER 10

Not an Activist, Tunde Wey, Detroit, Michigan, Part 1

He treated Detroit like an American science laboratory, a small-sample-size experiment where he could learn how Americans socialized and worked and played and ate. All of these things were fascinating, but the biggest thing he learned before he took those ideas and traveled around America feeding and talking and educating was that it was always about power. He knew that much.

Tunde Wey was born in Nigeria, more precisely in a suburb of Lagos called Ikeja, most precisely in a brick house on Alhaja Kofoworola Crescent, painted baby blue. His full name, Akintunde, means "the warrior that has returned." Both his mother and father had an entrepreneurial spirit that would stick with Wey throughout his life. His father had done everything from working in corporate marketing to starting his own general contracting business, to running a company that supplied chemicals to larger concerns, and another that fabricated and sold furniture. His mother, Beatrice, had worked in marketing as well, but also opened up a bakery, and then spent Wey's youth raising the kids.

There were four total. Wey shared a room with his older brother, Tope, and his younger brother, Seyi (Thelma, his older sister, had her own room). The

Weys lived upstairs because the bottom floor was his father Moses's office and showroom for his furniture business. When Wey was a child, his parents used to wake the children up and make them take cod liver oil and other vitamins, enticing them with the promise of Rice Krispies if they completed the task. Wey and his siblings would play soccer and basketball and stick fight and wrestle and watch mostly American and British cartoons: *Teenage Mutant Ninja Turtles* and *SilverHawks* and the one about the Native-American superhero who could conjure up the power of a cheetah and the strength of a bear.

When he was little he attended the National Airport Authority School, which, disappointingly, was not an adolescent aviation school but merely close to the airport. From five to ten years old, he went to Green Springs primary, and then to the Corona School. Corona shaped Wey's consciousness as a teen; it was the place where he made friends he keeps to this day, the place where he came to develop his own senses of security and insecurity. But the initial years were hard due to the sudden influx of responsibility and his dorm prefect, a sporadically violent bully named Stephen.

When Wey was thirteen, Corona tried to close down the boarding facilities at the school, and so his mom—sensing an opportunity—decided to open her own boardinghouse, after which Wey lived with thirty others in the dorm run by his mom. Though he wasn't as popular as his older brother (only a year apart, they both ended up in the same grade), Wey had a good group of friends with whom he would talk shit and make jokes and play volleyball and backyard soccer.

He also read a lot—mostly Sidney Sheldon, Famous Five, and Nancy Drew mysteries—and though his parents wanted him to focus more on the traditional sciences, he excelled in English and the "soft sciences"—social studies, composition, history—and ended up graduating from Corona when he was fifteen. The next year he spent back at home, living with his parents. He took some university prep classes and computer classes, but he mostly just messed around, playing video games and feeling aimless, wandering, going out to Lagos clubs with his older brother and cousin—adult, twenty-one-plus clubs, places where young professionals listened to grown-up adult music and did grown-up adult dancing and drank grown-up adult beverages and discussed the unrelenting monotonies of a grown-up, untethered life.

But Moses and Beatrice Wey didn't put their kids through boarding schools just to see them wander and go to clubs and play video games. Wey's mother's sister was a pharmacist in Detroit, and she was willing to be Tunde and his brother's guardian if they moved to America and went to school. His parents asked Wey and his older brother if they wanted to go, and—wanting to see something new and experience America—they agreed and flew out to Detroit in the fall of 2000.

Wey's first day in America was not the glorious one he'd been envisioning; during the drive back from Detroit Metropolitan Airport, he'd been expecting to see bald eagles flying along perfectly paved streets and green grass and happy people waving American flags and handing out free hot dogs, but there were just as many potholes as in Lagos and the grass was just as brown and there were no eagles or gratis hot dogs. He begged his aunt to take them to McDonald's, because he'd seen the Big Mac on television and dreamed of the glory that was two all-beef patties, special sauce, lettuce, cheese, pickles, and onions on a sesame bun, but again, the actual burger was just as dreary and average as the ones he'd had in Nigeria.

He spent the summer in Detroit getting acclimated, walking from his aunt's apartment by Six Mile and McNichols to the University of Detroit Mercy to go to the library, where he often sat at the computers for hours in MSN chat rooms, finding out, for better or worse, just what America was like online.

His parents had a simple plan for him while he was in America: go to community college and get the necessary credits to get into pharmacy school, finish pharmacy school and get into medical school, finish medical school and become a successful doctor. His aunt and her husband were both pharmacists, and his cousin was in pharmacy school, so he knew at least part of the path was attainable, and so he started attending Oakland Community College to try to get an associate of science degree, but then he just kept going to school . . . forever.

For six years he languished in community college, doing well in the English and history electives he'd chosen, but mostly failing all of the science classes. Frustrated, he signed up for Organic Chemistry II without first taking I, wanting to see if he could actually do it if he applied himself. He could not. But facing that failure freed him to finally tell his parents that he wouldn't be taking the path they'd laid out. They adjusted their expectations and told him it would be okay if he just got a bachelor's degree, and so he graduated from Oakland with an associate's degree in liberal arts and transferred to Wayne State University, where he was finally able to take classes he was interested in, like Mandarin and economics, without pretending he was on the way to a glorious future as a medical doctor. But after the first semester, his parents could no longer afford to keep sending him to school. With no other options immediately available, in 2008, Tunde Wey dropped out of college, lost his F-1 student status, and became an undocumented immigrant.

FOR THE NEXT COUPLE OF YEARS, Wey just lived. He moved in with friends and got a job at Costco handing out free samples. He started practicing Buddhism. He started a T-shirt company called Thelma's Revolution, designing a T-shirt with Mao and a star in the background with Chinese script on it, and went as far as taking it to the local hip clothing boutique and getting them to agree to sell it, though his business strategy was relatively unsound, as he never went back to see if they actually did.

Another time, upon noticing Costco didn't sell sushi rice, he tried to hook up with a wholesaler and get Costco to buy sushi rice through him, but the giant, multinational corporation of membership-only warehouse clubs didn't actually take his proposal to be their sole supplier of sushi rice seriously, and so, as revenge, he stopped taking his job serving free samples of quiche lorraine seriously, and the tension escalated and soon they fired him for writing poetry on the job. Generating no real income, he moved back in with his aunt and started focusing on Buddhist activities—meetings and chanting, etc. He was floundering, and resorted to just going out with his friends and partying and working odd, manual-labor jobs that barely covered his relatively paltry bills.

During that time, his mother flew out with some news: assets from the estate of his grandfather, who'd passed away sixteen years earlier, had recently been liquidated and the family had come into some money and wanted to set up Wey and his younger brother on a path toward completing their education. His mother paid for an apartment in Troy, Michigan, for a year, and got them a car, and they discussed school but came to the conclusion that the amount of money they had left wasn't enough to pay for all that schooling. But Wey had an idea to use the money to start a clothing line and make a bunch of money off said clothing line and then use that money on education. His mom's reply: No.

Mom was, however, okay with them starting a grocery store—in fact, the first licensed grocery store in an apartment building in the city of Troy. But the Troy Place Apartments Grocery lost money at an alarming rate from the beginning, and quickly drained all of their resources, and soon Wey and his younger brother were forced to leave their apartment.

Wey's younger brother moved in with his cousin, but Wey didn't want to ask his aunt to let him come back yet again, so he moved in with a friend of a friend he barely knew, and when that didn't work out, he moved in with another friend back in Detroit. At this point, he'd lost his car in an accident, and so he spent two months walking the streets, filling out job applications. When nothing worked out, he took a trip to Seattle, and when he came back, his roommate—who suffered from an anxiety disorder—wouldn't let him in the apartment or give him his things, saying Wey owed him for some Microsoft Paint software, and then started threatening to call immigration.

Wey didn't know what to do, so he spent the night at a homeless shelter. Not knowing what to expect, he called his parents to tell them where he was, just in case something happened, and hearing the sadness in his mother's voice when he said he was in a homeless shelter nearly broke him.

At five thirty a.m. the next morning, he left the homeless shelter in the bitter cold and waited outside the University of Detroit library. When it opened at eight a.m., he went in to get warm again and evaluate his situation. Just then, his aunt called and told him to come back to her house.

Appreciative of the reprieve, he started hustling, picking up a marketing job for five hundred dollars a month from a woman he'd met in his Buddhist practice, which allowed him to flex his writing skills. He also started reading about what was happening in downtown Detroit. Amid the rubble of the national narrative illustrating Detroit's demise, there were now small stories of idealistic, creative folks going back into the city and starting a revival in places like Corktown and downtown.

Wey started going out to the local art school and listening to talks, and going out to shows in the city, and he began to feel alive in a way he hadn't before, filled with energy from all of these inspiring, educated (mostly white) folks who were so interested in activism and entrepreneurship and the DIY movement. The opportunities in the city astounded Wey—people seemed to be making it up as they went along, creating urban gardens and art studios and restaurants. Wey wanted to get involved too, so he created a sort of local Kickstarter-meets-Groupon called Detroit BigAssDeal to fund local projects in exchange for coupons from local businesses. Though that ultimately floundered, the creative events and opportunities he kept finding filled him up, and he knew he needed to live in the city.

He found a friend who had a room to rent him for $350 a month, and he was ready to put down the deposit when his father talked him out of it. When he told his friend he couldn't do it, the friend relayed his own story about his own father telling him to always plant himself on fertile ground, and whether that was genuine or just a clever pitch to get him to rent the room, it didn't matter. Wey realized Detroit was his fertile ground, and so he went against his father's advice and headed for the ATM and took out all his cash and moved to the Woodbridge neighborhood of Detroit in 2011.

EDWARD LORENZ DEVELOPED a chaos theory term called the "butterfly effect," which more or less posits that a small change in an initial condition can eventually lead to a hugely changed outcome. It is also the name of a bad Ashton Kutcher movie. If Lorenz were charting Wey's initial condition, and made note of the small change involving Wey's move to Woodbridge, he would be unsurprised to find that this relatively minor move in location completely changed the trajectory of Wey's life.

Despite the fact that he was now spending nearly all his income on rent and a cell phone, Wey finally felt free. It was incredible to him that he could live in the city and buy a dollar can of Black Label beer and sit outside talking to interesting folks and just feel like he wasn't a college dropout, or a poor undocumented immigrant, but instead a part of a small community of people who were actually trying to change Detroit. He knew farmers and writers and artists and butchers and nonprofit workers and academics, and everyone went to the same bars and played in the same soccer leagues and went to the same parties. Most of these people were progressive white folks, folks who had come from relatively affluent backgrounds and gotten advanced degrees and yet still chose to come into the city. He watched the way they went about their business—the connections they seemed to effortlessly obtain, the friends of friends that they all seemed just one introduction away from—and he knew that was a special and rare sort of power, made all the more special by the fact that if you ever brought it up to them, they would protest, with embarrassed, pained looks on their faces, that they didn't even know what you were talking about.

Wey made a point to make those connections, to introduce himself to everyone. It was easy—he was naturally charming and funny and sarcastic, and people gravitated toward him. Eventually these connections helped him get into an entrepreneurship program where he was mentored by the CEO of a media company, and when that same CEO got a grant from the city, Wey was hired and paid $1,600 a month to write articles and profiles of people doing cool things to try and change the city. Finding subjects was easy—he was already living among them—so the job wasn't challenging, but as he continued to do it, and learned about the petty squabbles of some of the people looking to change Detroit, he got more jaded and his initial enthusiasm and energy surrounding its revival waned.

There was more to it: despite the fact that he was now making money, enough money in fact to move into his own two-bedroom place in Mexican town in Southwest Detroit and spend hundreds of dollars eating and drinking and doing other grown-up things he briefly witnessed as a wayward teen in Lagos, he felt vulnerable.

A few weeks earlier, his brother had called him, saying that some people had shown up in a car at his aunt's house, looking for him and claiming to be from ICE, and this incident shook him up. His status still in question, he decided that the worst thing he could do was just be quiet, so he started to talk publicly about his status and began work, with a friend, on a video project on immigration. His puff pieces on local entrepreneurs no longer felt important, and so he was searching around for something else to do when he had lunch with former roommate Peter Dalinowski, who said he wanted to open a restaurant. Wey, whose only experience in the restaurant industry at that point was a brief fortnight of employment at Wendy's, said yes.

He called up one of his friends, the economic director of a small city within Detroit called Hamtramck, and this friend showed Wey and his partner a suitable space. Wey had five thousand dollars saved up from a marketing project and put that together with another couple thousand from his room-mate, and within four months, in September 2013, they were open for business.

The idea behind the restaurant, called Revolver, was simple: each week-end they would have a different menu and a different chef. They would do two seatings a night, and be open Friday, Saturday, and sometimes Sunday. To attend a dinner, you bought a ticket. Though they knew enough people to get some initial community and alternative press, Revolver had trouble selling tickets and filling seats for the first few months. What they needed, Wey realized, was to get the area's biggest paper, the *Detroit Free Press*, to write about them. So Wey reached out to Sylvia Rector, the food writer, but she kept turning him down, saying she didn't write "about pop-ups." But Revolver kept pulling in high-level chefs like James Rigato, Kate Williams, and Marc Djozlija, and by the time they got hot young chef Andy Hollyday (who went on to open the highly regarded Selden Standard), she relented, writing a front-page story about this curious new kind of restaurant. Revolver, which depended on selling tickets for dinners through its e-newsletter, got a thousand new sign-ups that day. After that, they never worried about selling out dinners again.

But despite the success, Wey and Dalinowski's relationship began to deteriorate. Dalinowski was extremely meticulous and wanted to handle most of the details, which was great in some capacities, but it made Wey feel like he was merely an employee of his own restaurant, and so—six months in—he sold his share of the restaurant and left.

Wey wanted to do his own thing, and after running through several ideas, he finally realized what he really wanted to do was Nigerian food. On top of the depth of flavor being richer than American food, he knew that Americans didn't know the food well, and so he would be able to play with format and style and do pretty much anything he wanted to do and control the experience. At first he tried to find a chef, but that didn't work out, and then he tried to find investors, but they weren't really feeling his idea either, so Wey decided to go about it on his own. He talked to his mom about her own recipes, and went online and did more research, and just started cooking Nigerian dishes in his own home: *jollof* rice, *egusi* soup, stew, *okpa*, fried rice, yam pottage, *akara*, *moi*, etc. He figured he would just do pop-ups until he could figure out what was next, so, calling it Lagos Nigerian BBQ because he "was trying to get white folks to come too," he made flyers using modern fonts with faded black-and-white African people on them, shit that felt hipster and cool, and put them up. His first pop-up had a team of ten people and used a bar down the street from his place, and starting in May 2014, he produced one dinner a month.

The dinners did fine—the food, he thought, was okay at some points and kind of bad at others because he was still figuring everything out: how to cook all of these recipes for huge numbers of people, how to get things out in a timely fashion, etc. Feedback was mostly positive, but he remembered every negative comment like a blow to the gut: the guy who said the meat was too chewy, the woman who said the beans tasted like Sterno. And worst of all, as the dinners continued, interest in them waned. The first dinner was for around a hundred people, but then the next was for eighty, and then seventy, and, financially, it just started to not make any sense. With crowds that size, Wey had tried to be accommodating—figuring out vegan and vegetarian options—and found that he was compromising at every point and no longer really even doing the thing he set out to do. Frustrated, he shut down the dinners until one evening, feeling a burst of creative energy, he ended up just doing a dinner for twelve at his friend's restaurant on a night he was closed, cooking a goat's head stew all through the night, texting friends to roll through. The friends who showed up loved it, and he finally felt like he was reclaiming a little bit of what filled him up in the first place.

Once he and Dalinowski had sorted out the Revolver separation, Wey realized there was nothing keeping him in Detroit, and after meeting a Filipino chef who'd cooked in all fifty states, he decided he wanted to do that too. He'd always wanted to live a man-about-the-world type of life, and he realized that these dinners might be his chance to do that. Unsure of where to go first, he picked New Orleans because his former editor at the Detroit publication had moved there, and she and Wey had a connection. In order to publicize the dinner in New Orleans, Wey had a plan. He'd seen what the *Free Press* story had done for Revolver's business and he realized just how powerful the right media outlets could be in amplifying a message, so he sent emails to food writers and editors at NOLA's biggest publications—the *Times-Picayune* and *Gambit*—imploring them to write about him. Much to his surprise, *Gambit* actually did, and his New Orleans dinner sold out in one day.

He began picking cities nearly at random. He went to Minneapolis because he had a friend there, Buffalo just because he liked the vibe of the city, Philadelphia because he'd always wanted to see Philly. Each time, he would implement his own PR email strategy—first researching all the writers and editors at any print or online publications in the city that covered food, and then, in the manner of a singer on tour changing lyrics to give a shout-out to each city she was performing in, slightly altering the template of an email to offer up some sort of personal or city-specific angle to make it feel more intimate. Something like:

Dear [Food Journalist],

Man, that [local sports team] game was crazy last night! You watch that?

OR: That [topic of the most current story written by said journalist] story was great. How long that take you to research?

Lots of people used this strategy, of course, but the genius was actually the rest of the email, which truly did feel personal because Wey's personality couldn't help but sing through. It would be slightly bombastic, but also sarcastic: "I'm sure you're tired of writing about Nigerian food because you talk about this shit all the time, but I have a new angle and that new angle is—you guys don't talk about this shit ever!!!"

Editors and writers who received this email couldn't help but respond. Most of them said that the email stayed with them throughout the day or even the week; that even if they sensed they were being played, it didn't matter, because the enthusiasm and entertainment Wey provided felt so singular. They would write back and say, "I don't know you, but I like you. Let's talk."

One of the first writers from a big publication to cover Wey was *The Washington Post*'s James Beard Award–winning food writer Maura Judkis, who responded to his email with a phone call interview he conducted from Buffalo while sitting in a hotel room with a honeymoon-style hot tub. The *New York Times* food editor, Sam Sifton, also responded to Wey and called him while he had that hot tub room in Buffalo, which to Wey seemed to suggest that maybe having a heart-shaped tub was some sort of lucky omen, but either way, Sifton met him in New York City when he came to cook and asked him what he wanted to do. Wey gave the answer "change culture," which was vague and unsatisfying and in retrospect a little silly, but damn, Sifton kind of put him on the spot. Despite that poor answer, Sifton was interested in writing about Wey, and so he asked him where he was going to travel next, and Wey said, "Los Angeles."

At the time, he wasn't going to LA. Even now, he doesn't know why he said LA—he hadn't even started sending his famous template emails to folks in LA—but once he said it, he knew it had to happen and that it would force him to will some sort of dinner into existence. So he sent one of those emails to Roy Choi's restaurant Chego!, and within a few days someone from the restaurant must've forwarded it to Choi, because he responded and told Wey he liked his energy and should definitely come through. Once he got Choi locked in, Wey reached out again to Sifton and said the magic words "Roy Choi," and suddenly Sifton was sending an advance video team out to film him shopping for food, and booking a flight to LA to meet up with him for a story and video for the *Times*, and NPR had also gotten in touch about a potential story, and holy shit, it was all happening; all he needed to do was get out to LA.

Because he had no American identification, Wey didn't believe he could fly without legal issues, so he boarded a Greyhound bus to California from New Orleans. The problem with Greyhound bus routes from New Orleans to LA was that they went through parts of New Mexico, and the problem with parts of New Mexico was that they were within a hundred miles of the Mexican border, and the problem with being within a hundred miles of the Mexican border was that Border Patrol had jurisdiction over those parts, and the problem with the Border Patrol's jurisdiction was that they tended to frown upon discovering Nigerian immigrants in the country on expired student visas and without proper identification, and so two days before *The New York Times* and Roy Choi and NPR were supposed to use their amplifiers to make Tunde Wey famous, he was arrested and shipped to the US Immigration and Customs Enforcement El Paso Processing Center to await potential expulsion from the country.

CHAPTER 11

Pioneer Woman, Ree Drummond, Pawhuska, Oklahoma

T he folks in Pawhuska always called her by her first name.

"You come here to see Ree?" they'd ask.

The folks in Pawhuska liked to tell stories about Ree. How Ree randomly showed up at her restaurant/coffee shop/bakery/home goods store, the Pioneer Woman Mercantile, and signed autographs for two hours for free even though a lot of people in that position would've charged for that sort of thing. They told stories about her husband, Ladd, too. How he ate breakfast most days in the Merc and was always unfailingly polite and respectful, and threw a big Fourth of July party in the middle of town and set off the fireworks himself.

The folks in Pawhuska liked to tell other stories too.

BEFORE REE OWNED A TOWN, her parents owned a house along the seventh fairway of Hillcrest Country Club in the Tulsa suburb of Bartlesville. Ree Smith was the third of four, two boys and two girls, and spent her youth doing the things the daughter of an orthopedic surgeon does, drinking Shirley Temples in the Hillcrest clubhouse, dating boys at St. Luke's Episcopal Church camp, and practicing ballet. Ree was obsessed with ballet, with the grace and beauty and perfectly choreographed movement, and lined her walls with pictures of Gelsey Kirkland and Mikhail Baryshnikov.

By the end of high school, Bartlesville felt small and ballet wasn't going to be a career, so Ree went away to school, attending the University of Southern California. She planned to major in broadcast journalism and be an anchor someday, though at some point that dream took a left turn, and she ended up focusing on gerontology. Majoring in the study of old age only leaves you with so many work options, so after school she "helped wrangle celebrity guests for senior-centric consumer trade shows" and, perhaps as proof of her success in that field, once made out with James Garner in an elevator.

Eventually she returned to Oklahoma with vague plans to study for the LSAT and go to law school in Chicago. One night during her time at home, after purchasing a $495 wool gabardine winter coat in olive, she went out with her friends to the local J-Bar, where she met a young cattle rancher from Pawhuska named Ladd Drummond. They flirted and talked all night, and eventually she gave him her number, but Ladd was dating someone, so she didn't hear from him for four months. During that time, Ree played the field and made plans to move to Chicago.

But when Ladd settled his own affairs, he called, and they went out. And then they went out again, and again, and again. Eventually she stopped thinking about moving to the Windy City, and they began dating in earnest. They watched action movies and she cooked him linguine with clams, which he hated but ate anyway, because that's the type of guy Ladd was. She gave up being a vegetarian and started eating steak again. Soon after that, they got engaged. And soon after that, in 1996, they got married in St. Luke's, had a party at Hillcrest, went on a honeymoon to Australia, got pregnant, and moved onto Ladd's family's property.

TEN MILES FROM BIRD CREEK, past several dead armadillos, at CR 4461, sits the white gate for Drummond Ranch. Frederick Drummond came to

America from Scotland in 1882, and then—after failing to find success in New York City and Texas—ended up in St. Louis working at a dry goods store. One of the store's customers hired him away to work as a clerk at the Osage Mercantile Company in Pawhuska in 1886, where Drummond fell in love with a girl from Kansas named Addie Gentner and married her.

Drummond started his own Hominy Trading Company, which made its mark selling Pendleton blankets to the Osage Native Americans on the nearby reservation. Over the generations, the size of the Drummond land holdings grew. In 2010, *Modern Farmer's* "Land Report" listed the Drummond family as the seventy-ninth-largest owners of land in America. By 2013, they were number seventeen, one place behind Denver billionaire Philip Anschutz, with 433,000 acres. Ladd, along with his brother, Tim, owned a healthy portion of those lands under Drummond Land & Cattle, and aside from their private cattle ranching operations, the Drummonds also secured a Bureau of Land Management contract that paid them generously to host wild horses and burros on their land. The game behind the game had changed, but the Drummonds were still figuring it out.

For ten years, Ree and Ladd lived out on the ranch, and as he conducted the business, she raised and homeschooled their four children. But for some reason, in the early summer of 2006, Ladd offered to take all of those children out with him to work cattle in order to give Ree time to herself. Suddenly faced with actual free time, Ree thought that starting an online diary might help her stay connected with her mother, whom she'd had a strained relationship with since her parents divorced.

Ree didn't know what the hell she was doing with the blog, but quickly got savvy with the technology and, within four months of launching, talked knowingly of browsing her site meter and checking the list of referring URLs.

Ree established a public persona and a narrative around that persona before social media made everyone think about their public face. She was unique in the blogosphere at the time, because her life subtly encouraged and propped up the aspirational fantasy aspect of leaving your life to move to a ranch and the novelistic, romantic fantasy of having a smoking-hot cowboy husband waiting at that ranch who just happened to be one of the largest landowners in the country and progressive enough to help with the kids and give her time to herself.

Then, on December 23, 2006, she posted a beautiful shot of just baked cinnamon rolls. Her comments went crazy, with everyone asking if she'd post the recipe for the rolls, and soon she was regularly posting food shots and recipes alongside the pictures of kids and the stories of life on the ranch, and the blog took off yet again. She began winning awards—including beating out *The Huffington Post* for Weblog of the Year at the 2009 Bloggies—and yet again she adapted to her place in this world, hiring a Bay Area communications firm to manage her site and launching TastyKitchen.com, an online community where other food bloggers could join, comment, contribute, and search for recipes. More than four million unique visitors a month started frequenting her various sites.

In 2010, the Food Network had celebrity chef/television personality Bobby Flay do a Throwdown Thanksgiving Special, cooking against Ree at the Lodge on Drummond Ranch. Trisha Yearwood judged. Ree entertained the crowd with comments about wearing Spanx and told Flay she watched his show while breastfeeding and then beat him in the throwdown. The Food Network brass were charmed, and within a year, *The Pioneer Woman*, hosted by Ree Drummond, was on the air.

Her show gave her a new, even bigger audience, and the folks she mentioned in her blog were now live characters for the camera: her kids and husband; her best friend, Hyacinth; her developmentally disabled older brother, Mike; and people like Edna Mae and Pastor Ken and Ralph the Cattle Buyer. The critics didn't love it; *The New Yorker* wrote that Ree "comes off as nervous, stiff, and enervated, as if she can't muster up much enthusiasm for her own endeavor. She speaks in a near-monotone, pausing awkwardly between thoughts (not long enough here, too long there), and when she tells a joke, there's no oomph in her delivery. The show, a mere thirty minutes long, is thus surprisingly boring and difficult to follow."

But as with her blog, she—and her family—learned television quickly, and—critical darling or not—she had an audience, and they kept coming back. The show is currently in its twenty-first season.

On October 31, 2016, Ladd and Ree opened the Pioneer Woman Mercantile at 532 Kihekah Avenue in downtown Pawhuska in the former Osage Mercantile Building, the very same business Frederick Drummond worked in when he first came to town. They spent two years overhauling the building, and Ree documented the construction and recipe testing on her blog and Instagram, even asking for readers to weigh in on things like whether the French Dip should include cheese.

The space itself was incredible—an expansive mix of Ree's own well-thought-out aesthetic, with colorful Le Creuset pots in the background and elaborate wooden carvings and black-and-white photos of cattle on the wall; a down-home restaurant, with weathered-edge wood tables and vintage Cholula hot sauce holders that served Ree's own recipes for fried pork chops and chicken fried steak and tangy tomato beef brisket; coffee baristas marking up chalkboards with Ree's favorite single-origin drip Chemex coffees and cortados alongside signature drinks like the Spicy Cowgirl; a candy counter display that was part Willy Wonka and part Old Tyme Candy Shoppe, featuring a taffy tree; an upstairs bakery selling Ree's signature glazed scones stuffed with Red Hots candy; a downstairs home goods store selling everything from stacks of *The Pioneer Woman* magazine with Ree on the cover, advertising recipes for "Caramel Apple Sweet Rolls" and "Chili for Cowboys," to Charlie the Ranch Dog books and statues, to Ulysses S. Grant finger puppets, to vintage fabric doorstops that look like squirrels, all while Toby Keith and Garth Brooks and Tim McGraw hits played in the background.

The day the 25,000-square-foot combination restaurant/bakery/deli/coffee shop/candy and home goods store opened, the line of people waiting to get in ran for three blocks. The folks waiting to spend their money in the Pioneer Woman's place of business ran the gamut, from well-dressed retired women in floral scarves and gold earrings in from Dallas and Oklahoma City and Tulsa, to working-class women from the rural towns and exurbs in flannel shirts and comfortable walking shoes, to T-shirt-clad tourists from as far away as Alaska. The idea that folks from all over the world might come to a town two and a half hours away from Oklahoma City and wait in line for three hours to eat in what, more or less, feels like an upscale Cracker Barrel, as staged by the set designers of *Sweet Home Alabama* in collaboration with Williams Sonoma; that they might plan all their vacation time and spend all their money to participate in the ranch-inspired fever dream of an upper-middle-class suburban doctor's daughter, married to the biggest landowning cattle rancher in Oklahoma, only seemed crazy if you knew nothing of the way her rabid fan base Oprah-fied Ree.

Ree had managed to thread a needle through a hole so small only she could really see it. Her refracted interpretation of the Culinary Revolution felt aspirational yet achievable for a swath of mostly southern women who might think the Barefoot Contessa was too East Coast elitist, but wanted to relate to someone a little more elegant and suburb-friendly than Paula Deen. Ree's money and time away from Oklahoma gave her a cosmopolitan air that felt nearly exotic, but she blended it seamlessly into the narrative of being a cowboy's wife. She was a Magic Eye picture, inviting you to relax and look and see whatever it was you wanted to see.

The folks in Pawhuska appreciated what Ree and Ladd had done for their town. How they'd created more than three hundred jobs themselves, and how twenty businesses had opened since they built the Merc. How folks could now rent out their houses on Airbnb and get steady income all through the summer and fall. How the increase in tax revenue for the town meant they might be able to pave the road to the Tallgrass Prairie Preserve and develop Bluestem Lake. The folks in Pawhuska joked about them owning the town, but it was barely a joke. They bragged about how Ree and Ladd had just

Mosaic Oklahoma explores the landmarks, people and communities that epitomize Oklahoma culture. First stop? Pawhuska! Explore the history and heritage of the Osage Nation, the revitalization of downtown Pawhuska and the impact of "The Pioneer Woman." Interviews include Osage Chief Geoffrey Standing Bear, Osage elder Edward Red Eagle, the Tallgrass Prairie's Harvey Payne and "The Pioneer Woman" Ree Drummond.

Greetings from

Mosaic Oklahoma premieres during Festival on OETA!

OETA HD: **OETA OKLA:**
March 7 at 7 p.m.   March 8 at 6:30 p.m.
March 11 at 2 p.m.   March 12 at 7 p.m.
March 17 at 12:30 p.m.

Love the show? Call during these times to pledge your support! 1(800)288-9494

OETA
FOUNDATION

A Mosaic postcard found in Pawhuska, Oklahoma

opened an eight-room "cowboy luxury" hotel called the Boarding House, down the street from the Mercantile, in April 2018 and within weeks it was booked *through next year*, thanks to its beds (made up with the exclusive bedding collection Ree was selling through Walmart), themes like Tack Room and Drugstore Room, and the promise of exclusive access to the Merc.

The folks in Pawhuska marveled at the fact that she'd also just opened P-Town Pizza up the block in June 2018, serving wood-fired pizzas with three types of pepperoni and craft cocktails and desserts in mason jars, and was working on the P.W. Steakhouse & Saloon, which would be a fancier, reservations-type date spot, and also an event space for weddings and, as Ree put it, "hoe-downs." The folks in Pawhuska were a little bit wary that so much of the town's economy was based around the popularity of one woman, but if it meant steady jobs and money for school improvements and a new downtown, it was hard to be upset.

On the way out of town, next to T-Bone's Original Pig Stand and just past the American flag billboard from Pawhuska Elks Lodge 2542 reminding drivers to "Honor Our Flag," sat the old ALCO store. In the third season of her television show, Ree went shopping there for mousse and other fun hair products to put in a goodie bag for a high school reunion she was hosting at the Lodge on Drummond Ranch. Ree now owned the building but kept it closed, using it only as a storage facility. The folks in Pawhuska said it was the only existing building in town that could possibly hold all her merchandise.

CHAPTER 12

Freret Street, New Orleans, Louisiana, 2011, Part 2

Cure opened in February 2009 to little fanfare. Folks didn't know what Kohnke and Bodenheimer were trying to do. They didn't know why there was a dress code. Or why you couldn't get a Coors Light. Or why the bartenders gently tried to steer you away from standard bar drink orders to something new. Slowly, their "thing" caught on. They were lucky—New Orleans had a cocktail drinking history and bartenders like Paul Gustings, at Tujague's, and Chris McMillian, at the Library Lounge and Kingfish, to keep the cocktail flame lit. By 2011, *Esquire*'s David Wondrich had named Cure one of America's best bars. The place was now a destination.

Tentatively, things began to build around the bar. First came Sarita's Grill with its Cuban-influenced Latin food, Beaucoup Juice (sno-balls and smoothies with fresh ingredients), Village Coffee & Tea, and then, by the end of 2009, Freret Street Poboy & Donut Shop. Most of these were modest, walk-up affairs opened by relatively inexperienced owners, folks from the neighborhood who sensed it was changing and wanted to get involved. In the parlance of marketing textbooks, they would be in the chapter on early adopters.

But by 2011, there was a third wave. First, fancy hot dog joint Dat Dog opened in a tiny space not far from Cure; then Memphis native Chip Apperson and chef Adolfo Garcia (who'd worked together in New York City) teamed up in the old Bill Long's Bakery building to create a chef-driven southern diner. Garcia, who already had three restaurants in the Warehouse District, also partnered on the other side of their building with chef Jeff Talbot to open Ancora Pizzeria & Salumeria, featuring Neapolitan pizzas cooked in a Stefano Ferrara pizza oven imported from Naples and "hand-crafted with materials from Mt. Vesuvius."

On top of that, Adam Biderman, a New Orleans native who'd spent his high school years eating at Dunbar's, had just come back from two years in Atlanta cooking at national sensation Holeman & Finch. Biderman opened his much-acclaimed fast-casual cheeseburger restaurant, the Company Burger, at 4600 Freret. Then the Latin grocery store Supermercado moved down the block, and its old space became The Midway Pizza, a Chicago-style deep-dish joint with craft beer and cocktails. The local papers covered the spate of openings as an announcement of a new important food street in New Orleans, one titling their story "The Rebirth of Freret Street." The previously disbanded Krewe of Freret reformed and started making parade floats again.

And after a shooting shut Friar Tuck's down, there was a new tenant in the space. Origami Sushi featured a trio of master sushi chefs, plus "specialty cocktails, unique rolls, spectacular sushi, and sashimi platters."

CHAPTER 13

Gabriel Rucker, Portland, Oregon, Part 2

For Gabriel Rucker, the latter aughts blurred.

Le Pigeon was still a phenomenon, the kind of culinary aurora borealis that consistently packed three seatings into a Tuesday night, and Rucker, in his twenties, didn't really have anything else to worry about. His social life had remained almost stubbornly consistent: work, go to either the B-Side or Rontoms, drink Powers whiskey, smoke cigarettes, sometimes do drugs, have an after-party at his house with a soft cutoff of four a.m. primarily to showcase his continual improvement in mastering the ballads of Pavement, go to sleep, wake up, get a coffee with lots of cream and a breakfast burrito at Floyd's Coffee Shop on Morrison, and head to work by ten or eleven a.m. Even if it wasn't healthy, it was consistent. But then two changes—one work-related, one personal—altered the narrative course of Rucker's space-time continuum.

The first was Andy Fortgang. Fortgang was a born-and-bred Manhattanite who as a teenager started reading cookbooks and getting into cooking. His mother, while at a work event, was telling a friend about her son's nascent interest, and the friend mentioned that her friend's brother was a chef, and maybe Fortgang could come see his kitchen. The next week there was a phone call at the house for Fortgang. It was Tom Colicchio.

"Hey, Andy," he said. "I heard you like to cook. Want to come to my restaurant on Sunday?"

From then on, Fortgang spent nearly all his free time at Gramercy Tavern, doing whatever they'd let him do, until they finally hired him on for the summer. For college, he attended Cornell's hospitality school, with Colicchio helping him secure roles at other notable restaurants, like Jean-Georges and Aureole, in the summer. He'd always worked in the kitchens, but when he got a chance to learn the front-of-house roles, that excited him even more, and that became his life. He started as a manager at Gramercy, and looked into going elsewhere, but when Colicchio started Craft, he urged Fortgang to stay on as his beverage director. During that time he began dating his future wife, Lauren, who had been a pastry chef at Craft, and she convinced him there were opportunities outside of New York City.

While visiting Portland, he had dinner with Lauren at Le Pigeon. Fortgang was blown away by the meal he had, and it stuck with him all the way back to New York. Searching on Craigslist, he realized Le Pigeon was looking for a manager, so he got in touch with Rucker. Though Bruce Carey, the successful restaurateur who'd started Zefiro and now owned several restaurants in Portland, had offered him a job, he decided he wanted to try something that wasn't necessarily safe but exciting and new. And Rucker and Le Pigeon, especially during those fiesta days, were certainly that.

Two months later, Fortgang was the new manager of Le Pigeon, and quickly went about restoring (or, really, storing) an order that had been missing with Rucker's extemporaneous, ad hoc, improvisational jazz–styled management technique, including getting everyone health insurance, keeping proper records, having a list of the people they bought things from in a spreadsheet, and adding table and seat numbers so servers didn't have to ask each table what they'd ordered.

While Fortgang was whipping the restaurant into shape, Rucker fell for Hana Kaufman. She was from Battle Ground, Washington, twenty-five miles from Portland, just over the Washington border, and had come to Portland at the encouragement of her brother after briefly enrolling at the University of Nevada, Las Vegas. While at community college in Portland, she waited tables at Macaroni Grill and went out on a lunch date with a coworker, who took her to Gotham. Rucker's girlfriend at the time was her server. Kaufman had never seen anything like Gotham—the edgy, hip vibe, the food, the meat cleaver tattoos, any of it. Her mind sufficiently melted, she rode her bike home, went to Macaroni Grill, quit, and rode back to Gotham to apply for a serving job. She was hired that day. She worked the same shift as Rucker, but he didn't talk to her other than to offer her beef tongue once. She turned that down, and they didn't talk again.

After Gotham imploded, Kaufman worked for Naomi Pomeroy at Clark-lewis as a food runner, helped open the hip sushi joint Yakuza, and took shifts at Simpatica catering. When her best friend, Alise, went on vacation, she asked Kaufman to cover her shift at a new bar called Rontoms, and she just sort of stayed on working there.

But Kaufman didn't really get to know Rucker until she worked the last two infamous days at Colleen's, which involved screaming patrons, brunch orders piling up for hours, and Colleen allegedly getting in a fistfight with someone doing meth in the stairwell. Not long after, Rucker took over, made it Le Pigeon, and eventually broke up with his girlfriend.

At the time, Kaufman was constantly hanging out and saying hello to everyone at Le Pigeon on her way to work. Eventually she got Rucker's number and would text him when she was working a bartending shift at Rontoms or the Aalto Lounge. He started showing up. One day, while Rucker was en-tertaining a friend from out of town at her bar, he put his arm around Kaufman while laughing. Whoa, she thought. She could feel electricity. Not long after that, for the first time, they kissed.

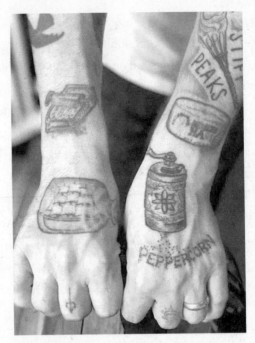

Gabriel Rucker's sardine and deviled ham tattoos

Another Gabriel Rucker Tattoo Story, as told by Hana Kaufman Rucker

We'd dated in secret for a while, but really, our first public date, aka the Most Portland Thing Ever, was a tattoo chef dinner, in which, I think, like, six tattoo artists and six chefs all got together for a dinner party, and the chefs all got tattoos of whatever they were making for dinner. Gabriel picked me up in this old Cadillac he'd gotten from his uncle, and we drove up to North Portland and made out and went in this hip-hop clothing store and tried on ridiculous outfits, then went to this dinner. I watched him get a tattoo of a can of sardines and a tattoo of canned deviled ham (note: watching your boyfriend get a tattoo is like watching him play *Call of Duty*, aka boring, not fun), and then he ditched me to go to the kitchen and cook his meal and left me with a bunch of random people I didn't know. So it wasn't exactly the most romantic first date, but the food and the make-outs were great.

They went on practicing a progressive form of restaurant-industry dating, which basically meant sleepovers at Rucker's house post-after-parties, but the turning point was a freak snowstorm in December 2008 that forced Rucker to close his restaurant for several days. Snowed in with nothing to do, Rucker and Kaufman spent the entire time watching all episodes of the epic *Lonesome Dove* TV miniseries, eating frozen pizza, and driving around in her ever-reliable Honda Accord, picking up friends, and bringing them back to the house to party. By Christmas, when she drove him to the airport to go home, they were in love.

Four months later, they were hanging in Colonel Summers Park on a Monday. Mondays were when the Burning Man–esque Portland punk bike crew would show up to the park with kegs on bike trailers, and stereo systems on bike trailers, and hallucinogenic drugs not on bike trailers, and so they used to go and check out the scene. While lying in the grass, drinking rosé, making out, and generally acting very French, Kaufman thought she was sighing, but in actuality she spoke words aloud to the effect of "I think I could see myself spending the rest of my life with you." Rucker asked her if she was proposing, Kaufman said yes, and Rucker said, "Hell yeah, I want to marry you." And then they didn't talk about it again, possibly ever.

Almost exactly a month later, they were in New York City for the James Beard Awards. By 2009, Rucker had already been nominated twice for the national James Beard Rising Star Award, given to a chef age thirty or younger "who displays an impressive talent and who is likely to make a significant impact on the industry in years to come," but lost that year to Nate Appleman of A16 in San Francisco. They wandered around the next day on Canal Street, and Kaufman was haggling with a merchant selling knockoff Louis Vuitton handbags when they spotted a beautiful white gold and diamond ring in a jewelry store window. When they went in the store, Rucker got down on his knee and proposed with the ring they just saw, and then they went to a hipster café for brunch and Fernet shots and called their parents. It was a glorious day.

On September 6, 2009, Gabriel Rucker and Hana Kaufman were married on the banks of the Clackamas River in front of a hundred of their closest friends. They had no idea what they were doing.

The date was chosen because Rucker only closed Le Pigeon on the Fourth of July and Labor Day, and they weren't turning around a May engagement for July. The Clackamas River location was the property of a friend of a friend of Rucker's, who promised to cut the grass by the river for the wedding. They got Simpatica to cater the event because they'd both worked there, and they were given the choice of hamburgers or hot dogs. They chose both, and managed to talk them into also providing corn on the cob and huckleberry pie. Kaufman spent every dollar she had on a Sarah Seven wedding dress she found on Etsy for five hundred dollars. Rucker had already bought his suit from Portland designer Adam Arnold for the James Beard Awards several years earlier, and just re-wore it.

The day of the wedding, it was pouring so hard that people pulled over on the side of the freeway, saying they couldn't see. Kaufman's bartender/hairdresser friend did her hair in the car. When she got to the wedding, Rucker had already opened a bottle of Jack Daniel's. They each took a swig and started setting up chairs. Kaufman was wearing a sweatshirt and jeans, and eventually someone had to tell her to put her wedding dress on. Her aunt did her makeup. Kaufman didn't actually see herself in her wedding dress until she was peeing by the side of a car and caught her reflection in the window. Right before the ceremony, the meteorologists and God shined their collective greatness down upon the Kaufman-Rucker espousal and it became incredibly sunny and beautiful. There was a rainbow.

An ordained minister friend who also happened to be Rucker's chef friend, Tommy Habetz, married them (it would take them two more months to realize that this was not a legal act and they needed to file paperwork to make it official).

The next morning, they got up well before five a.m. to go off on a honeymoon to Maui. They hadn't initially planned on it, but enough people gave

Rucker shit that he finally just booked a two-day honeymoon. Rucker remembered drinking cocktails by the pool and finishing Dennis Lehane's creepy novel *Shutter Island*. Kaufman remembered the hotel staff almost not believing these two pale, white-trash kids with tattoos all over the place could afford to go to this nice Maui hotel; that everyone looked at them as if they'd won the trip on a game show or something. And she also remembered that at the swim-up bar, this wealthy older guy came up to Rucker.

Wealthy Older Guy: Are you Gabriel Rucker?

Rucker: Yes?

Wealthy Older Guy: I absolutely love your restaurant. I go there every time I'm in Portland. I think it's the best restaurant in the country. Would you mind taking a picture with my wife and I?

BY 2010, THEY WERE RUNNING into what felt to Rucker like a good problem: the kitchen staff was growing, and he realized that his second-in-command, Erik Van Kley, was too damn talented to keep in the supporting actor role. He needed his own show. By now, with all the attention Le Pigeon was getting, Rucker and Fortgang (who in the previous years had bought into the restaurant as an owner) were receiving nearly an offer a week from different restaurant groups or investment groups or rich dudes from Tokyo to open another Le Pigeon in Vegas or New York or wherever. But Rucker had no interest in doing any of that shit—for one, he felt like they always had ulterior motives, and two, life at the time was overwhelming enough without bringing more people into the mix.

At the time, Rucker, Fortgang, and Van Kley all loved Keith McNally's Balthazar in New York; they loved its versatility, the fact that you could go there for a perfect breakfast meeting but also go late at night for drinks and all of it was exceptional. They felt like Portland really lacked that all-things-to-all-people, three-meal place, and so they decided—with the help of local investors—to do a sort of everything French bistro called Little Bird.

Van Kley and Rucker had ideas for the Little Bird menu, but they were still coming from Le Pigeon's model of freestyle creation, so they really didn't lock down an opening menu until they got into the kitchen there and started messing around. Said menu was mostly a departure from Le Pigeon's purposefully exotic, even challenging theme. There were a few Le Pigeon nods, like a crispy pig ear salad with a poached egg, and a deep-fried beef tongue entrée, but there was also a ham-and-Gruyère baguette, butter lettuce, Roquefort and tomato salad, coq au vin, and steak frites. There was a pork chop with a cabbage galette and the Le Pigeon burger. There were twice-fried frites. The narrative surrounding the place was same technique and ingredients, but simpler, more approachable, more accessible. And also two and a half times the size.

With Van Kley running the kitchen, and Su-Lien Pino as sous chef, Le Pigeon's entire senior structure, aside from Rucker, had shipped off to Little Bird. Andy Fortgang's wife, Lauren, also joined the team as pastry chef. The hype for the launch was deafening, at a local and national level. The food media frothed over the idea of getting a more approachable, casual Rucker menu for lunch (and downtown!), and Rucker loved the idea of letting Van Kley spread his wings more, and when they opened at the very end of 2010, the restaurant was jammed from the beginning, and looked like yet another Rucker success story.

But behind the scenes it didn't quite feel that way. There were grumbles in the press that Little Bird was just a watered-down version of Le Pigeon, that the formal atmosphere and service didn't mesh with the more casual food. Rucker, as an owner but not the chef, wasn't exactly sure how to act either, and so he threw himself into helping by doing (in this case, cooking the lunch shift), instead of overseeing and managing. He would come in and do the lunch shift at Little Bird, then ride his bike over the bridge to cook dinner at Le Pigeon, where he was now without his senior team. It was an unsustainable work schedule, and Rucker felt, for the first time in a while, that his identity was up in the air. The success of Le Pigeon and how it was so tied up in the identity of Rucker made Little Bird an extremely difficult situation to balance correctly, as Rucker wanted it to be Van Kley's kitchen and yet the superimposed narrative in the press would always say it was a Gabriel Rucker joint and judge it as such.

In an attempt to deal with the depression and stress, Rucker started sneaking nips of booze even during lunch, taking quick pulls from the bottles just like at Southern Exposure Bistro, and then drinking more openly at Le Pigeon during dinner, as that was just part of the Party Time Gabriel Rucker Show Experience. It was an extremely trying time, and then amid all of this, Rucker won the 2011 James Beard Rising Star Award.

There was nothing about that particular year that suggested the 2011 James Beard Awards would be special (except possibly the pending arrival of the Ruckers' first child, Gus, in July). Rucker had been nominated three times before, and at this point, the whole crew had a routine. Rucker and his wife and Fortgang and Van Kley would all go stay at Fortgang's parents' house on the Upper West Side. Because it was a formal event, Rucker put on a tuxedo, and because he was representing Portland, he wore purple Vans, and they sat in the Lincoln Center auditorium listening to Tom Colicchio, Ming Tsai, and Traci Des Jardins host the awards.

As the Rising Star came up, he heard the list of names announced: himself, Aaron London from Ubuntu in Napa, Thomas McNaughton from flour + water in San Francisco, Christina Tosi from Milk Bar in New York City, and Sue Zemanick from Gautreau's in New Orleans. It was a particularly competitive crew, and so Rucker settled in to clap for whomever he thought might win, with Vegas giving even odds between McNaughton and Tosi. But then, out of nowhere, they said his name, making Rucker the first Portland chef to ever win the Rising Star Award. He sat there stunned. Finally, Kaufman tapped him on his leg. "That's you, buddy. That's your name!"

The rest was a blur. The speech, the photos, the other awards. He just

couldn't fathom it. He fucking won. A national James Beard Award. To celebrate, they skipped the standard after-party to go down to the Lower East
Side, first to the wine bar Terroir and then over to Alphabet City because a
friend who used to bartend in Portland was now working at a dive bar in
Lower Manhattan. Fittingly, it was called the B-Side.

WINNING A NATIONAL JAMES BEARD AWARD helped everything. The res-
taurants were more crowded. Rucker's identity issues momentarily subsided.
And most importantly, the publisher Ten Speed Press really wanted him to
write a cookbook. Through his literary agent, he was connected to Meredith
Erickson, a Canadian writer who'd previously worked with the team behind
Montreal dining sensation Joe Beef on their acclaimed cookbook "of sorts,"
The Art of Living According to Joe Beef.

In many ways, Joe Beef was Le Pigeon's uncanny Canadian cousin. The
2005 restaurant from David McMillan, Frédéric Morin, and Allison Cun-
ningham started out as a small bistro in a scruffy neighborhood, but it began
to get a national (and then international) reputation with their daily-changing
experimental but fun-loving dishes, like a foie gras sandwich stuffed with
bacon, cheddar, chicken-skin mayonnaise, and maple syrup; or the smoked
meat croquettes; or the bloody steaks served with the marrow bones. And
their cookbook, which was not quite a cookbook but more a series of recipes
surrounded by essays and other playful service elements, like "Building a
Garden in a Crack Den," seemed like a great example of how to make a cookbook people might actually want to read.

After the Beard victory, the pressure to produce the book became more
intense, and over the next year, Erickson would visit from London for two-
week periods, to try to cram as much as they could into those days. Rucker
wanted the book to be weird and correct and to capture their spirit, but he
also knew he didn't have the sort of gravitas to just make a fancy coffee table
cookbook. If he was going to do something, he needed people to actually cook

the recipes inside; it had to be useful. But figuring out how to translate Le Pigeon recipes for home cooks proved really fucking hard. For one, he didn't really have any recipes saved—Le Pigeon prided itself on not repeating dishes, so when they went off the menu, they were gone. The best he could hope for was to find little notes he'd scribbled about dishes stuffed randomly into binders. Second, many of those dishes involved a four-day prep time, and some pretty ridiculous directions. Rucker could just see them trying to make his lamb's brain dish: *First, get a lamb head....* Well, it was hard for *him* to get lamb head, so how would they get it? And then, if they did get it, they would have to get the brain out. How did you do that? *Well, get a really big drill with a huge drill bit and drill the brain out. Don't have a huge drill? Well, just use a giant knife and a hammer!*

None of that seemed really feasible, so Rucker would spend hours sitting in the basement of their tiny house in Portland's Brooklyn neighborhood, at his computer, listening to the San Francisco Giants game on the radio, ripping through cigarettes as he desperately tried to craft single-day home-cook recipes out of weeklong-prep meals, his dyslexia ensuring the spell-check got a vigorous workout. Afterward, he would meet with Erickson to try to put it all together, getting a couple of whiskeys during their lunch meetings, which Erickson pretended not to notice.

As 2012 came to a close, Little Bird and Le Pigeon were both in better places, and the *Oregonian* had even named Little Bird its Restaurant of the Year for 2012, but Rucker continued to slide, and 2013 seemed like it might finally be too much. On top of running the two restaurants and having a kid at home and working on the cookbook, in the winter of 2013, the Ruckers found out they were going to be having a second child, whose due date would be right around the book release. But just like before, as the internal stress piled up, from the outside great things continued to happen.

At the 2013 James Beard Awards, Rucker won Best Chef in the Pacific Northwest. He'd so expected to lose that he'd been back in the kitchen, working up the dinner for the event in his chef coat and clogs, and just slipped out of the kitchen into the awards ceremony for his category. The ushers tried to kick him out, but he pointed up to the screen: "That's me—let me just see what happens." And again, to his surprise, he heard his name.

After three bottles of Krug champagne at Pearl & Ash, and a late-night after-party solo hang with Van Kley consisting of them finishing a bottle of Johnnie Walker Red and getting emotional, Rucker passed out.

On September 18, Rucker's daughter Babette was born. Two days later, mother and daughter were in attendance for the official release of *Le Pigeon: Cooking at the Dirty Bird*. The book was a true collaborative dance between Rucker and Erickson, and also Andy Fortgang (who added his own "Pigeon Pours" drink pairing suggestions) and Lauren Fortgang, who handled the book's dessert recipes. Erickson had pulled it off: it had all the eclectic touches you might expect from a Rucker project, but still felt functional as a serviceable cookbook.

With the birth of his daughter coming so close to the release, they planned a shortened book tour with four days in New York, kicking off with an amazing night at the Spotted Pig. April Bloomfield and her kitchen staff had decided to offer a few Le Pigeon dinner specials for guests to order off the menu while Rucker, freed from cooking, was supposed to act as a host and honored guest, going around the dining room talking to folks who'd shown up to celebrate the book's release. But Rucker didn't do much of that. He got so drunk he was forced to pass out upstairs on the third-floor bench. He'd completely humiliated himself in front of chef April Bloomfield on her own turf, thus embarrassing her too. He could feel the mortification on his coauthor Erickson's face as well, forced to apologize for this person she'd collaborated with on the book they were celebrating in front of her friends.

Rucker had always felt like his identity, the thing that drew people to him, was that he was the fun, cool chef, the guy who could get drunk while he cooked and still do a fantastic job, and everyone else would look at how much fun he was having while he was still making delicious food and they would be impressed, and in his mind, he was pulling it off, always pulling it off. But in September 2013, in New York City, the curtain was pulled back. The entire New York trip, Rucker was drunk, or maintenance-drinking in the morning because he was hungover and on his way to being drunk. He was drunk at Gramercy Tavern, and drunk at the Macy's demo kitchen. He looked like shit, and what's worse, he was performing like shit, unable to cook to even the standards of a middling chef.

Rucker hated what was happening to him. He hated the way it made him feel. On the flight back to Portland, he felt as low as he ever had. And yet he kept drinking.

He drank again on his trip down to San Francisco to do a cookbook event at Incanto. And he continued to drink back in Portland. Kaufman could see he was struggling. Perversely, part of the problem was Rucker didn't have a mean bone in his body, and when he got drunk, he wasn't nasty or destructive or cruel; he was just dopey and over-polite and silly, like a big puppy. It was always easy to forgive someone like that.

He'd tried to stop drinking before, but at the time, the other chefs around him at the festival event had laughed his declaration off as unserious. "Okay, man," they'd said. "Well, once you decide to stop pretending not to drink, you can meet us at the bar."

Rucker and Kaufman never said unkind things to each other—it was part of what made them work; they were both genuinely nice people—but in avoiding unkindness, Kaufman knew that she was also avoiding telling Rucker how she truly felt about his drinking. Now, when he got back from New York and she saw how depressed he was, she felt emboldened.

"Your kids are getting older," she said, "and they're going to start noticing this change in you, how daddy is one way when he's sober and another when he's not. Do you want that?"

Rucker knew he didn't, but he felt almost helpless to change that. It went on for a few more weeks. And then finally, on October 28, 2013, after yet another night of drinking too much, Rucker sat down briefly with his parents and Kaufman and his kids as they ate dinner at Little Bird, and asked his dad a question: "Hey, Dad, will you take me to an AA meeting tonight?"

His dad paused for a second. "Yeah," he said, "of course."

That night they found a meeting on Northeast Glisan Street, at a place called 12x12 Club Portland. It was a serious crowd—there were talks about getting out of prison, and losing kids, and it was a far cry from the Burning Man punk bicycle-park scene thirty-year-old Rucker was used to—but Rucker liked the honesty and the structure.

As they were leaving the meeting to head back to his house, Rucker's father turned to him. "Gabriel, if you do this and I help you, it will never be the same for us. If you go down this path, I won't be okay with you casually drinking around me again." His father patted his arm. "I'll help you, but our relationship will be different."

The next night after work, when Rucker got home his entire house was asleep. He hadn't had a drink that day, but the idea of going to sleep without some sort of substance in his system terrified him. Remembering that his old roommate had made a bunch of weed butter and stored it at their house, he opened the freezer and broke some shards of the frozen butter off the green hockey puck and swallowed them. Almost immediately he had buyer's remorse, and made himself throw them up. It was absolutely miserable.

The next two nights, he did the exact same thing.

On October 31, 2013, Rucker woke up early. He wanted to get to Little Bird to start his day by eight a.m., but he really felt like going to a meeting. He'd always assumed AA meetings were just at night, with coffee and cigarettes, the type of thing you see in *Fight Club*. But while searching around the Internet, he came across the Eastside Sunrise meeting, which took place in a church on Division Street. It was six forty-five a.m. when he found it, and he noticed they had a seven a.m. meeting. He went straight there.

Rucker was ready for a change, ready to give in to the process, and really didn't want to lose his restaurant or his family. He was blown away by the people in the meeting. Everyone was so clear, and the group felt very welcoming. In AA, they call the meeting you frequent most your "home group." Rucker had found his. That day, he got himself a sponsor, and Rucker has checked in with him every single day since then.

October 31, 2013, is Gabriel Cameron Rucker's sobriety date.

CHAPTER 14

Behind the Curtain, Anonymous Restaurant Publicist, USA

S he'd wanted to be a chef.

That was her plan, anyway, but her parents made her go to college first, so she picked a school in a city with a great food scene and found an internship with a public relations firm that specialized in hospitality. While there, she met a bunch of chefs and realized that she'd never be able to cut it in the kitchen (making her parents happy), but she wanted to stay around food, and so when she graduated, she applied and got a job as an account coordinator at a large PR firm that worked with restaurants in a big city.

An account coordinator was the lowest on the chain. Up top there was the executive director—the most powerful person, the person who goes to the big meetings but doesn't actually do any work on accounts—and then the account supervisors, who manage the work of account executives and account coordinators but are also responsible for finding new business, and then the account executives, who at least get to take meetings themselves and create agendas.

Account coordinators did not do any of that. Her day-to-day as an AC basically consisted of culling through magazines, online publications, and newspapers to find editors and writers to pitch and then writing pitches for every client nearly every single day: the new wine program at this restaurant, a St. Patrick's Day event at this bar, a new spring menu over here, etc. They used the company Cision's database, a crazy-expensive service that provided profiles of countless journalists, listing their specific beats, phone numbers, and emails.

Each day, using the database, she would send the same pitch to fifteen to twenty writers using an email system that would BCC everyone and hopefully enter their first names in the correct prompt, but of course this didn't always work and so writers occasionally received emails with wrong names or just [ENTER WRITER'S NAME HERE], which those writers would then tweet out as further evidence of PR people's stupidity. She knew in her heart of hearts that most of these email blasts were actually stupid and ineffective and that she wouldn't get a response, but the emails weren't about the actual writer so much as being able to show the client a lengthy monthly report showcasing any media results naming the client, and any stories in the works, but also stories pitched and the outlets they'd been pitched to. Sending out these mass pitches was crucial for padding the report.

While the day-to-day was boring, one of the perks of being at a big firm was that they worked with some amazing people—James Beard winners, Michelin-starred restaurants, etc.—and almost every night there was something to do. The majority of her coworkers were female, and the rest were gay men (in all her time on the job, she'd met just one straight male restaurant publicist). Of that 90 percent majority of women, 75 percent usually fit the same profile: white, attractive, under thirty-five, often sorority-experienced communication majors who really, truly loved food and wanted to be around its creation and innovation. Also, because entry-level gigs in these major cities often paid shit while expecting you to go out to events at night and look glamorous, mostly everyone tended to come from upper-middle-class families who could help subsidize expensive apartments and nice clothes. From that perspective, at least, the perception of the industry was more or less the reality.

SHE WORKED HER WAY UP IN THE BIG FIRM, and the job got infinitely more interesting. Initially, she was shocked by how much power she had to essentially turn chefs and bartenders into these fascinating characters who didn't really exist, for the sake of a marketable narrative. When she first started working with new clients, she would interview them and ask them to tell the story of their upbringing and how they first got into cooking, and often those stories would be boring, so she might push them a bit:

Her: So maybe your grandmother took you to a bakery when you were young?

Pastry Chef: Yeah, I mean, I guess that probably happened?

Her: Great, so basically you're a baking prodigy whose passion for creating perfect pastries was stoked by early memories of traveling to quaint bakeries with your stern but loving grandmother and the memories of the dough and flour seared into your brain almost before you were old enough to walk, and you instinctually knew you had no choice but to pursue this passion, that pastry was your lifeblood, and that you'd rather die than disrespect those childhood memories of you and your grandmother sitting in rocking chairs on her ramshackle porch, hungrily tucking into hot crossed buns, listening to the rain patter down on her tin roof as you learned what it meant to truly love something more than yourself.

Pastry Chef: My grandmother was a bank manager.

Her: All right, maybe don't mention your grandmother.

She quickly learned that there was a hierarchy of "gets" in the industry, both awards and placement in publications.

At the top sat the national James Beard Awards. With eighteen judges sorting through tens of thousands of restaurant and chef submissions the James Beard Foundation was also the hardest to actually influence, but she had certain strategies, including doing any and all James Beard fund-raisers, cooking at the James Beard House whenever possible, and trying to get into the top food festivals—Feast Portland, Pebble Beach, Aspen, Charleston, etc.—so that more and more judges could honestly say they'd tried your food. On top of that, she would send an email out to all the people she could find who were former Beard winners, but make it a casual email from the chef, humble-bragging about any and all "accolades I was lucky enough to receive" in order to get some name recognition.

After the Beard Awards were the national Best Of lists in notable publications. *Bon Appétit*'s Hot 10 list, written primarily by Andrew Knowlton (though Knowlton seemed to be phasing himself out), was the top get, both in terms of prestige and needle-moving, followed by Jordana Rothman's Restaurants of the Year at *Food & Wine*. After that it was basically a tie between the two major men's magazines (*GQ* and *Esquire*) with their Best New Restaurants lists, compiled by Brett Martin and Jeff Gordinier respectively, followed by *Eater* national critic Bill Addison's list (Addison has since decamped for the *Los Angeles Times*). From there you got down to the more influential local critics: Pete Wells and Adam Platt in New York City, Tom Sietsema in Washington DC, Brett Anderson in New Orleans, *New York Times* California critic Tejal Rao, Michael Russell in Portland, Hanna Raskin in Charleston, Alison Cook in Houston, Craig LaBan in Philadelphia, Kathleen Purvis in Charlotte, Phil Vettel in Chicago, Hal B. Klein and Melissa McCart in Pittsburgh, Soleil Ho in San Francisco, and others. In the kitchen of every restaurant she worked with, she would place pictures of all the major national critics and the significant local ones.

Local critics played a doubly important role, though, as they also acted as tour guides for the national critics when they came to town. So if Bill Addison was in Pittsburgh, he might hit up Hal B. Klein and ask him which four restaurants he should try while in the Steel City, thus giving Klein the power to act as a gatekeeper to publications he wasn't even directly involved with. And even food writers who were lucky enough to have their meals all over the country paid for by their publications weren't immune to influence, especially if it meant a comped room in a local boutique hotel, with a welcome basket filled with local booze and other goodies from clients. And if that local boutique hotel also just happened to have a new cool bar and restaurant where these writers might sneak in a snack and drink before they went out around town, well, that was never a bad thing, right?

She was still shocked when her mom would send an email after one of her clients was named in a Best Restaurant list and think it got there *only* on the merits of its food. And she truly felt bad for ambitious, interesting restaurants in smaller cities that couldn't afford PR and thought they were playing a game that wasn't at least partially rigged.

AS THE YEARS WENT BY, the job changed. At first, it was traditional: pitching stories and getting them into magazines, newspapers, and online publications; trying to get your clients on television; and to the "right" food-focused nonprofit events, especially ones with other high-caliber chefs and fancy people who might be potential investors for projects or James Beard voters or both.

But as social media took off, the job became less about media itself and more about controlling the chef's or the restaurant's social media. As the food media world moved more and more toward roundups of best breakfasts, best burgers, best places to visit, there was no longer an interesting story or compelling angle to pitch; it was just about getting your client on that list, and even then, there were so many damn lists that it was more just another notch in the belt to put in the monthly report. To combat that, she realized she could control more stories if they went right to the source, so she started encouraging her clients to use Instagram and Facebook and encouraging her restaurants to create their own e-newsletters.

Meanwhile, the nontraditional media changed as well. When she'd started, bloggers and Yelp Elite members wielded an almost shocking amount of power, and their ability to quickly get up posts meant restaurants could no longer quietly open and hope for a few weeks to get things right, so restaurants began doing "media preview" dinners, an ironic thing to call a dinner mostly featuring prolific Yelpers and people with their own personal food blogs who had no qualms about accepting freebies. She would be there too, to help control the meal and to make sure the right food was coming out and the stories behind the dishes were being told, that the best servers took care of the table, and that the chef came out and played his part and seemed charming. She hoped that after giving these bloggers something free, they in turn would give her something, either a first-look preview of the place or a chef profile or whatnot.

But now blogging was over. Everything was Instagram based. She often got emails from Instagram "influencers"—or, better yet, other PR agencies representing Instagram influencers—who flat-out asked for free stuff. Something along the lines of, "In exchange for a complimentary meal for me and three friends, I will provide an Instagram post and two photos on my Instagram story." She originally thought this sort of thing was ridiculous, but as social media evolved she began to realize that these folks actually delivered, and there was a return on that investment, and there was none of that fake dance of actually pretending these food bloggers were real journalists. Instagram had stripped away the veneer from that enterprise, and she found it simultaneously disgusting and refreshing.

THERE WERE PARTS OF HER JOB SHE LOVED. She loved the fact that she could get cooking advice and products from chefs, and be around hyper-passionate people all the time, and eat for free at incredible restaurants. She loved helping small businesses stay solvent and support a staff, and it was really cool and rewarding to watch something you'd designed or a story you'd shaped get the recognition it deserved, especially if she actually liked her client and knew they deserved good things. And often they were good people, but sometimes they were not, and they put you in an uncomfortable position or looked to exploit the fact that hers was a workforce primarily made up of younger women boosting older men.

THIS HIGHLIGHTED A FLIP SIDE that the #MeToo movement was starting to expose. These men, the good and the bad, thrived in the spotlight because the food media wanted them there. And now, she felt like there was some hypocrisy hidden in food media coverage of #MeToo. The restaurant industry was the most unprofessional professional industry in the world, and that was a well-known and documented fact, provided by the food media. They'd loved the stories of "bad boy" chefs and loose cannons. Mercurial people made for good copy. Didn't people read Bill Buford's *Heat* before 2017? And suddenly within two weeks the paradigm flipped and the food media acted as if it had been this triumphant investigative body from the beginning. Or journalists might reach out and ask if she had any clients that were women or people of color. It seemed cynical, or some insulting form of tokenism. Where were these requests before?

And yet, despite the issues, she still was drawn by it. She knew there was an expiration date on the PR side, and that going out most weeknights wouldn't be tenable with kids and a marriage. She had a plan, though.

One day, she thought, she'd love to open her own restaurant.

CHAPTER 15

Anjan and Emily Mitra, San Francisco, California, Part 2

By 2007, DOSA on Valencia's success started to create some good problems. It took six months just to deal with the surge of people coming in from the *San Francisco Chronicle*'s positive review. So many Indian families were driving up from all over the Bay Area that they would regularly get requests for tables for ten or fifteen people on a weekend night, and because they could see that a lot of times it was an entire family, from the grandmother down, they had a policy, even in their sixty-seat restaurant, that they'd seat parties of any size. It might take two hours and take up 30 percent of the restaurant, but they couldn't possibly turn anyone down. On top of that, catering calls were regularly coming in, for special events and weddings and everything else, and they just didn't have the capacity to fulfill that kind of a request. Also, at this point, with Anjan having left his daytime job, they occasionally ran into the issue of having too many bosses in the room. Pretty soon it was clear: they needed a bigger restaurant.

To try to understand what a new space might mean, they spent a lot of time in restaurants like Slanted Door and NOPA, both of which were absolute dining sensations in San Francisco at the time. NOPA was especially a unicorn, an all-things-to-all-people place featuring a huge bar with an ambitious cocktail program, upstairs and downstairs dining, and an incredible late-night industry scene, all while maintaining the feel of a neighborhood restaurant in a corner space. Seeing these places succeed was a confidence builder for Anjan and Emily, and so they decided they would put out the word that they were looking for a restaurant space 5,000 square feet and up. As DOSA on Valencia was only 1,600 square feet, they wanted something that would triple the size.

As fate would have it, a month after they'd started to officially look, Emily was closing the restaurant one day when her friend, a local chocolate maker, came in with another friend, Judith, who owned a building on Fillmore where they were looking to expand. In a strange coincidence, Anjan had worked out of an office space for two years on the same block and had long admired that building's architecture. It seemed, for a minute, like a perfect match.

Of course, it wasn't that easy. Judith had a partner in the building, her ex-husband, who rejected them outright and ended the conversation. They felt frustrated. The things he was asking for, they just couldn't rationalize. They didn't have investors; they only had the profits coming in from the other restaurant. After getting nowhere, Emily tried a different tack. She wrote the ex-husband a letter, telling him as honestly as possible why they couldn't afford to accept his terms, and if he ever changed his mind, to let them know. She heard nothing for a while, and figured the deal was dead. They started looking at other spaces, one by Urban Outfitters down in the Marina, and another in Mint Plaza that they came pretty close to signing a lease on. With the Mint Plaza lease papers sitting on her desk, the ex-husband called back. He was willing to make them another offer, this one much closer to what they had in mind. They quickly signed the lease on 1700 Fillmore, at the corner of Post.

The space took a year and a half to open. There were several speed bumps. They had to file for change of use. And it was also in the redevelopment district, which meant more hoops to jump through. But for whatever reason, compared to the panicked stress of Valencia, opening Fillmore felt like a breeze. Again they decided to do the interior design themselves, with the help of their architect, Jim Maxwell, who would help fill in the blanks in the spaces they couldn't understand. Certain elements were vital: they wanted an element of Bollywood glamour to it, as a call back to Anjan's childhood growing up in Juhu Beach around the people from that industry. They also wanted to make sure their signature rust color played a prominent part. But most importantly, they had to have the correct bar. On dates, Anjan and Emily always sat at the bar when they could—for one, because they weren't planners, but also because the bar at any restaurant always offers the best seat in the house: the pressure was off to order conventionally, you could people-watch easily, and you could engage in conversations with bartenders and peer into the soul of the restaurant. Plus . . . bar snacks!

At this point, the craft cocktail movement was sweeping through San Francisco, and Anjan and Emily were eager participants, quick to sample innovative drinks being introduced at Rye, Range, NOPA, Alembic, and Slanted Door. Because it was all they could afford at the time, DOSA on Valencia only had a beer and wine license, so they were determined that Fillmore would not only have a liquor license but also a cocktail program, and one that wouldn't just ride the trend of craft cocktails but would actually make sense with the South Indian food they served. To help execute that vision, they tapped Jonny Raglin, a longtime SF bartender who'd worked at Stars Bar, Incanto, and influential craft cocktail pioneer Absinthe. Raglin and Anjan developed the Spice Route Cocktail Menu, a gin-focused lineup of ten unique cocktails. One of the distinguishing features in Raglin's menu was that many of the drinks didn't just add spices to existing cocktail schematics, but actually incorporated complex nectars with the help of the cooks in the DOSA kitchen, like the black cardamom tincture in the Smoked Cup, and the curried nectar in the Bengali Gimlet. There was a Laughing Lassi cocktail with Bols Genever, Straus yogurt, cucumber, grains of paradise, agave nectar, Angostura, and mint. And the Juhu Palm, a gin drink with coconut milk, kaffir lime, bird's eye chili, and a "spanked" curry leaf.

Armed with a stunner of a cocktail menu; a bigger food menu, with entrées like whole fish and lamb chops; and more desserts and appetizers, DOSA on Fillmore seemed like it was well positioned for a huge opening. And then the economy broke.

Lehman Brothers went bankrupt. AIG failed. The bank bailout bill didn't pass the House, sending the stock market spiraling down 777 points, the most of any day in history up until that point. In September alone, 403,000 jobs were lost. By the end of October, the Bureau of Economic Analysis declared that America was officially in a recession.

Friends started to caution Anjan and Emily against opening the restaurant. "No one is spending money at restaurants right now!" they told them. "Everyone is just eating cereal and Wheat Thins!"

"Don't they realize we've been working on this place for eighteen months?" Anjan would ask Emily. They didn't have a choice. They'd sunk $2.5 million into the Fillmore space. They needed to open now.

On Friday, November 28, they finally opened their doors. Two days before, a series of coordinated terrorist attacks began in Bombay that ultimately killed 166 people and wounded more than 600. The day it started, Anjan was driving into work when he heard about it on the radio. He immediately called his mother to make sure she was okay and, once he knew she was, went into the restaurant to check on other people's friends and family. At the time, the chandeliers had just arrived in big wooden boxes from London and were being installed. It was the first time he'd ever seen the chandeliers up twinkling at night, alongside their artwork and photographs of India. With all the trauma being inflicted back home, he felt weirdly conflicted, as if enjoying the beauty of the finished restaurant was not proper in the moment, but decided it could be an escape, a place to forget for a minute and celebrate the good things.

They braced for a disappointing weekend, but Fillmore was packed from the beginning.

The cocktail menu was a huge hit. A few days before opening, influential cocktail writer Camper English posted the drink menu to his *Alcademics* website under the headline "The Craziest New Cocktail Menu in San Francisco." Other cocktail bloggers picked it up and started writing their own stories. That one of the most ambitious and original cocktail menus in the city was at a South Indian restaurant blew minds. On top of that, across the street from the restaurant, at the Sundance Kabuki Theater, *Slumdog Millionaire*—the sleeper-sensation, Academy Award–winning film starring Dev Patel as a boy from a Juhu slum not far from where Anjan grew up—opened the very same week, well before it was released nationally. The rousing success of the small film, which grossed $378 million off a $15 million budget, meant that it stayed in the theater for many, many months. The dinner-and-a-movie crowd became a staple.

In a strange way, the economy proved to be a boon to their success. With so many other new places pumping the brakes on their openings or scrapping the projects altogether, DOSA on Fillmore and Gitane, a romantic Spanish restaurant, were the only new shows in town in the second part of 2008. The food truck/pod revolutions taking place in Los Angeles and Portland had yet to really gain a foothold in San Francisco, and after so much depressing news, folks were genuinely happy to be a part of something that felt fun and optimistic and that was actually succeeding. Every night, the restaurant was doing between 300 and 400 covers, with a 375 average. They were also finding that with the opening of a bigger, more ambitious second restaurant, they were getting an entirely new level of respect in the industry. Restaurateurs no longer considered them one-hit wonders, lucky civilians who'd ridden a novelty to success as some sort of a fluke, but possibly savvy operators who needed to be taken seriously. There was something else about opening in Pacific Heights as opposed to the Mission: Anjan and Emily started appearing in the society pages, and were touted in *7x7* magazine as one of the "Bay Area's Power Couples."

Anjan had taken to his role as liaison between the kitchen and the front of the house, the guy who would fully explain the cultural history and ingredients in a new dish and go through how to explain it to a guest. Emily controlled the host stand, but still, she felt a bit scared every time the door opened, not knowing what she was going to face that night. In Valencia, she was used to being in control of sixty seats; it felt manageable to check on servers and tables and make sure all the trains were running on time and everyone was getting what they needed. But in a place triple that size, any sense of control over the staff and the bartenders and every guest's experience felt ephemeral. She'd look at one table and notice something missing, or something they were waiting on, and by the time she'd made sure that was taken care of, she'd spot three more issues elsewhere. And that was before she'd even gone upstairs.

BY 2011, ANJAN AND EMILY found that their original DOSA on Valencia was suffering. Overshadowed by the newer, bigger, fancier Fillmore location, Valencia was no longer getting the big out-of-town Indian families visiting from all over the Bay. With two locations in such different neighborhoods, they never thought they'd be cannibalizing their own business, but there it was. On top of that, they started to face competition in the neighborhood. Like, lots of competition. Aslam's Rasoi, from chef Mohammed Aslam, opened in 2006 two blocks down on Valencia, featuring Pakistani and Indian foods. Udupi Palace, the same South Indian fast-casual chain that had bid against them for their original Valencia space, had opened a location on the street in 2008. And the owner of the Amber India restaurants, Vijay Bist, had just gotten approval to open Amber Dhara, a 6,000-square-foot, 275-seat, upscale Indian restaurant with a full liquor license, three blocks down on Valencia.

People would come in to Fillmore and ask, "Oh, did you keep Valencia open?" Anjan and Emily felt like a family where the second child becomes famous and everyone forgets they have a first. Not wanting to give up on the place that got them there, they decided to recommit to Valencia, applying for a liquor license and doing a total renovation.

But the hits kept coming. DOSA restaurants with very similar logos and styles began to open in the Bay Area, something that originally got on their radar when someone told them about visiting their restaurant in San Mateo. They eventually won cases against these new restaurants, but the legal headaches and fees just to protect their intellectual property added up.

Determined to stop for a moment and enjoy their lives and two kids (in October 2010 their second daughter, Milaan Madelyn, was born), they spent 2013 and 2014 essentially on pause, focusing on making sure both restaurants' menus were current and improving internal logistical things and, finally, looking elsewhere. They took a trip to New York City and ate at every modern Indian restaurant there. They ate and drank around San Francisco. Every night out felt at least a little like a research trip: Why is this place crowded? What are they doing with their drinks? How are they delivering the food? How is the menu set up? Their brains had officially morphed into industry brains, even in so-called down moments or date nights; there was no going back. By the end of 2014, they were both getting restless. They liked being entrepreneurs and problem solvers—in fact, it was what they prided themselves on—but if they were just trying to solve the same problems day after day, that's when it stopped being interesting.

When they were alone, over a glass of wine, they started talking philosophically about why they got in the business in the first place. Emily had fallen in love with the food that Anjan's mother had cooked in their home and with the delight and surprise (and terror) of eating a dosa for the first time. Anjan had wanted the pride of knowing he was spreading the lesser-known elements of Indian food to Americans, while also giving Indians a place to be proud of that felt culturally like their own in an environment they could visit with their friends and family.

"How do we scale this?" Anjan asked. They evaluated their most central issues. The biggest was consistency. With all the ingredients, Indian food was extremely sensitive to demand. People would come into Fillmore and say they liked the sambar better at Valencia, or they liked the batter in the dosas at Fillmore, or the spice in the masala potatoes, and this had always exasperated them. It's the same recipe, damn it! But if they were being honest, it was true—you couldn't truly regulate such complicated spice mixtures unless you had a central kitchen making all those core ingredients.

If they got a commissary kitchen, they reasoned, they could stabilize the consistency of recipes in the restaurants, reduce specialized labor, and start to grow. They put the word out and quickly another San Francisco restaurateur friend confided that he'd just leased a huge commissary space in South San Francisco and didn't need all the square footage. Anjan and Emily agreed to split the space with him, and suddenly they had their commissary.

Around the same time, one of the owners of Café Spice in New York reached out. He said he had an arrangement with Whole Foods to do premium Indian food within their stores, but he couldn't manage the West Coast and wondered if Dosa would partner with him. The idea of working for someone else didn't appeal, so Anjan offered to buy him out after an introduction and they struck a deal. Emily was especially excited; she'd loved Whole Foods from her time wandering the store in the early nineties, so partnering with them was a dream.

In 2014, they launched the fast-casual Dosateria in Cupertino, inside the Whole Foods flagship store. It was six hundred square feet with fourteen seats around it, a little DOSA satellite inside Whole Foods prepared-food Disneyland. Soon after that, they got tapped by Cisco Systems to put three Dosaterias on their campus, each able to serve a hundred people an hour over two hours in three buildings, five days a week. Within three weeks, they'd built their Cisco Dosaterias as well and they were ready to go, thinking this was just the beginning of Dosateria's international dominance.

They got their asses kicked.

Everything about the process was different. They instantly felt like they had before they opened DOSA on Valencia: amateurs in way over their heads. They hadn't realized they would have to go from being professional restaurateurs to professional food manufacturers. This wasn't just about having a place to make gigantic batches of sambar or dosa batter. In order to satisfy Whole Foods and perfect the process, they had to figure out how to make the food, chill the food, bag the food, and drive the food to all locations without anything spoiling. And if you got a message from a restaurant that something did spoil, you needed to have it all tracked exactly so you could recall that exact bag, figure out what batch it was from, and then make sure none of the other parts of that batch were also spoiled. This meant every item of food had to be coded and sample-saved, with a neat paper trail. It meant hiring real commissary general managers and production people, folks who liked the process and were used to working two a.m. to two p.m. in cold rooms.

From the beginning, the Cisco deal was especially difficult. Cisco's campus featured a majority Indian or Indian-American population, and so they'd put the Dosaterias front and center. But because the same people were coming to the cafeteria each day, Anjan and Emily quickly had to develop an extensive line of foods, including fifteen to twenty different curries, and snacks. On top of that, the compensation model wasn't great. Cisco workers didn't get free food on campus—they had to pay for food, but prices were usually low, as the food outlets were heavily subsidized by Cisco. But Dosateria wasn't subsidized, so in order to basically break even, they were forced to charge regular prices, much to the chagrin of the workers, who incessantly complained about the prices. Communication was also not ideal. Cisco would email the night before to let them know that there would be a convention that week and that food trucks would be parked outside and likely no one would come to the Dosaterias, and they had to be like, "Okay, but are you still going to pay us for the five hundred pounds of food we just made for you?"

Anjan was frustrated with the deal from the beginning, but they recognized that if they weren't going to make any money from Cisco, at least it could act as a testing ground for the commissary. After eighteen months, once they felt like the commissary kitchen finally had its legs, they left.

The Dosateria in Whole Foods, however, was exactly what they needed to help prepare for their next move: a stand-alone fast-casual version of DOSA. It would have to be cool and efficient, and, judging by the insane costs, definitely not in San Francisco.

CHAPTER 16

Mayor, Flavortown, Guy Fieri, Santa Rosa, California

How do you really feel about Guy Fieri?

Do you have opinions on his flame shirts and American muscle cars and bleached hair stuck up in a sort of real-life Bart Simpson impression? Do you have strong feelings on goatees or Evel Knievel tattoos?

Where do you fall on his catchphrases, like "bomb-dot-com tasty" and "Flavortown" and "put it on a flip-flop" and "serve it on a trash can lid" and "Funklicious" and "gangster" and "that's bananas, and bananas is good"?

Would you be shocked to know that Fieri's parents were hippies who, in 1968, drove a Volkswagen bus out from Columbus, Ohio, to Ferndale, California, in Humboldt County, where they had both a saddlery and designed and sold candles out of a store named after a Santana album? Or that his younger sister, Morgan, had cancer when she was four, and Fieri spent many days and nights in a hospital being bored and scared and angry before he finally watched her get better and leave the hospital and be able to live and play like a normal little sister?

Would your mind touch the void if you knew Fieri was a talented horseman and that Morgan used to ride and show horses, or that Fieri's father's time in the navy made him more worldly and inclusive and curious and eager to try new things? Would you be struck by the fact that his mom was a prodigious cook, and that the Fieris experimented with the macrobiotic movement and gave young Guy sushi and tofu in the seventies? Can you juggle that mental image together with Fieri and his family eating breakfast at the Samoa Cookhouse near Eureka, the type of place with one menu item and three prices dependent on your age?

Do you know anything about the soft-pretzel food cart Fieri started when he was ten, after checking the dumpster of the pretzel guy in town to see who provided him with pretzels? Would it surprise you to learn that the cart became a fixture at various fairs throughout Humboldt County? Could you have possibly assumed that a man who often pronounces "Worcestershire" as "Washashasahshashasha" would have gone to a junior college to study French when he was fifteen in order to get his parents to agree to let him spend an entire year of high school in Chantilly, France, living in a single room in a boardinghouse with a family who spoke no English?

Could you ever have imagined that his francophone experience eating snails and traveling around Europe would have the Alice Waters–like effect of pushing him into his first restaurant job at the Red Lion Inn in Eureka, and into majoring in hospitality at the University of Nevada, Las Vegas, before joining the Stouffer Corporation to develop restaurants? Or that his name was actually the even more unrealistic-sounding Guy Ferry until he married in 1995 and switched his last name back to the original spelling his grandfather used in Italy?

Was his heritage on his mind when he opened his first restaurant, Johnny Garlic's, in 1996, an Italian-American joint known for dishes like Guy-Talian Spicy Sausage & Penne? Did his next venture, a sushi and barbecue collab called Tex Wasabi's, attempt to hedge the Asian fusion trend of the late nineties with an eternal favorite like barbecue, or is that overthinking it? Do you believe that when he told his hairdresser to do whatever she wanted to his formerly long hair and she dyed it platinum blond, it would eventually become part of his signature brand?

Were you struck by how easily Fieri seemed to coast to victory in Food

Network's *Food Network Star* reality competition in 2006, or how his energy never flagged during his first show, *Guy's Big Bite*, as he cranked out recipe demos for penne with hot links and chipotle shrimp, Bloody Mary flank steaks, and cornbread-stuffed meatloaf? Could you even fathom that his next show, *Diners, Drive-ins, and Dives*, was actually just supposed to be one special featuring him eating a *cabrito* burger in Tarpley, Texas, especially now that there have been thirty seasons? Did you know that he's a Dale Carnegie fan? Or that the first thing he does when he hits a new town is find the local art studio?

If not for Fieri, would anyone else have told the world about the drive-in on the Hawaiian island of Oahu serving ahi cakes, or the Burbank, California, restaurant Chili John's, or the Nepalese-Tibetan bites at a Columbus, Ohio, grocery store, or the Mexican bakery La Panadería in San Antonio? Would Vida Cantina in Portsmouth, New Hampshire, or the Table Cafe in Louisville, Kentucky, or the Smoking Swine food truck in Baltimore, Maryland, still be kicking if Fieri didn't enthusiastically recommend them?

Would the phrase "Triple D" mean anything if there wasn't an entire digital boomtown built around Fieri's travels, especially FlavortownUSA.com, a fan-created searchable database of the thousand-plus restaurants that have appeared on Fieri's shows?

Were you one of the millions of people who lustfully shared *New York Times* restaurant critic Pete Wells's famous 2012 disemboweling of Guy's American Kitchen & Bar in Times Square, adding a fire emoji in the "retweet with comment" section of your Twitter timeline as Wells put the restaurant over his knee?

Would it shock you that Fieri believes Wells knew exactly what he was doing when he came in during the first few weeks of service, especially since it is normally standard for the *Times* food critic to wait two months? Is it that crazy that Fieri believes it wasn't even really about his restaurant but instead just a safe space for Wells to punch down?

Could there be an argument made that the very act of singling out a restaurant that didn't fit the description of what is normally reviewed in the *Times*, that wasn't meant for the *Times*, is exactly the type of snobbish behavior that people in other parts of America hold up as evidence of a growing divisive elitism?

Might you look at Wells's later positive review of Señor Frogs as a way to make himself feel less guilty about the fact that he'd become famous primarily by showcasing his skewering sophistry taking down a place that wasn't even parked within a mile of his readers' wheelhouse?

Would you be surprised that Anthony Bourdain also weighed in on Fieri's Times Square restaurant and called it a "terror-dome" that "turned the neighborhood into the Ed Hardy district"? Or that British comedian John Oliver compared Vladimir Putin to Fieri?

Would you care to posit a guess as to what so angers food elites about Fieri?

Is it that his sixty-three restaurants all over the world (and even on Caribbean cruise ships) feature menu items that are puns, or that his relentless capitalistic pursuit of financial success and his willingness to plaster his face on a variety of products of ranging values seem a bit uncouth?

Is it that the folks who tend to publicly, non-ironically support him also tend to favor calf tattoos, and to come from California's inland empire, or the Gulf Coast of Florida, or even sometimes Nevada? Is it that his supporters tend to use their vacation money on Caribbean cruises, that they view a one-hundred-ounce frozen mango daiquiri in a souvenir cup at a walk-up bar on Beale Street as a pretty good deal, that they seem to be fascinated by the more approachable parts of motorcycle culture? Are food elites embarrassed by them because they think they represent the uglier side of the world's American stereotype, because anyone supporting someone who approaches things so viscerally without any sense of irony, who willingly dyes their hair unnaturally and actively seeks out attention via eye-catching T-shirts and loud cars and crazy catchphrases, who seems to be having fun in public too loudly (especially at *that* age), is part of the American experience they wish didn't exist?

Does the fact that a former producer claimed that Fieri was homophobic reinforce that feeling? Does it even matter that Fieri officiated more than a hundred gay weddings in Miami all while wearing a purple tuxedo? Or that he tapped his sister, Morgan, a lesbian massage therapist, to run his foundation before she passed away at the age of thirty-eight from metastatic melanoma? And that he's made it very clear that his tattoo of Botticelli's *Venus* is in memory of Morgan and is by far the most important tattoo on his body? Does that, coupled with his quiet work helping to feed victims of the terrible fires in Northern California, illustrate a depth of character and nuance you might not expect from a person who has also permanently inked his body with a picture of a platinum grenade?

Or was it all just an act?

CHAPTER 17

André Prince Jeffries, North Nashville, Tennessee, Part 2

On the day of our nation's founding, 2007, at noon in East Park on Woodland Street in Nashville, Tennessee, everything changed.

That was the day of the first-ever Hot Chicken Festival, the final item in Nashville mayor Bill Purcell's hot chicken world domination master plan. The free event was an attempt by Purcell to showcase hot chicken to a larger variety of Nashvillians, and nothing attracted a large cross-section of Nashvillians like the promise of free food and music.

The original party featured three hot chicken establishments: Prince's Hot Chicken Shack, Bolton's Spicy Chicken and Fish, and the upstart 400 Degrees, started in 2006 by Aqui Hines.

Hines grew up in North Nashville and first ate Prince's in elementary school, falling in love with the heat. Craving it on Sundays and Mondays when Prince's wasn't open, she started experimenting with a recipe to cook for her family, and eventually quit her job selling ads at the *Tennessean* to open a little, eight-seat, seven-hundred-square-foot spot on Clarksville Highway. With no food-service or cooking experience, Hines enlisted the help of her mom and a few folks who knew the food business and went out on her own guerrilla marketing campaign, printing flyers and taking them around her North Nashville neighborhood, telling folks they wouldn't be disappointed if they checked it out. Hines, pretty and charismatic and confident, ended up being a natural marketer, and folks started coming in, and then they started coming back. She knew she really had something when the white folks came—musicians and Vanderbilt professors and doctors—and within three months she covered all her costs. By the time the festival came around, Hines's hot chicken business was the young darling of the scene.

When Purcell had asked André Prince Jeffries if her restaurant could captain the event, she was dubious at first, but ultimately figured that much free publicity was probably a good idea. Jeffries spent the morning cooking up a small batch to give away at the festival, and Semone and Mario and a few others drove it over. But within a half hour of the festival kicking off, Jeffries got a frantic call from Semone. "Mom, you better make some more. We're already running out."

Semone and the rest of the crew spent the entire festival driving back and forth between East Park and Ewing Drive to pick up more chicken, until finally Jeffries shut it down. "I'm not going to give all my damn chicken," she said. "I'm the one paying for it."

The event was a rousing success. Hundreds of locals turned out for it, braving hour-long waits just to get a taste of the spicy chicken even many longtime city residents had never tried. Eventually, Prince's, Bolton's, and 400 Degrees ran out of chicken.

After that day, Jeffries noticed an impressive uptick in new folks coming into the shack, many of them white. At the festival, the line for Prince's had dwarfed the lines for the other establishments; even if lots of Nashvillians hadn't tried the food before, there was name recognition that associated Prince's and hot chicken. They were inextricably linked. But that soon would change.

The 2007 Hot Chicken Festival was pivotal because it brought Prince's recognition from two demographics that were also inextricably linked: white people and media. The year before, at their summer symposium, the Southern Foodways Alliance, a section of the Center for the Study of Southern Culture at the University of Mississippi that aimed to document and study "the foodways of the American South," run by the influential journalist and academic John T. Edge, had released an entertaining ten-minute documentary by Joe York on Prince's, titled *Prince's Hot Chicken*. Edge, who had lived in Nashville in the late eighties, had written about Prince's before, first in his 2000 book *Southern Belly*, then again in his 2004 book *Fried Chicken*. His goal with the documentary was to honor folks like Jeffries and others who helped define Nashville's food culture but got little credit.

In the documentary, Jeffries tells what soon became one of her signature stories, about the lady who, every weekend, would bring her suitors in to eat hot chicken as a sort of foreplay before sex. One night, Jeffries explained, the woman was so worked up from the spice that she couldn't wait and they ended up doing the deed on the hood of the car right in front of the restaurant. "Hey," Jeffries said, shaking her head and laughing, "different things turn different people on."

As the documentary proved, Jeffries was a skilled raconteur, able to entice an audience quickly with a series of slightly provocative, possibly exaggerated, good-natured stories, many of which were punctuated by her signature boisterous laugh. And almost as soon as the festival was over, Jeffries was able to start putting that charm to use frequently, as more and more stories about Prince's started showing up, first in popular food blogs like *Cook Eat Fret*, *Ulika Food Blog*, *Menu in Progress*, and, of course, *Good Fatty, Bad Fatty*. In 2008, NPR's Audie Cornish stopped by to conduct an interview with Jeffries for the network's Diversions section. Influential southern magazine *Garden and Gun*'s 2008 story "100 Southern Foods You Absolutely, Positively Must Try Before You Die" contained a write-up on Prince's by none other than Edge, who said, "I fear the apocalyptic burn of the skillet-cooked and cayenne-swabbed chicken dished by André Prince Jeffries the way I fear the wrath of the Lord. So should you. One taste of a Prince's drumstick rouses me from a twelve-pack stupor."

Even restaurants in other parts of the country started to stand up and take notice. The wildly popular Ann Arbor restaurant Zingerman's Roadhouse began doing "Nashville Hot Fried Chicken Tuesdays" in late 2008, becoming one of the first places or publications anywhere to characterize hot chicken as something connected directly to the entire city of Nashville.

And then, in 2009, there came the Hoodie Awards.

THE HOODIE AWARDS were the brainchild of comedian and syndicated radio and television host Steve Harvey and his former manager, Rushion McDonald. Started in 2001, the awards sought to spotlight businesses and other pillars of the community that maintained "a positive presence in the 'hood." Categories were all over the map, from best nail salon, to best church, car wash, soul food, and fried chicken. Voters in communities with affiliates tied to Harvey's syndicated radio show would vote for the finalists, who were then invited to come out to Las Vegas for the actual show.

On a Monday in March 2009, Semone Jeffries was handling some paperwork in Prince's when she saw a professional-looking woman knocking on the door. Semone poked her head out to inform the woman they were closed, but she wasn't interested in eating.

"I've been trying to get in touch with you!" the woman exclaimed, explaining that her name was Monica and she was a producer on Steve Harvey's radio show. Semone told her she wasn't really familiar with Harvey's show, as she usually listened to Tom Joyner. "Never mind that," the woman said. She told Semone she'd been calling for weeks, but because she was never able to get in touch with anyone, they'd finally flown her out from Atlanta just to drive over and talk to Miss André Prince Jeffries.

"That's my mother," Semone said.

"Well, tell your mom she's nominated for a Hoodie Award for best fried chicken in America," the woman told her. "We're going to fly y'all out to Las Vegas for the ceremony in August."

Excited, Semone called Jeffries and told her the news.

Semone: "Mom, we got nominated for a Hoodie Award for best fried chicken, and they're going to fly us out to Vegas for the awards!"

Jeffries: "That's great. [Pause.] What are the Hoodie Awards?"

In August 2009, Jeffries and her two daughters flew to Las Vegas. Her brother, Martin, who lived in California, drove over to meet them. The Harvey people treated them right, putting them up in a hotel room in Mandalay Bay Resort and Casino and offering them a gratis rental car if they wanted it. They got to see the Gap Band's Charlie Wilson perform, plus Musiq Soulchild and Jazmine Sullivan. They got to do meet and greets and take pictures with celebrities like Mo'Nique, comedian Tommy Davidson, *The View* cohost Sherri Shepherd, and BET *106 & Park* cohosts Rocsi and Terrence J. At the actual awards ceremony, Jeffries was seated by herself next to the other finalists in the Fried Chicken category. The rest of the family was up a few rows. A Finer Touch Nail Spa in Grandview, Missouri, finally won for Best Nail Salon. Showroom Shine in St. Louis took Best Car Wash/Detail Shop. And then it was time to announce the winner of Best Fried Chicken.

Steve Harvey introduced comedian Lavell Crawford (best known for his role as Saul Goodman's unenthusiastic bodyguard in AMC's *Breaking Bad*) as well as the Gap Band's Charlie Wilson. After some jokes, they listed off the nominees:

Bourbon Street Fish in Los Angeles

Prince's Hot Chicken in Nashville

Carey's Cuisine in Washington, DC

Green Acres Cafe in Birmingham

After a brief pause to demand that a five-piece chicken meal be delivered to his hotel room, Crawford let Wilson read off the name of the winner. Wilson said, "Prince's Hot Chicken Shack of Nashville, Tennessee, baby!"

What followed established André Prince Jeffries as a national icon.

A Brief Rundown of the Exact Events that Occurred Slightly Before, During, and Directly After André Prince Jeffries's 2009 Hoodie Awards Acceptance Speech for Best Fried Chicken

As she heard her name, Jeffries reached her hands up to the sky, then balled them into fists, and then opened her hands and raised them again. She slid out of her seat and reached backward for Semone, who had come down the aisle from her seat to escort her to the podium. As they walked up together, holding each other in a hug, Crawford said, "Hey, I took a picture with that lady."

Jeffries got to the top of the podium and a model handed her the plaque commemorating her win. She set herself in front of the microphone and then she shrieked.

Jeffries: "GLORY!!!!!"

She paused, her left hand stretched out toward the sky. Then she shrieked again, louder and longer.

Jeffries: "GLORRRYYYY!!!"

She paused again, her left hand still stretched out toward the sky. Then she let out a sound that was at the upper register of what humans can possibly hear, a shriek clearly intended for a higher power.

Jeffries: "GLORRRRYYYYYYYYYYY."

She paused a final time. Her hand dropped. And in a normal voice she spoke.

Jeffries: "To God."

The camera cut away to Steve Harvey, who had a look of simultaneous disbelief and amusement on his face, and he started to faux-walk away from his own podium.

The crowd lost its collective mind, the cheers roared for fifteen to twenty seconds, uninterrupted until Jeffries started to speak again.

Jeffries: "It is no secret what God can do. I thank you, Steve Harvey, for working your idea. I thank all of those who voted for us. And those who had a desire to vote for us, but didn't have the means."

Jeffries paused again, as people laughed and clapped. She was warming to this, and she began to recognize that she was in control of the crowd. She lifted her left hand to the sky.

Jeffries: "I want you all to know . . ."

She paused again. She was the master of pauses. She could quite possibly control the time-space continuum.

Jeffries: "There is no me."

Another pause! Was this even legal? She was treating the world like her own personal DVR.

Jeffries: "Without you."

Left hand still in the air. Somehow ANOTHER pause. The world was no longer in prograde motion. The tidal effects of the moon didn't register. Atomic clocks all burst into flames.

Jeffries: "Thank you."

As she walked off, Crawford shouted "Glory!" into the microphone again, trying to mainline some of Jeffries's energy back to himself. It was impossible. Like in the ocean, the noise was coming in waves of three. When the camera finally cut back over to Steve Harvey, he shook his head for a long time and smiled. Possibly in an attempt to pay homage to Jeffries, he paused too. Finally he spoke.

Harvey: "That's somebody's mamma right there. That's a churchgoing woman right there."

BY 2010, MORE RESTAURANTS in Nashville joined the hot chicken conversation. That year, Isaac Beard, a white Nashville native, opened a small two-man take-out joint on Gallatin Pike in East Nashville called Pepperfire Hot Chicken. Beard, a former photographer, car salesman, and massage therapist, had first tried hot chicken about ten years before, and, after he finished his first meal, wasn't blown away. But that night he woke up thinking about hot chicken, and couldn't stop. He began eating at different hot chicken establishments every week, and then—for the three years before he opened Pepperfire—nearly every day, trying out different restaurants and experimenting in his own kitchen to try to perfect a recipe of his own.

After developing cognitive issues following a collision that occurred when Beard's car was hit during a high-speed cop chase, Beard spent six months in the Vanderbilt hospital trying to keep his wits about him, studying Christmas trees and triangles and trying to decipher the difference between them. When the May 2010 flood hit, soaking Nashville with nearly fourteen inches of rain in thirty-six hours, causing two billion dollars in damage, and destroying three hundred businesses, Beard's own massage business closed. When the money finally came in from the collision, Beard was able to open his own hot chicken place in a tiny wood and stucco building on the Gallatin Pike.

Unlike most hot chicken shacks, Pepperfire offered chicken tenders, an addition Beard made reluctantly when he discovered many of his friends and family were turned off by bones in chicken. Also, mostly on a lark for his kids, he had thrown a special kind of deep-fried grilled cheese he'd once found in a King's cookbook on the menu. On the first day they sold four grilled cheeses, and Beard had every intention of pulling the item from the menu, as it was a huge pain in the ass and had to be made to order each time. But *Nashville Scene* writer Chris Chamberlain had shown up that very day and, in his write-up of the restaurant, spoke highly of the Fried Peppercheese, calling it "perfectly golden and crispy on the outside and velvety and melted on the inside." The next day, they sold fourteen, and the Fried Peppercheese—and its eventual evolutionary successor, the Tender Royale, a combination of those hot chicken tenders and the grilled cheese—became its most famous and popular dish.

But while others continued to slowly enter the hot chicken market, Jeffries continued to see a steady rise in national exposure. *The Washington Post* restaurant critic Tom Sietsema dined at Prince's in late 2010, ordering the extra-hot chicken and describing it thusly: "Ever tasted molten iron? Kissed the sun? Me neither. But 'extra hot' at Prince's is what I imagine those sensations approximate. Like dynamite, the spices from Prince's most volatile dish explode on the palate, torching every taste bud in their path in wave after wave of assaults." He also talked about French Laundry chef Thomas Keller being denied a chance to try the extra-hot because he was "a virgin to their chicken." In the summer of 2011, the Travel Channel's popular *Man v. Food* show aired an episode featuring host Adam Richman attempting to eat the extra-hot as he sat next to Jeffries.

Around the city, elements of the Culinary Revolution were showing up. Chef Tandy Wilson opened his award-winning Germantown restaurant City House in 2007. The Goldberg brothers, Ben and Max, had launched their Strategic Hospitality business in 2006 as well, with a rethinking of the honky-tonk (Paradise Park), before opening Nashville's first New York–style cocktail bar in 2009 (Patterson House), and a slew of other restaurants, bars, and work spaces. Not far from Bolton's, in the Five Points neighborhood in East Nashville, chef Margot McCormack had opened Margot Café & Bar in 2001, many, many years before the rest of the city started to think of the area as an eating destination; by 2010, the hip Winnebago Mas Tacos por Favor had a brick-and-mortar restaurant in the vicinity, craft cocktail bar Holland House had opened, and the Pharmacy Burger Parlor and Beer Garden was beginning its buildout (and would open the following year).

By 2012–13, everything changed. The US Census Bureau estimated Nashville to be the tenth-fastest-growing metro area in the country. The show *Nashville*, featuring *Friday Night Lights* star Connie Britton as a famous country music singer, debuted to fantastic critical and audience ratings, and propelled certain Nashville landmarks like the Bluebird Cafe into the type of TV tourism usually reserved for *Sex and the City*. The Culinary Revolution was in its prime, with Germantown's Rolf & Daughters being named the third-best new restaurant in the country by *Bon Appétit*, national food media darling chef Sean Brock returning to the city where he first made his name at the Hermitage Hotel to launch the second iteration of his world-famous Charleston restaurant Husk, Deb Paquette opening Etch downtown, and both Lockeland Table and Treehouse opening in East Nashville.

But for Nashville's hot chicken scene, nothing was bigger, more game-changing and ultimately more controversial than the summer 2012 opening of Hattie B's in Midtown.

ON AUGUST 9, 2012, Nick Bishop Sr. and his son, Nick Jr., along with chef John Lasater, softly opened Hattie B's at Nineteenth Avenue and Broadway in Nashville's Midtown neighborhood.

The Bishops had a restaurant-industry bloodline: Nick Sr.'s father, Gene, had been CEO of Morrison's Cafeteria, a restaurant chain that specialized in cafeteria-style spots, often found in malls, and that had in the early eighties also acquired the Ruby Tuesday chain. After working at that company himself, Bishop Sr. then went into business with his son, Nick (who'd previously been in the music business), to open Bishop's in 2007, a meat and three in the Nashville suburb of Franklin. Fans of the classic hot chicken joints, the father-and-son duo began experimenting in the Bishop's kitchen with a spicier version of their own popular fried chicken. By 2011, they were ready to put it on the menu at Bishop's, and they were pleasantly surprised to find it was a huge hit, eventually becoming the most popular item, responsible for nearly a quarter of all orders.

Confident they had something special, the Bishops decided to open a restaurant focused strictly on the chicken, which they wanted to call Hattie's, after Nick Sr.'s grandmother and Nick Jr.'s daughter (the *B* was added after the fact, when they discovered there was already a Hattie's Chicken Shack in Saratoga Springs, New York). Around this time, thanks to a city kickball league, Nick Jr.'s sister, Brittany, had started dating chef John Lasater, a French Culinary Institute grad who'd been working at the Capitol Grille in the Hermitage Hotel and the Porter Road Butcher. Following the couple's engagement, Lasater was brought into the fold at Hattie B's, where he helped fine-tune and streamline the hot chicken recipe and the side dishes.

Their Midtown location put Hattie B's close to both tourists staying around the quickly developing Gulch area and college students at Vanderbilt and Belmont. They offered beer, a rarity for hot chicken joints, and meticulously curated the local craft selections on the menu. To help spread the word, they hired French Laundry chef/owner Thomas Keller's former director of publicity. And she was good at her job—the number of different media outlets that covered Hattie B's opening was staggering. But most important, the entire enterprise marked a crucial transition.

If Prince's and Columbo's represented the first iteration of the hot chicken shack (as originators who both at least stemmed from the same place), and 400 Degrees and Pepperfire represented the second evolution (non-professional fans doing their own interpretations of the original), Hattie B's represented hot chicken's third evolution: the world of professional restaurateurs.

Others followed in a similar vein. In 2014, Austin Smith and Nick Jacobson, along with chef Bart Pickens, opened Party Fowl, the first full-service hot chicken restaurant and the only one (at the time) with a full liquor license and cocktail menu. Smith was a former wine and liquor distributor who'd grown up in Nashville (his father was Dolly Parton's bandleader for twelve years and met Smith's mother when she moved to Nashville to sing at Opryland). He'd held every job in the restaurant industry, from valet and dishwasher to general manager, but really noticed a change in the types of restaurants he was selling wine to in 2011, from generalized Americana pub concepts to more focused conceptual fare: scratch pasta restaurants, Basque tapas joints, dumpling shops, etc.

As hot chicken started to creep into the general Nashville consciousness around that same time, he noticed that none of the 129 restaurants he was selling to had hot chicken on the menu. Sensing an opportunity, he got in touch with Jacobson, an industry veteran he'd met back at local wine bar the Grape. With Pickens, a talented chef who'd opened the Southern Steak & Oyster downtown, they came up with twelve different plays on hot chicken, added a brunch menu and a valet, and quickly positioned themselves as the hot chicken favorite for the downtown partying bachelor and bachelorette set.

The floodgates had opened. As Hattie B's began to develop a Franklin Barbecue–esque line down the block, Nashville's ever-growing ranks of restaurant professionals seized on the momentum. East Nashville ramen shop Otaku South added hot chicken *bao* buns. Breakfast favorite Biscuit Love offered it inside a chicken biscuit. The Sutler Saloon put Nashville Hot Nuggets on their late-night menu. Mexican restaurant Saint Añejo did hot chicken tacos. Hell, even Husk put out a version for their lunch menu.

It didn't stop in Nashville. Conveniently coinciding with a similar national obsession with hot sauces exemplified by the cultish madness surrounding sriracha, hot chicken places were popping up all over the country. Peaches HotHouse and *The Chew* cohost and former *Top Chef* competitor Carla Hall's Southern Kitchen in Brooklyn. *Top Chef* contestant Kevin Sbraga's Fat Ham in Philadelphia. Budlong Hot Chicken and also Leghorn Chicken in Chicago. Hot Chicken Takeover in Columbus, Ohio. Rocky's Hot Chicken Shack in Asheville, North Carolina. Joella's Hot Chicken in Indianapolis. Former Husk Nashville cook Johnny Zone's Howlin' Ray's in Los Angeles. And then Kentucky Fried Chicken got in the game.

Starting in late 2015, KFC had been quietly testing a Nashville-style hot chicken at Pittsburgh restaurants, and after the initial testing phase proved successful, they launched "Nashville Hot" with the tagline "A spicy bird with a savory burn" nationwide in late January 2016. *Food Republic* called 2016 "The Year of Hot Chicken." Its fourth evolution into a mass-marketed commodity was upon us.

Jeffries watched her family's invention explode into a national phenomenon with a sense of bemused detachment. She was still getting publicity—she did *Mind of a Chef* with Sean Brock and Erik Anderson, and won a James

Beard America's Classics Award—but what was most perplexing to her was how quickly the name had morphed into something that represented the city as a whole when ten years before most of the white people even in Nashville hadn't heard of it. She wasn't surprised about the KFC thing—she'd heard rumors Colonel Sanders had tried to buy her uncle's recipe back in the seventies—but she expected a certain amount of respect and recognition as these places took her family's idea and ran with it. She liked that Peaches HotHouse in Brooklyn had talked about Prince's when they launched, and that the owner of the Columbus restaurant had invited her to come out for the opening and had put her picture on the wall. That was showing respect. But it was this name everyone was using, "Nashville Hot," that bothered her. "Originated in Nashville." She felt the family was being pushed to the side, in their little corner of North Nashville, as the city took over ownership of hot chicken.

But, Jeffries reasoned, that was the American way, wasn't it? The ones with the money are going to do what they want to do.

Anthony Bourdain ✔
@Bourdain

Following ⌄

Fucking Cadillac . Greedy venal #travelchannel ad sales motherfuckers.

6:49 PM - 5 Nov 2012

288 Retweets **192** Likes

♡ 68   ⟲ 288   ♡ 192

In 2012, Anthony Bourdain tweeted after a series of Cadillac commercials using his likeness ran without his permission during his Travel Channel show *No Reservations*. Bourdain left the channel to go to CNN soon after the feud.

CHAPTER 18

Phil Ward, New York City, New York, Part 2

By 2008, the Death & Co cocktail list had grown so big they ended up breaking it down by spirit, and then into shaken and stirred drinks. It was unwieldy. But Phil Ward wanted to make it even bigger.

In his opinion, the thing about cocktail menus was that even for a menu with ten drinks, there will always be people who look and say "Ugh, I can't read all those drinks" and then talk to the bartender. And for the other people, no matter how big the menu was, he felt like he could narrow them down to five drinks with two questions: "What spirit do you like?" and "Do you like your drinks more refreshing and shaken, or boozy and stirred?" And then, while they were waiting on the drink, they could have fun perusing the menu. If you thought about it as an entertainment while you wait, your idea of what size a menu should be changed dramatically.

But one thing he couldn't stop noticing was that, despite the fact that there were so many drinks and spirits available, 25 percent of all the drinks would inevitably come from the agave page, either tequila or mezcal. Ward had always had a soft spot for the agave spirits, because he felt like they got unfairly pigeonholed.

Tequila had, forever, only been consumed two ways: in shitty shots or in margaritas. No one sipped it straight, and it was always being blunted with salt and lime, or sugar and fillers and lime, or frozen into oblivion in what looked like a corner store Slurpee machine. Even at places like Death & Co, where the more serious and knowledgeable folks would come, knowing they were getting legit drinks, they would often hear a description of a tequila drink and say, "Sooo . . . it's basically like a play on a margarita?"

With the possible exception of rum, no other alcohol had that sort of stereotype. You didn't look at every gin cocktail and say, "Sooo . . . that's like a martini?"

The other thing Ward liked about tequila was the challenge of creating something new from something so old and known. It's one thing if you're working with a green peppercorn tincture and unicorn tears, but it's another if you're trying to create new drinks from bottles that have been behind that bar for a hundred years.

So when Ravi DeRossi stood outside Bourgeois Pig with Phil Ward and asked him if he wanted to open another bar, and Ward said "Hell yeah." Ward had a very clear idea of what he wanted that bar to focus on: tequila and mezcal.

(DeRossi remembers it differently: that they were definitely outside the Pig and definitely drinking beers and definitely agreeing on opening a bar, but that it was actually David Kaplan who had the original idea for a tequila and mezcal bar. Kaplan did not venture an opinion either way.)

DeRossi got to work finding a place, and because he was de facto mayor of the East Village and had partied or at least shared a cigarette with every single person who lived, worked, or graffitied the alleys in the neighborhood, it didn't take long for them to find 304 East Sixth Street. Their landlord, an Estonian who allegedly owned a tech company, offered them a decent deal for the bottom two floors of his building, so they took it, got the keys on October 27, 2008, and started the buildout. The space had been a somewhat claustrophobic Moroccan restaurant before, and because Ward was tall and his head was basically touching the ceiling, the first thing they did was to get rid of the drywall ceiling, and in knocking it out they found these incredible wooden beams.

Being an artist, DeRossi had a creative eye for spaces. He spent some time in Seville, got obsessed with balconies, and decided they should cut a hole in the upstairs floor to look down like an internal balcony. Ward thought he was crazy, but when they actually did it, he had to admit it looked pretty damn cool, especially with the church-esque stained glass windows. They imported tiles from Mexico, but found the ones for their bar top on a random supply run to a local Brooklyn Home Depot knockoff. After reading about tarantulas reproducing in agave, DeRossi fashioned the upstairs chandelier to look like a spider. They played around with different names, things like La Verdad, but in the end they kept the religious undertones of the space and its mission and named it Mayahuel, after the Aztec agave goddess.

The buildout was not without issues. Their contractor was usually drunk, so Ward essentially played foreman, and when all else failed, he would wait for everyone else to leave, get a cheap six-pack, roll a joint, put on Pink Floyd, and start staining wood. There was always more wood to stain, and there was something relaxing to Ward about having a bar to himself with some sort of simple, mindless task; it reminded him of his days on the south side of Pittsburgh in that little bar in the back of a coffee shop. It was amazing what you could accomplish if nobody bothered you.

For his opening team, Ward tapped a roster of folks he knew from the still-small circle of cocktail bars around New York, and by April 2009, he had the staff he wanted, the bar equipment installed, and the produce and refrigeration all up to code; they'd also finally convinced the New York City Department of Buildings to give them the proper licensing, a harder-than-expected task once they found out their landlord had outstanding fines. The place was basically ready to go, except for one thing: Ward hadn't written the menu.

There was a swashbuckling element to Ward at this time. Having reached the heights of his powers at Death & Co, he no longer worried he wouldn't be able to come up with cocktails on demand. And so the weekend before Mayahuel opened, Ward went on a four-day bender, experimenting with different cocktails and tasting and tasting and tasting until he was drunk with the

An early version of the art for the cocktail
menu at Mayaheul, created by bartender
Phil Ward

power of creation and also with the alcohol he was putting into them. When
the dust settled, he had his opening list of twenty tequila and mezcal
cocktails.

Separating them into five categories (Strange Stirrings, Tea-Killa Cocktails, Vino en Mi Copa, Punch-o Villas, and Agave de Fresco), Ward sampled
all around, including the Division Bell (mezcal, Aperol, a Croatian mara-
schino liqueur, lime, and a grapefruit peel), calling out the Pink Floyd album
he listened to most frequently while staining wood; a play on sangria called
La Vida en Rosado, with strawberry-infused blanco tequila, rosé, and elder-
flower; and the sherry, mezcal, and grapefruit Smoked Palomino, which cost
them only $1.73 to make and, with those fantastic margins, earned the moni-
ker "rent maker."

By the second week it was open, there were already two *New York Times*
stories mentioning it, including a Dan Saltzstein piece on mezcal trying to
get out from under its college worm-in-the-bottle reputation, and an Eric
Asimov–introduced Q and A with Ward answering questions about mezcal.
Eater breathlessly covered both the actual opening and the initial blogosphere feedback, including two different reactions from Yelp. NYC Food Guy
loved it.

Aside from the Palomino, the undisputed champion of the menu was the Watermelon Sugar. With a spiced salt/sugar rim, fresh watermelon, tequila, mezcal, and citrus, it was a simple and easy introduction to what they were trying to do, and though most people just thought Ward had run out of creative drink names, it actually referenced his favorite postapocalyptic novel by Richard Brautigan.

Quite unexpectedly, they managed to thread a tough needle, appealing to the Death & Co regular cocktail head nerds alongside the People Who Enjoyed Hot New Bars, alongside the East Village regulars, alongside Crabby Old People Who Always Drank Tequila on the Rocks and Finally Had a Place to Go That Understood Why. That first year was magical, with almost unfettered access to both local and national press, who couldn't quite get over the fact that they were essentially a single-spirit-focused Death & Co. Or at least that was how they had to keep Mayahuel in their head, as the old single-spirit models—the dusty-bottle whiskey joints, or the margarita joints that just kept a hundred bottles of tequila on the shelves and never planned for the day when someone might ask to open them—were not fair comparisons.

Before opening Mayahuel, Ward had never been to Mexico. He'd meant to go, and even had a trip planned, but then swine flu happened and that trip got scrapped. But after they opened and every single publication in America started singling them out for evangelizing craft mezcal in America, the invites lined up. His first trip, with Tres Agaves, was to Jalisco, and it was fascinating, but the true mind-melding journey came on his second trip, a ten-day voyage to Oaxaca with the founder of Del Maguey mezcal, Ron Cooper, "wine geek" and spirits scholar Steve Olson, and—using Ward's highest complimentary terminology—an all-star cast of degenerates that included some of the most influential cocktail bartenders of the era, including San Francisco's tequila pioneer Julio Bermejo, former Harvard Divinity student turned mescal missionary Misty Kalkofen, South African San Francisco bartending legend Jacques Bezuidenhout, and prominent Los Angeles cocktail bartender Eric Alperin.

Cooper took them out to the beautiful Oaxacan hillsides, and this is where Ward saw his first *palenque*, a basic distillery that consisted of one little still, four wooden fermentation vats, a hole in the ground where they cooked the agave, and a molino to crush said agave. It was so simple and yet so perfect.

At each *palenque*, Ward would have Cooper ask the people making the mezcal how long their families had been doing it, and each response was similar. The man would start counting on his fingers, and usually stop somewhere between four and seven. This wasn't years, Cooper told him. They were counting generations.

As more and more of these families gave the same sort of answers, Ward had an epiphany. The reason this mezcal was so damn delicious was because these poor farmers had every intention of drinking it all themselves, they never thought about selling it, and thus never thought to change the recipe to be cheaper. In fact, they could hardly fathom why a bunch of stupid gringos had showed up to basically fall into ecstatic shock tasting a thing they'd been making as long as anyone could remember.

Ward had almost no time for people, and tended to be distrustful and cynical about even his own friends' intentions, but the folks he met in the Del Maguey villages were so fundamentally nice and warm and welcoming, it nearly made him start believing in the human race again. After that second trip, Mexico became his happy place, and in the ten years since that first trip, he's been back at least fifty times.

OVER THE NEXT FEW YEARS, Mayahuel continued to shine, and Ward grew its cocktail list like a weed plant in an enterprising yet troubled teenager's attic. One of the things that annoyed him about Death & Co was how much of a pain it was to change the menu. As for Mayahuel, Ward's girlfriend at the time, Katie Stipe, just had a program on her computer where she could amend the menu really quickly, and so Ward would often go to a coffee shop, add a drink he'd been playing with the night before or that morning, Stipe would save it on the program, and then they'd get the new menus printed up that day.

One day Ward walked into the storage room in the kitchen and came across this giant bag of ancho chiles, which their chef was using in various salsas. Ward found himself constantly returning to the storage section and smelling chiles. There was something about the smell that was weirdly familiar to him. Finally, it came to him: muscatel sherry! Maybe because both the grapes and the chiles were sun-dried and dry-aged, the aromas were incredibly similar, but either way, it motivated him to infuse mezcal with said chiles and create a chile de árbol mezcal. With this delicious new weapon in the quiver alongside the jalapeño blanco they'd previously made, Ward added an entirely new section of the menu made up exclusively of spicy cocktails like the Killer Cortez with the new chile mezcal, pineapple-infused mezcal, tamarind sangrita, cumin syrup, and yellow pepper. The *Times* critic Pete Wells lavished praise on the sneaky heat of jalapeño in the Pilot Punch. Every drink seemed a hit.

As the bar continued to pack in customers night after night, Ward looked to go deeper and deeper into the mezcal and tequila worlds. He had no interest in building one of those stupid libraries of tequila for the sake of saying that they had X number of bottles. That, to him, seemed like the bar equivalent of someone insecure about his manhood buying a giant Hummer SUV. He only wanted to acquire interesting spirits that they would actually use in drinks. Under his watch, Mayahuel would never be a drink museum.

But DeRossi, the human equivalent of Robert Fludd's perpetual motion machine, already had a wandering eye for another project. Ward thought he knew what would make sense. During the early days of Death & Co, he'd gone to England with David Kaplan and seen just how creative, cool, and cost-effective serving large-format boozy punches could be (also interesting: Ward drank so much punch on that trip he hallucinated in his hotel bathroom). When they came back to the States and added them to the Death & Co menu, the punch bowls immediately took off. Ward and DeRossi began to talk about the idea of a rum punch–based bar, and DeRossi even found a space on East Sixth Street. When it became clear this project was moving forward, Ward kept trying to engage DeRossi in discussing percentages, and when DeRossi finally offered up just 10 percent, he was taken aback.

"That's less than the deal here," said Ward. "Why would I take a step backward?"

But DeRossi didn't budge on the offer, so Ward dropped out of the project. In the spring of 2010, in a second-floor location above DeRossi's Cuban sandwich joint Carteles, Cienfuegos opened. It was a throwback 1950s Havana-esque rum joint with a speakeasy vibe—you had to walk through the back of Carteles and up a metal staircase to enter. The bar was focused almost exclusively around rum, but the real signature was its punch bowls.

At the 2010 Tales of the Cocktail, an incredibly influential industry cocktail conference held in New Orleans, Death & Co won Best American Cocktail Bar, but Mayahuel won Best New Cocktail Bar in the World. It was a signature moment for the bar and should've been a feather in the cap for both Ward and DeRossi, a chance for them to celebrate all they'd accomplished with this little East Village bar. But it was not to be. They barely spoke.

After Cienfuegos, DeRossi and Ward's relationship was never the same.

RESTAURANTS ARE PUTTING AS MUCH THOUGHT INTO THE RESTROOM AS THEY ARE INTO THE DINING ROOM. I VISITED THE HYPER-DESIGNED LOO AT THE PASS & PROVISIONS IN HOUSTON FIVE TIMES—JUST TO HANG OUT. | Nduja (en-DOO-yah), the fiery pork paste from Calabria, Italy, is everywhere. | Sorry, Instagrammers, but you will not be posting shots of your steak or salad, because a footnote on the menu reads "Photography is not permitted." | *No more chasing your lunch all over town: Food halls are the new food trucks.* | I was an early supporter of the bacon boom. But now we've reached Baconageddon: bacon on brussels sprouts, bacon on steak, bacon on dessert, and in (and on) pretty much everything. It's become a culinary crutch. Don't know how to make that chicken dish thrill? Add bacon! | "IN 5 YEARS, OCTOPUS WILL BE THE NEW PRAWN," PREDICTS JOE RIEKE, OPERATIONS DIRECTOR FOR OPPER MELANG RESTAURANTS. | *Starting tomorrow, this round, glazed thing you see before you will be added to the permanent collection at Dominique Ansel Bakery. Because it's part croissant and part doughnut, the pastry chef is, appropriately, calling it a cronut.* | Things are getting confusing in Cannes with two films titled *Chef* being shopped, so Sony Pictures (which controls the Bradley Cooper *Chef* film) has sent a cease-and-desist letter to Aldamisa (which controls the Jon Favreau *Chef* film).

2013

Chef John Tesar's now infamous 2014 1 a.m. tweet to *Dallas Morning News* restaurant critic Leslie Brenner after she negatively reviewed his Dallas steakhouse Knife

CHAPTER 19

South Again, Mashama Bailey, Savannah, Georgia

First, there was fire.

When Mashama Bailey was four, she would go into the closet, light a match, and watch it burn. Bailey liked the idea that perhaps she could master this uncontrollable flame, that only she could decide when to blow it out, so she would watch it burn down to her fingers, the heat getting more intense until it was unbearable, and then she would snuff it out. Later on, she would speculate that this also went on in the kitchen, and that the idea of controlling flame innately appealed to her on a childlike level. But at four, living in an apartment off University Avenue in the Bronx, lighting fires in the closet was an issue.

Bailey's mom was from Waynesboro, Georgia, county seat of Burke County, the "Bird Dog Capital of the World." During Bailey's pyro stage, her mother gave birth to her younger brother, and the family moved from the Bronx in New York down to Savannah, Georgia, to be close to her family. Bailey's mom got a job at the Red Cross and her father in social work, and they got a little house in the Baldwin Hills neighborhood on Forty-Second Street off Waters Avenue, past the two Spanish moss–wrapped magnolia trees that shrouded over the street corner, making it look like the stage entrance to a cave.

Bailey spent five years in Savannah as a child, and remembers her neighborhood being full of kids her age: the girl across the street with the tribal marks, three scars that rode down her cheeks—a rite of passage, she told Bailey, as she described the ash they put on the marks afterward to help the healing process.

There is a food memory that sits locked in her brain from this time, during a road trip she'd taken with her parents. They were visiting friends somewhere else in the South and they were all sitting around a kitchen table, and her parents' friends brought down this 1970s yellow Tupperware pie plate and unveiled a cake like nothing she'd ever seen. It was red, with white icing and pecans stuck all over it, and when she got her slice and bit in, she tasted chocolate and coconut and sugar and the crunch of the pecans. Her parents were chatting away with their friends, but she couldn't hear a word. The rest of the world got blurry and might've stopped for all she knew. Until she was done, it was just her and this magnificent, improbably red cake.

EVENTUALLY, IN THE SUMMER OF 1986, they moved back, searching for the better job opportunities New York City provided. First her dad and her brother left, and soon after, she followed with her mom and younger sister. Everyone moved into her grandmother's house, a big home in Queens off of Hilburn Avenue and Farmers Boulevard. Her grandmother was a well-respected nurse, and among her generation, lots of African-American artists, musicians, and poets, and other middle-class professionals would keep apartments in Harlem but have homes in this section of Queens. Her grandmother's house had three stories, with a furnished two-bedroom basement, another four bedrooms in the main house, and a finished attic space.

The move back changed Bailey. The schools were bigger and more rowdy, and the city life was completely different. She got to be extremely protective of her little brother and sister—she was always really tall and lanky for her age, so kids didn't mess with her—and this new environment gave her a new

sort of survival lockdown mentality. When her family moved in, her grandmother was already housing two of her older cousins as well, and they were
out in the streets, break-dancing and going to block parties, but that wasn't
Mashama. During the week, especially the first few years attending P.S.
192 in Queens, she just kept grinding. With her parents and grandmother
working, it was her responsibility to get her brother and sisters home, set
them up with their homework, and make them English muffin pizzas or
Philly cheesesteaks.

On the weekends, when her grandmother was off work, she would organize a structured activity for all the grandkids. This could be anything—
going and walking around Sears all day, or heading out of town to a Native
American reservation—but Bailey's fondest memory is of the day her grandmother took everyone into Manhattan to go to Zabar's.

She remembers walking in, and smelling the vinegar and the bread baking and the salty, cured meats. She remembers the people handing out little
samples of all sorts of glorious treats, and staring up at the food in those glass
cases and hanging from the ceiling like cartoon animals stuck in traps. That
day, her grandmother bought bagels, two types of cream cheese, lox, and crab
dip, and spread everything out picnic-style for the kids, so they could take
bites of the salty, doughy bagel with the tangy cream cheeses. Bailey remembers sitting and eating the spicy, salty, slightly fishy flavors of the crab dip
and feeling like this was the way you were supposed to live.

High school didn't do much for Bailey. She had passing interests—the
clarinet, track—but never stuck to anything. Part of that was because her
commute to Grover Cleveland was an hour on two buses each way, and she
didn't have time to stick around for practices, but another part was that
whenever something got hard, she would quit.

She'd wanted to attend the historically black university Wright State, but
she didn't have the grades to get in and couldn't afford the early summer
program she'd need to catch up. So instead she attended junior college upstate. She'd planned on majoring in the sciences, but again it got hard, so she

quit and picked liberal arts. She had a physical therapy internship at a local hospital, but stopped that too. The one thing she liked to do that didn't stop was cook. The school mostly attracted city kids from all five boroughs—West Indians, Puerto Ricans, Jamaicans—and everyone at the school with housing had a kitchen, so she and her friends would go to the local ShopRite, look for cheap deals, and put together feasts. Being around kids with all of these diverse backgrounds meant she got to try all sorts of flavors—jerk chicken, cassava cakes, *boka dushi*, *sofrito*, *mofongo*—and slowly her palate expanded.

At home on break, she used leftover chicken wings her mother had in the fridge to put together a stewed chicken dish, and her mom was blown away.

"You need to do this," her mom told her. "This is your thing."

But Bailey wasn't feeling it. "I don't want to stand on my feet all day," she said. The dream stayed dormant.

INSTEAD, SHE TRANSFERRED to Brooklyn College to finish her degree, majoring in psychology because her parents had done the same thing and she thought she wanted to get into social work. She still thought she wanted to get into social work when she graduated and followed her cousin down to Jacksonville, Florida, and started working in a homeless shelter. But when she finally did an honest self-scan, she realized she didn't have that fire, at least not in the way you need to make social work your career.

She dated a guy in Jacksonville whose family threw big potluck dinner parties. Bailey got into being a part of these dinners, buying recipe books and flipping through them and testing recipes. Her go-to moves were always Thanksgiving-based: baked mac and cheese, with sweet potatoes, sliced long and layered with butter, brown sugar, cinnamon, and cayenne, and then cooked down until they were crispy and bubbly. His family would go nuts. This feedback gave Bailey the confidence to talk to a caterer down there about working for them, but just as she seemed to secure a job, she got homesick and moved back to New York City in 1999. Again, too worried to branch out, she got a job at a homeless shelter, but she still didn't have the energy for the work, and right around Christmas they let her go. This was the push she needed. She immediately left, filed for unemployment, and applied to the Institute of Culinary Education's work-study program.

For six months she worked as a stage or assistant to the instructors, heading down to the industrial kitchen in the basement to get olives or cayenne or butter or olive oil, making the dishes alongside the instructor in class until she paid off her tuition and was officially allowed to enroll in classes. It was hard work, and normally Bailey shied away from hard work, but something about cooking was different. Despite the physical and mental grind, it left her feeling full instead of empty.

Bailey got an externship at Aquagrill. The head chef there was a yeller, the type of person whose eyes would bulge out of his head as he screamed, and Bailey remembers watching one girl just get up and walk out after he tore her up. But even after she, too, faced his wrath for attempting to plate broken cookies in a dessert, she empathized—the yelling seemed to come from a place of frustration and helplessness, of knowing that people would cut corners if you weren't on top of them.

After Aquagrill, she just kept working—for the "Tri-State's Premier Wedding & Event Caterer," Abigail Kirsch's operation in Chelsea Piers, then as a line cook for a small Carroll Gardens restaurant called The Grocery, then making strange, fat-free meals from a Texas spa cookbook for a high-powered producer at CBS, sketchily meeting her on street corners to pass along Tupperware containers.

Of all the gigs, Bailey loved cooking at The Grocery the most, but they couldn't afford to pay her more, so she looked for different work. Eventually she found herself working as a personal chef to a wealthy family on the Upper East Side at Park and Seventy-Third. The job was easy; the couple were in their late sixties, with grown kids out of the house, and every summer she would go with them to the Hamptons from Memorial Day to Columbus Day. She loved being in the Hamptons in the fall when all the summer folks went home. She would wander the farmers markets, and find beautiful corn and sorrel and squash, and try to incorporate them in the couple's meals, even though they'd just as well prefer she make tuna fish sandwiches or veal marsala.

The job kept her comfortable and earning decent money, and suddenly one year as a personal chef turned into three and then four. But Bailey knew if she stuck with the gig any longer, she would never go back to the restaurant world. On a whim, she applied for an externship in France at Anne Willan's La Varenne Cooking School. The gig lasted for six weeks, with another month-long internship at a restaurant in France, all set up through the program. Bailey had applied late, and was told the program was full, but at the last moment a girl dropped out and she was admitted. Within a couple of weeks, Bailey quit her job, sublet her apartment, and headed to France with nothing more than a half-filled giant suitcase.

For the next couple months she lived with five other women in a chateau on a hill outside the village of Sens, going to the market and cooking dinner and assisting Willan in making classic French dishes for their cooking classes. In her spare time, Bailey sat around the house leafing through Willan's incredible collection of cooking books, reading everyone from Edna Lewis and James Beard to M. F. K. Fisher. At the end, the students were all given a cooking exam that consisted of getting a basket of food and seeing if you could turn it into something delicious. Bailey did well on the test, and Willan pulled her aside after and asked her what she wanted to do. Bailey hedged, saying she thought maybe she wanted to go into food writing.

Willan was firm. "No," she said. "You have natural ability. Most people don't. You need to cook."

Bailey was flattered, but didn't think much about it until a few days later. Willan's husband had had a stroke, and so this was going to be the last year she would do the cooking classes. As the women readied to leave, they also helped pack up the chateau. As Bailey was breaking down the library, she came across *The French Laundry Cookbook*. Inside there was an inscription from Thomas Keller to Willan. Keller thanked her for her advice, saying that, had he not listened to her, he wouldn't be doing what he was today. If one of the greatest chefs in the world had listened to her, Bailey thought, maybe she should too.

WHEN SHE RETURNED FROM FRANCE, she jumped right back into restaurants. She wanted to work at a crazy-intense spot, a boys' club with a bunch of twentysomething, ultracompetitive dudes, and see if she could handle it. She got what she asked for at davidburke & donatella. While applying, she figured by this point she was at least on the sous chef level, but the chef looked at her résumé and told her, "You left the restaurant world doing salads; we kind of need to start you back there." Bailey, at thirty-two, found herself working as garde manger, working with nineteen-year-olds, doing two hundred covers a night, working twelve-hour days, commuting all the way from her apartment in East New York. It was a mental and physical grind. So when the executive chef left to start working at The Plaza and poached Bailey, she eagerly took the gig. Aside from a shorter commute, the kitchen environment was a thousand times better. Though working for a hotel was "corporate," that meant they had HR and rules and regulations about sexual harassment and general decorum. Later for that *Lord of the Flies* boys' club bullshit.

Bailey thought she would work at The Plaza for a while, but less than a year in, a guy she worked with told her his buddy was leaving Prune and a line cook gig was opening up over there. Bailey didn't know Prune chef Gabrielle Hamilton personally, but she knew her by reputation and the buzz that was surrounding her memoir *Blood, Bones and Butter*. She applied and got the gig and was thrilled to see that there were a bunch of old heads in the kitchen, but mostly she was just blown away by Hamilton's management style. Everything they cooked had a purpose. Hamilton would lead discussions of the food—not only asking about the ingredients themselves, but where the techniques being used to cook the food came from too. Not only did everything come with a works cited, but if you wanted to do it differently, you had to articulate your argument. If you wanted to make creamed Swiss chard, you had to tell Hamilton why you would do that over creamed spinach. The questions were logic-based: Why does this make sense to you? Why would this make sense to the diner? Even if you were just cooking the family meal for the staff, you had to show and prove.

Hamilton's ability to recognize early on that taste was only part of a dish's story, that the narrative and history mattered too, was eye-opening to Bailey. She had moved back in with her now declining grandmother in Queens to help keep an eye on her, and working downtown often meant she wouldn't get back until two a.m. or later, but cooking under Hamilton kept her going because she was learning so damn much. At Prune, you kept track of time by season, and once Bailey worked all four seasons there three times, she started to itch. Bailey had worked her way up to sous, but once there, she didn't have anywhere else to move up—Hamilton was rigid about chain of command, and there were several people who'd been around even longer than her. They had talked about another project, about doing essentially a more affordable version of a Dean & DeLuca–type store in Bed-Stuy, but that got stalled. Bailey was learning so much at Prune, but she could feel her wheels spinning.

About that same time, John O. Morisano was doing a lot of driving. A venture capitalist from New York, he'd fallen in love with Savannah and purchased a home there, and later bought the old Greyhound bus depot on Martin Luther King Boulevard across from the Chatham County Courthouse. His plan was to turn it into a serious restaurant, and so he hired a restaurant designer and started work on the space, but they still didn't have a chef. During his drives back and forth from New York City to Georgia with his massive Rhodesian ridgeback Flounder, he listened to Hamilton's book on tape, and began reaching out to her, writing her a letter and emails and generally being a pain in the ass until she agreed to meet.

When they got that face-to-face and he explained what he was doing, she mentioned Bailey. Hamilton wasn't someone who selfishly kept good cooks who had outgrown her space, and she told Morisano that Bailey was ready to do her own thing and set up a meeting. Morisano asked Bailey to meet him at the National Arts Club, a rickety, old-money private club in the Samuel Tilden Mansion on Gramercy Park. Bailey, intimidated by the setting, came awkwardly dressed like she was applying for a job at a bank, but when she realized Morisano was just a quirky, nice, kind of geeky white guy, she settled in. After a few more meetings he offered her the job as head chef of his new restaurant, The Grey.

THE BUZZ STARTED almost as soon as they opened, and you could see why. The narrative was tidy. Here was an African-American chef whose own grandmother would've used a segregated bathroom at the Greyhound station, and now she was running this beautiful place. Her brief time as a child in Savannah and her mother's Georgia upbringing meant it could be considered a homecoming, and gave her the local street cred. The meticulously restored restaurant was beautiful and had a retro-ish vibe and just the right amount of nods to its past, with the old ticket counter as an open kitchen and the original skylight glass salvaged for partitions. It photographed extremely well.

In October 2014, Howie Kahn mentioned The Grey in *The Wall Street Journal Magazine*, heralding Bailey's return to Savannah. Then in November, Julia Kramer's *Bon Appétit* Checklist name-checked it as well under the heading "Say You Have One Night in Savannah." From there, the snowball gained mass. In *Elle* magazine's February 2015 issue, The Grey was ranked as the seventh-best restaurant in the country with a woman chef or owner. That same month, *The Washington Post* and *Architectural Digest* put out their own stories on The Grey. And then *Atlanta* magazine followed suit. And two months later, Jeff Gordinier from *The New York Times*.

Bailey was overwhelmed by the national press, especially because the truth was, she felt lost. She had never been a head chef before, and was still learning how to handle staffing and management. People were motivated differently in Savannah than they were in New York. She had to adjust the way she communicated with folks she was hiring, to figure out if they were just looking for a job or a career.

On top of that, she was confused. How could *Elle* name her as chef of the seventh-best woman-operated restaurant in the country, ahead of April Bloomfield and Ashley Christensen and other incredible, legendary chefs, when she'd been open for two months and was mostly just trying to survive, genuinely concerned about whether someone would actually clean the building or a grill cook would show up?

How could they omit Hamilton and Prune from that list when Hamilton was the person who gave Bailey feedback on her first menu and told her it was all over the damn place?

How could all these publications shout out her Country Captain dish as evidence of her southern heritage when she only felt comfortable with it because she'd actually gotten a vegetarian version of that dish on Prune's menu a year before? Bailey felt like the narrative had gone beyond her—that it wasn't actually about her or what she was really about, but more about this stapled-on homecoming racial redemption story; that, taken another way from a geographical perspective, the narrative could've been very different, about a New York venture capitalist coming down to Savannah, buying a building, then contracting a New York design firm to build a restaurant run by a New York chef. Because of this, the accolades and the initial outpouring of press felt undeserved, or at least a bit hollow.

Bailey became extremely self-conscious. She would count the African-American diners each night, and worry about what they thought of her food. She tried to do too much, overthinking the menu and making sure everything was approved by her.

Eventually, Bailey had to give in to the process. The media had moved on to newer narratives, and the pace of the restaurant slowed, which allowed her to step back and evaluate exactly what the hell she was doing. She got better at training her cooks. She realized, to survive, she had to leave herself exposed and surround herself with capable and opinionated sous chefs. She recognized that when you're in the weeds every day, you can't actually see what you're doing, so she stepped back and let Jesus or the sous chefs take the wheel, and somehow it didn't all fall apart. The food got better, more focused and nuanced. The menu less eclectic. If some sous or line cook came to her with an idea, she would ask them to explain the why and not just the what. She could hear a dish and know whether it was something that made sense on her menu. Mashama Bailey found her point of view.

In the fall of 2017, *Eater*'s national food critic, Bill Addison, came back to the restaurant. Addison had been there when Bailey first opened and he'd mentioned that those original menus felt like Bailey was "still searching for something more in her cuisine." She saw Addison come into the restaurant for lunch on a Saturday and asked him what he was doing in town. "I'm here for you," he told her.

"Great!" she said, but inside she freaked out a little bit, mostly because she had to be in Atlanta that weekend and couldn't be there to cook for him that evening. She called her most trusted sous and told him to taste every single thing going out that night to make sure it was right. This will be a test, she thought, of how much I truly trust these guys. Addison dined at The Grey Saturday and Sunday night.

A few weeks later, Bailey was having coffee with a friend when Morisano called her over and over. When she finally picked up, he told her Addison had done more than just a story about the restaurant. He'd named The Grey Best Restaurant in America for 2017.

Bailey drove to Morisano's house, past the twin magnolia trees sitting at the edge of Forty-Second Street and the county courthouse where her parents wed, and when she came upon Morisano, she could tell he'd been crying. He got up and gave her a hug. Soon, Mashama Bailey was crying too.

CHAPTER 20

Souvla, 517 Hayes Street, San Francisco, California, Winter 2014

In the back of Souvla, next to the rotisserie simultaneously cooking sixty-four chickens, there was a backsplash that looked like Martha Stewart's orderly vision of a Greek kitchen, with three shelves lined with items like bottles of ouzo, copper pots, and little fern potted plants, plus a lantern and mirrors possibly salvaged from a 1950s movie submarine.

There was a ten-seat communal table and more seating along the walls and several high-top tables, plus more tables outside. By noon on any weekday, all of these chairs would be filled with people waiting for their food next to black stands holding blue-and-white numbers. Up front, there were two lines. The first was made up of delivery drivers, from Uber Eats and Caviar and DoorDash and the rest: white dudes with dreads wearing rust-colored half-pants, Latin women in soccer jerseys and backpacks, and unknown Vespa riders wearing leather gloves with their helmets still on. The other line was mostly white people in weathered jeans and expensive boots and nice button-downs and mountain couture Patagonia vests or corduroy jackets, because San Francisco weather dictates layering versatility.

The menu was simple: choose pork, chicken, lamb, or vegetables, and decide whether you want it as a wrap or a salad. There were also four sides, and frozen Greek yogurt. And Greek wine, beer, and soda. Other than the first and last hour of service, the lines did not flag for nine straight hours. People came in, ordered food and drinks up front, and then had them delivered at their seats. Most ate quickly and left in under thirty minutes. By the end of the day, Souvla had sold nearly a thousand meals.

The Greek motif was everywhere. Items were delivered in blue-and-white cups or on blue-and-white plates. Sandwiches came wrapped in brown paper with Greek vines. The folks behind the counter wore blue aprons and white shirts. Black-and-white murals against the wall depicted an older Greek man chugging ouzo, and a Greek Marlboro Man with an impressive, feathery, wide-angled mustache and a cigarette. It was very much a restaurant of the times. The bright splashes of blue and little quirky details were perfect backgrounds for what the Instagram folks called "capturing moments." The food itself, with its dark, pink, pickled onions, artful drizzles of bright white Greek yogurt, and leafy green pea shoots, also performed well in the battleground of social media imagery.

But it was also of the times for a different reason. Whereas the beginning of the Culinary Revolution revolved around the fine casual dining model, Souvla was a strange hybrid born in the fires of the costly cauldron of opening a restaurant in San Francisco. Fine, fast-casual dining. In the years after Charles Bililies opened in 2014, this new "fine" fast-casual model, in which restaurants looked incredible and served thoughtful food and eliminated wait service, was heralded by industry folks as a possible antidote to the rising tide of labor, food, and rent costs.

In 2018, *The New York Times* ran a story about Souvla and the increasing number of restaurants like it. In it, Bililies, who had three San Francisco locations, mentioned that he planned to go to New York City next. Most small-scale restaurateurs sought out changing neighborhoods for their affordability, but this wasn't Bililies's concern. His plan, as he told the writer, was to plant his flag in "iconic streets in iconic neighborhoods in iconic cities."

CHAPTER 21

A Story About Rosé, aka
The Fat Jew Interlude

His preferred moniker wasn't wrong, necessarily. He was overweight, and Semitic, as his given name was Josh Ostrovsky, son of Saul and Rebecca Ostrovsky, of the Upper West Side of Manhattan Ostrovskys. The nickname came from his time with the rap group Team Facelift, which he started with friends at Skidmore College and whose musical oeuvre he described on MTV as hip-hop you could play for "quiet Asians, a dentist on his day off, orphans, quadriplegic transvestites, gothic Puerto Ricans [and] middle-aged moms with short shorts and big T-shirts with polar bears on them."

He was often in a thong during live performances, and wore his hair as a 'fro or, later, in a tight top-of-the-head ponytail that stuck straight up like a janky lightning rod, or in a knotty, Princess Leia–style bun. He had the *New York* magazine logo tattooed on his chest, as well as a tattoo of a ghost who appeared to be skiing on his arm. He was a Personality. For a while that meant he was on real television, on the E! network, but later it meant he had an interview web series on a defunct fashion and entertainment site called the *Crosby Press*, and got to occasionally appear in indie movies with Mischa Barton and reality shows such as *The Real Housewives of Beverly Hills*. Attempts to characterize him as something other than a Personality didn't really take, as evidenced by his rhetorical response to a 2014 *New York Times* question about going on tour like a traditional comedian: "Why would I do that when I can roll myself into a giant burrito, take a picture, and get paid?"

He was an early adopter of Instagram and used it as a repository of jokes, videos, memes, and screenshots of text message conversations. Many of these jokes, videos, memes, and screenshots of text message conversations were not his original material, and he faced a Carlos Mencia–esque plagiarism scandal and several weeks of what crisis PR teams call "bad pub," but ironically, in the backward logic of social media scandals involving intellectual property and the fascination with Knowing What Is Going On, that only brought him more followers. He had no issue being the silliest, most outlandish person in the room (as long as he knew you knew it was all being done in a winking manner), was incredibly savvy at self-skewering, and built an audience of more than ten million followers as a person skilled at mining the shallow caves of irony to comment on self-image, hipsters, #basic girls, standard-template East Coast progressive political burns, zany sexual relationships captured on dating apps, morning pizza cravings, the mundaneness of office work culture, and famous naked, pregnant women magazine spread poses. He was a marketer and a capitalist, and he was intent on capturing the zeitgeist of his moment, standing in front of one of the biggest social media megaphones, the post-blog millennial version of Stuff White People Like. And in the world of 2015, this meant rosé.

If you had created a specific 2015 product that would fall directly into the center of the Approval Matrix on the back page of the magazine Ostrovsky had tatted on his chest, it would've been rosé. For decades the chilled pink wine lay dormant, mocked as suburban housewife wine and most commonly associated with Sutter Home's white zinfandel, which acquired that pink color in 1972 when its founder, Bob Trinchero, was experimenting with ways to intensify the flavor in his white wines and increased the ratio of red grape skins to the clear grape juice. When the Bureau of Alcohol, Tobacco, and Firearms required he label his new blush-pink wine in English, he changed the name from Oeil de Perdrix ("eye of the partridge") to White Zinfandel, and for thirty years, Sutter Home white zin was one of the most popular wines in America, though it also scared off most serious wine makers and drinkers from attempting anything with that pink hue. France didn't have this self-consciousness, of course, and the rosé wines of Provence slowly leaked back into the American market in the mid-aughts, as hipsters and food industry folk discovered the twin delights of the taste and cheap price of the delicious dry French version, its redemption song only augmented by its embarrassing past.

By the time Ostrovsky, his manager (Alexander Ferzan, a former Warner Music exec), and the authors of the White Girl Problems Babe Walker books (and popular Twitter handle) teamed up to create White Girl Rosé under their Swish Beverage label, the wine had reached a saturation point in #basic culture rivaled only by avocado toast and the stationary biking and positive life affirmation exercise class SoulCycle. The facile rhyming derivatives off of "rosé" allowed for the easy branding of sub-trends, like frosé (literally frozen slushie-style rosé) and brosé. The very idea of brosé, more an Instagram hashtag lifestyle statement than an actual product, encapsulated the essence of the Fat Jew ethos, as it was really just guys publicly, faux-ironically drinking rosé, superficially to be like "aren't we silly, winkingly emasculating ourselves?" but really just because they thought it was kind of delicious but felt they needed to rationalize it. Ironically, the wine that became cool again because it had been so uncool was yet again reaching a point of unfashionable ubiquity.

White Girl Rosé aimed to take full advantage of that omnipresence. Central Valley winemaker Claudio Basei developed the wine, a mix of 30 percent sauvignon blanc and 70 percent white zinfandel, with a bright coral color. Sommeliers who tried WGR for wine site VinePair described it as having a "gorgeous salmon color" but tasting of "watermelon Jolly Ranchers" and "powdered cement."

On Sunday, July 12, 2015, White Girl Rosé threw its launch party at "the

Beach" in the Dream Downtown in New York City. There was White Girl Rosé merchandise sponsored by Tablelist, an app marketed as sort of an Open-Table for clubbing. Internet Person Who Takes Photos of NYC Nightlife Nicky Digital was there. So was DJ Jonny Famous. And Kirill Bichutsky, who calls himself the "Slut Whisperer," has an Outback Steakhouse tattoo on his arm and a million Instagram followers, and was wearing a "Thank You for Being a Slut" tie-dye shirt. Girls in bikinis sat in pizza inner tubes in a pool teeming with pink and white beach balls. Ostrovsky was wearing a sleeveless denim vest with no shirt underneath and had his hair in that signature vertical ponytail that gave the impression he was somehow always hanging upside down. Page Six reported that as the party wound down, he went "full monty on the balcony steps" and "brazenly" pushed his "Jew jewels" against the glass of the balcony window.

Eventually, White Girl Rosé would go on to be distributed in thirty states. Swish Beverages would switch producers to O'Neill Vintners & Distillers and produce a canned sparkling rosé called Babe Rosé with Bubbles, another sparkling rosé in a champagne bottle called Pink Party Rosé, and a pinot grigio called Family Time Is Hard. There would be a line of clothing featuring a ladies' one-piece swimsuit that said "Rosé, Bitch" and "YAAAASSSSS." The wine, they'd report to the *San Francisco Chronicle*, would become the most photographed alcohol product on Instagram.

CHAPTER 22

Not an Activist, Tunde Wey, Detroit, Michigan, Part 2

The processing center was set up like a minimum security prison: there was a dorm with a row of bunk beds, and a yard for exercise, and a library with computers that basically only provided access to legal information. As Wey walked in, he saw a bunch of men in street clothes staring back at him, and it was nerve-racking because he couldn't tell what they were about—who was a gangster and who was just a regular working man. He tried to get Buddhist about it and tell himself "whatever will be will be," but the unknown scared him. He tried to ask a guard, "Is this a violent place?" but the guard just ignored him.

They didn't take his phone initially, so he started reaching out to people as soon as he could. He called his former editor-turned-girlfriend and asked her to tell his family. He emailed Sam Sifton and NPR and told them where he was. Sifton promised he'd call *The New York Times* immigration reporter to find out what was happening. Other folks promised to come down and see him.

The Border Patrol overheard him talking, got suspicious, and asked Wey if "he was a press person," and by the tone of their voices, it sounded, for the first time, like there was deference. Earlier, he'd been in a room with another immigrant who couldn't speak English and he'd overheard the agents making fun of the man and his tongue ring and joking about him getting raped and it made Wey paranoid. Were they just being mean? Was this a prison-type situation he was walking into?

In the days that followed, though, he realized it was the opposite, one of the least violent and aggressive places he'd ever been. Even playing soccer, if someone knocked you down, he picked you back up. There was a reason for this, of course: men in the processing center wanted to stay in the United States, and the quickest way for them to get sent away was to be labeled a troublemaker. After twenty days, Wey's parents hired a lawyer and put together six thousand dollars for his bond and he was released (two years later he had to return to court, but then his deportation case was closed).

HE FIRST MET JOHN T. EDGE at his Nigerian food stall Lagos in St. Roch Market in New Orleans in the late spring of 2015. Before his detention, he'd been offered space in the new St. Claude Avenue food hall, but after his parents put together that money for the bond, they had no more money to lend him, and so he flailed around searching for the ten thousand dollars he needed to open. On a whim, he met a random friend of a friend and within twenty-four hours secured the money and the space. At the same time, his relationship with his former editor-turned-girlfriend, Claire Nelson, had become more serious, and they got married.

But almost from the beginning, the stall struggled. Rent in the market was high, and he just didn't have enough regular customers coming through to sustain the business and a staff of five. After five months, he was forced to close the stall. He now had ten thousand dollars of debt, and was still undocumented, making no money, and trying to sort through the highs and lows of a new marriage all while feeling like he wasn't contributing. It was a depressing point in his life, and Wey struggled, hopelessly treading water. In an attempt to settle his mind, he started reading more and more, and found himself continually drawn to stories and essays surrounding the Black Lives

Matter movement. As he continued to seek more, he was put in touch with a politically active African-American couple in New Orleans, and they pointed him past the news and into the realm of academic papers and studies. Wey, who'd always thought himself intellectually lazy, realized he just hadn't found something that truly interested him before, and he became a voracious consumer of any and all literature surrounding race and racism.

Four months later, completely reenergized, he launched a new series of dinners. These would serve the same sorts of Nigerian food Wey loved to cook, but this time, the focus wasn't the food. The dinners would have a point—exploring blackness in America—and he would bring in a special guest to discuss the topic. For Wey, the dynamics of the dinners were their own sociological experiment. He realized quickly that he really only needed to introduce the topic and guest speaker, and then—if they opened up the room—the conversation could go into places he hadn't imagined. He also noticed something else: African Americans at the dinner who spoke out tended to just want to air grievances, have a chance to be heard, but the white people in the audience—often politically active, self-identified liberals or progressives—felt they needed to introduce a solution or some way to fix it. There were often uncomfortable pauses as folks carefully chose their words. But instead of wanting to ease it, Wey was intrigued by the discomfort. And then John T. Edge asked him to dinner.

IT WENT DOWN LIKE THIS. In early 2016, an *Eater* writer in New York named Hillary Dixler wrote a story titled "How Gullah Cuisine Has Transformed Charleston Dining" and used a Gullah descendent named Michael Twitty as her primary source. Twitty spoke of how many of the restaurants purporting to be the cause of Charleston's culinary renaissance (Sean Brock's Husk, for example) did not pay proper homage to the marginalized people who helped invent those cuisines. Twitter lit on fire as folks argued back and forth about authenticity and who even had the right to speak on this topic, and the situation got ugly.

Enter John T. Edge. John T. (as he's known) was driving down to New Orleans and started calling folks like Twitty and Brock in an attempt to help moderate the increasingly caustic conversations. In doing so, he started thinking about how he might shape his own response in his *Oxford American* column to some of the bigger topics being addressed, and he called Wey and asked him to dinner.

Over drinks at Compère Lapin and dinner and more drinks at the Ace Hotel, they had a frank discussion of race. Wey was both charming and challenging, and as John T. remembered, he felt like the conversation always teetered on the edge of chaos, and it was both a beautiful and dangerous place to dwell. They decided they would use John T.'s column to have a public conversation addressing some of the discussion points that the Dixler story brought up.

It took about a week to come together, but with editorial guidance and feedback from *Oxford American*'s editor in chief Eliza Borné, the column was shaped, mostly in the form of emails back and forth. John T. remembered telling his wife his heart was in his throat the entire time he worked on the piece.

On June 3, 2016, the *Oxford American* put the piece online. Within hours, in the food geek social media circle, there was almost an audible gasp. Wey's words, which he'd usually written late at night after a glass of whiskey, were poetic, but the poetry of the prose didn't hide the fact that he'd basically eviscerated John T. in his own column.

> White privilege permits a humble, folksy, and honest white boy to diligently study the canon of appropriated black food, then receive extensive celebration in magazines, newspapers, and television programming for reviving the fortunes of Southern cuisine.

John T. has decided to share this column with me—why the fuck would I not accept half his column wage when I have these debts to pay? Brock has decided to accept Twitty's invitation to share a kitchen and cook together—shit, get some money out that pot, Michael, Sean seems good for it. But each of course will eventually retreat after this gesture to the safety of his own privilege: John T. to his writing and non-profiteering, Sean to his celebrated kitchen.

Unless we keep them honest and desperately uncomfortable.

At the end, he posed a question:

John T., you have endorsed and celebrated the appropriation of black Southern food without consequence, and the consequences have compounded with interest. You have to return what you took to the place where it was, to the people to whom it belongs. And, after this principal has been repaid, the interest is due. You have to strip yourself of the marginal benefits of this appropriation willingly, with grace, or unwillingly by force and with shame. You're a graceful man, John T. So what will you willingly give up to ensure the Southern food narrative services properly and fully the contributions of black Southerners?

The piece went viral, quickly becoming one of the most read *Oxford American* stories of the entire year. Nationally, as election season continued to devolve into ugly spectacle, there was a hunger out there for people to question the status quo, or at least bring up hard questions, and no one was doing it as eloquently or forcefully as Wey. John T. invited him to a race summit retreat and introduced him to an entire world of people involved in the food world, people Wey hadn't even really known existed. He hadn't made the connection that academics and food journalists and activists and farmers might all know each other, and run in these circles. More important, he realized that these circles were the arbiters of ideas that then get consumed as trends by the greater masses. He thought about it one day as he sat in a random hotel in Charlotte and watched as they served him a random style of food he'd recognized from high-end restaurants and glossy food magazines, which had now trickled down to this hotel. This, he realized, was where the power was.

Quickly, Wey started making connections to people in these powerful circles. John T. made him a fellow at the Southern Foodways Alliance, and through that he met North Carolina chef Andrea Reusing and Toni Tipton-Martin and the executive vice president of the James Beard Foundation. He started to hear from literary agents about writing a book. Through John T. he met La Cocina executive director Caleb Zigas, who introduced him to Paolo Lucchesi from the *San Francisco Chronicle*, and just like that he had a column in the paper. From his perch at the *Chronicle*, Wey kept attacking privilege, going after Daniel Patterson and Roy Choi's Locol, and the white people at *Bon Appétit* who chose white-owned sandwich shop Turkey and the Wolf in New Orleans as their number one restaurant in America. He attacked Anthony Bourdain for his privileged *Parts Unknown* episode in Nigeria. He appeared in conferences in Washington, DC, and as a talking head on the popular Netflix show *Chef's Table*.

He could see his power growing, but it wasn't enough. So he did more: he started a social experiment in the form of a food stall in New Orleans that charged white people thirty dollars and people of color only twelve dollars for the same food, then offered to give the extra eighteen dollars to the black folks. With his newfound connections, press was easier, and soon the experiment was being written about in the pages of *GQ* and he was being interviewed by German radio stations and Australian newspapers.

For his next project, Wey tried to move beyond conceptual arguments to leveraging actual resources. In North Nashville, he set up what he called "Hot Chicken Sh*t," a project funded through a stipend from the city, to try to raise money to help fixed-income seniors secure home ownership in gentrifying areas. He was tremendously optimistic and ambitious when he began, and thought his target should be eleven million dollars. But in the end, the local press didn't respond, and except for one recently divorced woman, the rich folks he'd met in Nashville weren't giving him anything. Still, he managed to raise more than a hundred thousand dollars, which he planned to use for mini-grants, given to those fixed-income seniors to help them pay rent and taxes and fines so they could stay in their homes.

He wasn't done. In early 2019, Wey planned to go to Pittsburgh to do a series of dinners between immigrants and citizens to see if any of the immigrants could make a love connection, get married, and get their citizenship. The time for incremental ideas was over, Wey said. There needed to be a revolution. The power structure needed to change.

As he became better known, his desire for that power only increased. Real power wasn't just getting things for himself, but bringing others on. Despite being granted legal resident status in January, 2019, he still didn't feel safe, didn't feel like he could let his guard down. In order to do that, he needed more people who looked like him to have voices in newspapers, to be on television, to have well-known restaurants, or to run conferences. He needed people who had gotten so used to being in power they didn't even notice it to start feeling uncomfortable, until they were willing to relinquish some of that power.

But until then he'd keep it moving.

CHAPTER 23

111 N. 12th Street, Williamsburg Neighborhood, Brooklyn, NY, September 2016

The William Vale hotel

The 183-room William Vale is now open here in the Williamsburg section of the borough. The property features architecture by Albo Liberis and interiors by Studio Munge.

The amenities and guest services include the longest hotel pool in NYC at 60 ft., according to the company; Vale Park, an elevated 15,000-sq.-ft. green space atop street level; 24-hour in-room dining;

twice-daily housekeeping service; complimentary Wi-Fi; a fitness center; valet parking; business work stations; Frette linens; L'Occitane en Provence products; smart TV systems; and Brooklyn Roasting Company coffee available throughout the property. Gunn Landscape Architecture designs all outdoor spaces and greenery.

"We believe the William Vale will reinvent Brooklyn, and we felt it was the right time to bring this resort-inspired hotel to the neighborhood, as it is quickly emerging as the go-to destination," said Sébastien Maingourd, GM of the William Vale.

The hotel's wide range of spaces sets the stage for its calendar of cultural programs, which are open to both hotel guests and locals. Each event is meant to connect the property with the surrounding community, whether it's through book launches for Brooklyn authors, rooftop yoga, opera performances, indie movie screenings, painting classes with local artists, or group meditation, according to the company.

Chef Andrew Carmellini of NoHo Hospitality Group oversees the hotel's distinct dining destinations and in-room dining, including Leuca, a Southern Italian restaurant with wood-fired cuisine, opening this fall, and Westlight, a 22nd-floor rooftop bar serving rare spirits and craft cocktails with skyline views.

Carmellini and the NoHo team also serve a menu of light snacks and cocktails at Vale Pool and oversee all private event menus for the property's event spaces, which include a 4,000-sq.-ft. ballroom, two boardrooms, and two conference rooms.

The hotel is close to the Brooklyn Brewery; dining options include Bedford Avenue, the Brooklyn Bowl, the food festival known as Smorgasburg, and indie Nitehawk Cinema.

CHAPTER 24

Downfall, John Besh, New Orleans, Louisiana

He used to be a hero.

A Gulf War veteran Marine and Culinary Institute of America graduate from Slidell, Louisiana, Besh first came on the national radar in 1999 for his cooking at Artesia, a restaurant in a picturesque old home in Abita Springs. That year he received a Best New Chef in America award from *Food & Wine*, alongside big hitters in big cities like New York's Rocco DiSpirito and Philadelphia's Marc Vetri.

In 2001, August "Duke" Robin, a legendary New Orleans businessman and athlete, converted an old tobacco warehouse on Tchoupitoulas Street in New Orleans into a restaurant, a place where he could throw parties, but he needed a chef who could execute his vision. He found Besh at Artesia and hired him away after spending days fishing and hunting with him, talking to him about food. Robin wanted the restaurant to cook the types of meals locals loved, be it steaks or buster crabs and grits. Besh wanted to cook more challenging, fancier dishes, the types of things that would keep him on the national radar. The restaurant they opened together, Restaurant August, eventually did both, becoming just as known for its fried buster crabs on a lost bread crouton as it was for its cold foie gras trio.

In 2003, the *Times-Picayune* restaurant critic Brett Anderson gave the restaurant five beans, the highest possible rating, and Besh's star rose even further. He opened another restaurant, a steakhouse, in Harrah's Casino, installing a young, promising Israeli chef named Alon Shaya in the kitchen. At Harrah's, he was reunited with Octavio Mantilla, a Nicaraguan-born New Orleans local whom Besh first met in 1991. By 2005, Duke Robin was tired of the aggravations of running a restaurant and wanted to sell August. He offered it to Besh, and Besh went to Mantilla, and together they pooled all their resources, purchased August, and formed Besh Restaurant Group.

Then came Katrina.

ON AUGUST 29, 2005, Hurricane Katrina hit the Gulf Coast, its 140-mile-per-hour winds and heavy rainfall breaching the seawalls and levees that held back Lake Pontchartrain and Lake Borgne. More than three-quarters of the city evacuated, but those left over—mostly poor families stuck in low-lying areas—were stranded amid a water-soaked city, 80 percent of which was in some way underwater.

Besh had ridden out the storm in his cousin's Alabama cabin, drinking the Krug champagne he'd haphazardly grabbed during the evacuation and plotting a return. All of his savings were tied up in the restaurants, and he knew that if they were destroyed, he likely was too. As soon as he could, he and Shaya returned to the city, along with several of his former military buddies. Besh's two skill sets—cooking and being a former marine—all of a sudden became usefully intertwined. He went out on amateur rescue missions on private boats, guns and water and medical supplies in tow. Using propane burners, he started cooking red beans and rice for the National Guard, triage hospital, and others around the city, packing it into coolers and lugging it wherever they thought it was needed.

Soon folks began talking about this former marine celebrity chef who was feeding the hungry folks in New Orleans, and he started getting government and private catering contracts, which helped pay for the reconstruction of his restaurants and keep him afloat. Though conversations in intellectual circles and op-eds in national newspapers raged about the viability and intelligence of rebuilding a city that was already mostly under sea level, Besh doubled down on the city, opening two more restaurants in the next two years and becoming the unofficial national spokesman for New Orleans recovery. He embarked on an exhausting tour of the country, and spoke to any food journalist, television show, or blogger that was willing to keep the NOLA conversation going.

He was a man who had served his country in war, and then literally served his city in crisis, and on top of that he was handsome, in an ex-high-school-quarterback kind of way, and married to a whip-smart and beautiful lawyer from his hometown named Jenifer Berrigan, and had that Slidell accent that sounded like it was marinated in buttermilk and smothered in hot honey, and on top of that, he was a great chef. Besh seemed like an easy person to root for in a city that needed all the help and encouragement it could get. He won a James Beard Award in 2006, for Best Chef in the Southeast, and began to be featured in tourist board ad campaigns. New Orleans began to climb back.

Fresh narratives of its resurgence as the culinary capital of America started to pour out, and Besh pushed further, opening more restaurants with Mantilla and partnering with Alon Shaya to open Domenica, then Pizza Domenica, and then Shaya's namesake, a modern Israeli restaurant that lit the national food press on fire when it opened and won the James Beard for Best New Restaurant in 2016. By now he had sixteen restaurants in New Orleans, plus others in San Antonio and Baltimore. He had two television shows and four cookbooks and a foundation that provided microloans to farmers. The publisher of the *Times-Picayune* awarded him the first-ever T.G. Solomon Excellence in Innovation Award as someone who is "an exemplar of civic-minded entrepreneurial success." He emceed Whole Foods–branded fishmonger face-off competitions in Aspen. He was a hero.

And then he was not.

ON OCTOBER 21, 2017, Brett Anderson, the same restaurant critic who'd given Besh the highest possible review fourteen years earlier at August—the same guy who'd run into him in the days after Katrina as Besh, gun in hand, wandered off into the darkness of Harrah's to see what had become of his restaurant—broke a story he'd spent eight months investigating: twenty-five current and former female employees of the Besh Restaurant Group claimed Besh and Mantilla fostered a culture of sexual harassment.

Nine women allowed their names to be published in the story, which was also backed up by two Equal Employment Opportunity Commission complaints, including one detailing how Besh "continued to attempt to coerce (her) to submit to his sexual overtures" during a months-long affair that started when she was twenty-four. When she attempted to stop the sexual relationship, the EEOC document noted, Besh "asked (her) to help him find her 'replacement.'" There were descriptions of "pool days" at a certain supervisor's home, which women felt obligated to attend while wearing swimsuits and drinking, and a "bro-culture" in the kitchens that turned a blind eye to harassment even as women complained and ultimately quit. The entire story cannonballed through the food world, helped, in part, by the fact that *The New York Times* and *New Yorker* had both published their Harvey Weinstein exposés just two weeks before. And just as the Weinstein story encouraged others in the entertainment industry to speak out against other bad actors, the Besh investigation did the same for the restaurant industry.

Soon after, Mario Batali, one of the most famous chefs in America, was accused of sexual misconduct. Then Ken Friedman, the restaurateur known for his ownership in the Spotted Pig and his partnership with chef April Bloomfield. Then former Chez Panisse chef Charlie Hallowell. Then Washington, DC, celebrity chef Mike Isabella. And well-known pastry chef Johnny Iuzzini.

The #MeToo movement exposed the incredible cognitive dissonance that existed in the restaurant industry between the public-facing world that, for so long, traded in access to fawning profiles and TV interviews and Facebook Live chats in exchange for silence, or at least a tolerance of what they knew to be a brutal industry, and the inside culture of ubiquitous drinking and drug use, chronic misogyny, verbal abuse, and rampant sexual harassment. That most of the restaurants made popular during the Culinary Revolution happened to be chef-owned, with tight budgets, meant there was no institutionalized human resources department, and the critical shortage of line cooks ensured that shitty people who were competent cooks were rarely let go.

As for Besh, once the story was out, new lows hit seemingly every day. Harrah's cut ties with him, and within days his Besh Steak restaurant was quietly turned into BH Steak and then The Steakhouse. Across the country, his cooking shows were taken off the air. He got into a public and ugly trademark dispute with Alon Shaya, his formerly close friend and protégé, over the name of the Shaya, the restaurant they once owned together. Shaya lost the dispute and opened Saba, a similar spot a mile down the same street, and instituted an employee training program focused around harassment prevention.

Besh stepped down as CEO of his restaurant group, which rebranded itself as BRG Hospitality, making way for Shannon White, a longtime employee. He stepped down as a board member of Notre Dame's Center for Ethics and Culture. *Top Chef* reedited an episode of their show to remove him as a judge. But Besh retained part ownership of the restaurant group. (As I write this, Mario Batali is the only famous chef outed in the #MeToo movement who has severed ties with all of his restaurants.) He went back to Slidell, to try to repair his relationship with Jenifer and his kids.

In October 2018, his eponymous foundation announced its plan for a "rebirth" and a name change. It would now be known as the Made in New Orleans (MiNO) Foundation. Under "Event Details" on the website, promoting the first event at Felicity Church, in bold letters, they defined rebirth: "rē'bərTH is defined as the action of reappearing or starting to flourish or increase after a decline; revival."

JOHN BESH RESTAURANTS FOSTERED CULTURE OF SEXUAL HARASSMENT, 25 WOMEN SAY. | MARIO BATALI STEPS AWAY FROM RESTAURANTS AMID SEXUAL MISCONDUCT ALLEGATIONS. | Ken Friedman, Power Restaurateur, Is Accused of Sexual Harassment. | Oakland chef Charlie Hallowell steps away from restaurants as 17 women accuse him of sexual harassment. | LAWSUIT ACCUSES CELEBRITY CHEF MIKE ISABELLA OF "EXTRAORDINARY" SEXUAL HARASSMENT. | *4 former employees accuse celebrity chef Johnny Iuzzini of sexual harassment and abuse.*

2017

CHAPTER 25

Anjan and Emily Mitra, San Francisco, California, Part 3

By 2016, owning profitable independent restaurants in the city of San Francisco was becoming a more and more difficult feat to pull off. In 2011, two years after DOSA on Fillmore opened, there had been 3,600 restaurants with permits to operate in the Bay Area. By 2016, there were 7,200. The 100 percent increase in restaurants meant there was that much more demand for skilled hospitality workers, but thanks to the tech boom, real estate prices and rents in the city had also skyrocketed, meaning most hourly wage employees, especially back-of-the-house workers like line cooks and dishwashers who legally couldn't share in the tip pool, couldn't afford to live anywhere near the places they worked. The increased demand for skilled workers, coupled with more and more of them opting to take jobs closer to their homes in more affordable parts of the East and North Bay, created a crippling back-of-the-house shortage. What's more, thanks primarily to an effort by many of the South Bay tech businesses to return to the city and get closer to their workers, commercial real estate prices had skyrocketed over the last five years, and landlords increased rents with the irrational confidence of drunk teenagers.

The increasing unpredictability of the weather, with droughts followed by monsoon-style rains, challenged the farm-to-table mantra as never before, as food costs increased. But it wasn't just competition from other restaurants and the cook shortage and the taxes and the rents that worried Anjan and Emily. There was also the rise of online food delivery businesses. Naturally, because they all seemed to start in Silicon Valley, San Francisco was their testing ground.

The online food delivery game had been around for a while, starting with Seamless and Grub Hub. Seamless had existed since 1999, and Grub Hub since 2004, acting first as online menu repositories and then slowly working their way into taking online delivery orders for restaurants. But starting in 2012, when Caviar entered the San Francisco market, the business started to speed up quickly. Grub Hub, backed by venture capital investment, went on a buying spree, picking up Allmenus and Campusfood. Seamless acquired MenuPages and then merged with Grub Hub in 2013. Caviar, also backed by venture capitalists, had upped the game, with a more curated lineup of places (only four stars or above on Yelp) that usually didn't deliver, GPS tracking, and their own line of drivers, something that felt completely crazy at launch. The year 2013 also saw the launch of (venture-capital-backed) DoorDash, which essentially played the same game, also using their own line of drivers; they entered the San Francisco market in 2014. That same year, Uber, the king of venture capital backing, started playing around in the space, launching Uber Eats first as a service you could select through their main app (instead of, say, an UberX, you'd choose Uber Eats) and then as a separate entity two years later.

For most of these businesses, the sell was the same: let us add you to our roster of restaurants, give us 15 to 30 percent (in Uber's case) of the total cost, and we will deliver business you normally wouldn't be getting. To Anjan, it felt like a trap. For one, half of the food sales were going to regulars who might have just done takeout with no fee before, and the other half, the new business they were bringing in, wasn't really helping their bottom line enough to make up the difference. Two, there was a serious branding problem. In the same way that Facebook diluted a news organization's brand once everyone began getting their news from social media, once everyone began ordering off these apps, DOSA wouldn't appear to be any better or worse than any other Indian restaurant on these sites. The effort and time they'd spent building their brand and reputation with food quality and innovation was all for naught if people were simply choosing by price among random restaurants with tiny JPEG logos. But at the same time, they couldn't ignore the game altogether, because these online delivery apps had effectively wiped out all the independent delivery systems restaurants had set up on their own.

And if that wasn't enough, there were the food delivery businesses that competed against you. Anjan and Emily had to factor in places like Sprig, Munchery, Blue Apron, Eat Club, Zesty, and the like, each with its own commissary kitchen and venture capital backing. These businesses were burning through millions of dollars in losses a year, but because they had that crucial VC money, they could afford to keep on churning, and that meant poaching line cooks by offering them wages well above what a restaurant could afford, and poaching customers who might potentially have ordered takeout in the past.

There was a new kind of gangsterism in the way restaurants had to operate in the modern world. Whereas in the old days you might have to pay off the "Italian Businessmen's Association" and donate heavily to the Policeman's Union Fund and the campaign of whichever local city official had jurisdiction over your neighborhood, those funds now went toward improving your Yelp visibility and paying OpenTable, Yelp, or Resy for reservations, and Uber to deliver your food. Even for successful restaurateurs like Anjan and Emily, owning independent restaurants in the city could feel like death by a million small cuts, and San Francisco had the sharpest edges in the country.

But though it felt good to vent, it was pointless to wallow in self-pity about the challenges of running restaurants in the city, especially as so many others continued to dip their toes in the game. And then suddenly, twelve years after DOSA on Valencia opened its doors, something unexpected happened: South Indian food became "hot."

The Babu Ji Problem

The trend articles really started in October 2016, with Vignesh Ramachandran's "Why Indian Cuisine Is Having a Fast-Casual Moment Right Now" on *Eater*. Though the crux of the story tackles the fast-casual movement and Indian food's place in it—including significant mentions of Curry Up Now, the San Francisco–based fast-casual chain that had started out as a DOSA twin—South Indian food meanders into that conversation toward the end, during a discussion of Biju Thomas's Colorado-based restaurant, Biju's Little Curry Shop, which opened in early 2015. "Thomas's dishes feature ingredients reminiscent of the Kerala region in South India: fresh coconut, ginger, garlic, and curry leaves," the story points out, going on to mention that "Thomas's plan to bring South Indian flavors to the masses is getting attention" and that he'd opened a "chef-driven concept with his regional style of Indian cuisine inside one of its [Whole Foods] Boulder stores," and he was looking to expand to California, Washington, and Texas. It also says that "Curry Up Now is even expanding its menu to offer craft cocktails."

A full year later, in November 2017, *Food & Wine*'s Charu Suri put out "South Indian Food Is Having a Major Moment in America." The story mentioned that only forty of the four hundred Indian restaurants in New York City "serve typical South Indian dishes and snacks" but "that number is poised to grow." In the section under the header "The West Coast Embraces South Indian Cuisine," Suri mentioned Campton Place, a Michelin-starred Franco-Indian restaurant from Srijith Gopinathan, which the story says "has inspired locals with its 'Cal-Indian' cuisine." She also talked to the chef at Paper Dosa in Santa Fe, New Mexico, who, though it's not mentioned, actually started his career as a waiter and was trained in the kitchen for the first time at DOSA on Valencia under the tutelage of DOSA's opening executive chef Senthil Kumar.

In another section, the chef from Junoon in New York commented on the difficulty of making sambar and dosa:

These types of complex sauces often take a lot of time to get just right: "It's easier to train someone to make a roti (a dry bread, typically found in North Indian cuisine) than to make a good dosa," he continues. These steps involve the fermentation of the rice, leaving it overnight and then making a rich, thick consistent batter to produce crisp dosas. "Also, good South Indian cooks are hard to come by," he adds.

At no point is DOSA referenced.

The Huffington Post weighed in as well in 2017, with Sonam Joshi's "Can South Indian Food End the Hegemony of Curry and Chicken Tikkas in the UK, US?" also quoting the Campton Place chef. "Indian food was equivalent to north Indian food for the longest time," Gopinathan says. "It is only now that regional chefs are travelling and cooking their own regional food."

As the trend stories piled up, with other aggregating sites often just using these stories as the building blocks of their own, the narrative built into an unassailable truism. None of this would have been that upsetting to Anjan and Emily if they'd played some part in this narrative, at least in a qualifying statement like, "Though San Francisco's DOSA has been doing seasonal South Indian cuisine since 2005, it has just recently started to take off." But it felt almost as if they were too early to work with the current talking point, because it might throw off the thesis. Anjan and Emily had to remind themselves that online food journalism was a young person's game, and many of the writers might've been in high school around the time they opened. New restaurants were shiny objects to food writers, and by 2017, there was a trifecta of new, on-trend Indian restaurants in San Francisco ready to take advantage.

The first was Babu Ji, the third iteration of chef Jessi Singh and partner Jennifer Singh's Australia and New York City restaurants, known for being party-friendly and having self-serving beer fridges. The teal and gold space had installations from a local artist, a cocktail menu from a respected NYC cocktail bartender, and a menu "melding Bay Area ingredients with traditional Indian flavors." This was quickly followed by August 1 Five, ex-Google employee Hetal Shah's restaurant featuring an Indian chef who used to work at Washington, DC's beloved Rasika, doing what *Eater* described as "California-influenced Indian flavors" alongside cocktails designed by a local SF bartender. Three months later, SF's nouveau Indian trifecta was completed with Rooh, a lounge-y restaurant in the SOMA area and first US restaurant from Good Times Restaurants Group, which owned nightclubs and eateries in India. Again the themes sounded familiar—"progressive versions of Indian dishes using Northern California ingredients and modern techniques"—though this craft cocktail menu came from the group's beverage director in India.

Anjan and Emily's original DOSA restaurants, now open for eleven and nine years, respectively, were being left out of the narrative just as South Indian food appeared to be on the cusp of becoming an actual American trend, or at least being willed into one by the press.

Ever since Chef Kumar had left five years earlier, Anjan had taken the role of executive chef. He could define the visions of different dishes, and he'd always try to get the line cooks to talk about dishes their mothers had made them in an effort to suss out more home cooking that could be used in the restaurants, but while he had an intimate understanding of the food and the palate for the spices, he wasn't a chef or on the line every day. He wasn't trained, and he didn't have the technique or the know-how to push it up the hill even farther. He had looked around over those five years, spending thousands of dollars traveling to India and attempting to help secure visas for some notable Indian chefs. But the American government made it extremely difficult to get a visa approved for an Indian who wasn't in the tech, engineering, or medical fields, and so eventually Anjan gave up on the India search.

If they were going to find someone, it would have to be in America. For the sake of DOSA and the security of the restaurants going forward, it was time to find a new voice.

ARUN GUPTA WAS GOOD AT CHESS. Really, really good at chess. Growing up in the Battery Park City neighborhood in Manhattan as the son of an Indian father and Polish-American mother, Gupta had gone on to be an English and public health major at Tufts, before moving back to New York City and teaching chess. In college, he'd spent a summer in France living with a family, and was touched by how much they gave a shit about their food, and how the dad and sons used to leave their jobs every day to come home and have these simple, fresh, ninety-minute lunches, and that sparked an interest for him. During his chess teaching days, he started cooking more and more on his own, and throwing big dinner parties at his parents' apartment, and eventually he realized this was what he wanted to do. Through a connection he was able to trail chef Mike Anthony at Gramercy Tavern, and after Anthony witnessed him slicing his own finger while merely cutting bread, he hired him on, and Gupta went through every single station at Gramercy over the next five years before leaving to open the upscale southern restaurant Maysville with Kyle Knall, who'd worked under legendary Birmingham chef Frank Stitt at Highlands Bar & Grill. Gupta spent four years there, first as sous chef and then as chef de cuisine. But after a while he yearned to leave New York. He was married and had a young daughter and didn't like the grind of the city.

Gupta's cousin lived out in the Bay, knew Anjan, and would brag to Anjan about his cousin who worked at Gramercy Tavern. Remembering that, Anjan asked to be put in touch. Anjan and Emily explained they were looking for an executive chef to oversee their two Indian restaurants, and own the ingredients, the creativity, and the vision. They wanted someone who could usher in a new era to the cooking and see things with new eyes. They explained their vision, how the restaurants were primarily South Indian, but they wanted to look deeper into different, relatively unexplored regions of the country.

Gupta was curious. Even though he was half-Indian, he'd always felt out of place as someone of mixed race, not Indian enough for the other Indians in college, and yet not white enough to avoid characterization as Indian by outside forces. He expressed his doubts to Anjan: He'd never cooked Indian food professionally, so how would this make sense? Anjan told him not to worry and that he and the other Indian cooks would help him with the spice, but Gupta would also help them by bringing the techniques he learned at Gramercy: the proper way to braise a goat for seven hours, to fry a chicken, to smoke a fish, to make a spiced vinaigrette for a salad. Hopefully as an Indian American, Anjan said, you will be able to respect the tenets of Indian cooking without feeling imprisoned by them. Why don't you come out and cook a meal?

Gupta flew out to San Francisco. He used spices from Anjan's own kitchen, but also scoured the SF Farmers Market and was predictably blown away by the breadth of produce, so much so that he started taking pictures of vegetables to text back to his chef friends in New York. That night he made an asparagus soup with *raita* yogurt, sable with a fresh spring onion and star anise sauce, a smoked lamb shoulder, and dal cooked like grits. Anjan and Emily were extremely impressed and offered him the job.

As he'd gotten older and watched his parents get older, Gupta had felt a sense of nostalgia about traditions, and he realized that taking this job would allow him to seriously explore a side of his heritage that he'd only sort of considered. He accepted the job as executive chef and moved out to San Francisco with his family in July 2017.

In preparation, he began looking for ways to immerse himself, but he quickly realized that there wasn't a ton of literature out there. When he started, Gupta decided he would treat it almost like his trailing of Chef Anthony at Gramercy: he would watch the cooks operate and talk to them and ask them questions and eventually he would be able to figure out ways to tighten or change techniques, or at least start to evolve the kitchen. But it would take some time. As he attempted to make it more his own kitchen, Gupta's tendency was to simplify, but Anjan had to remind him that this wasn't Western cooking.

"I know you want to keep it simple, but it's making it flat," he'd say. "Simplicity doesn't translate well to Indian food; it's about balance and textures." To drive that point home, Anjan had a plan: he'd take Gupta on a research trip to India.

The trip was for two weeks, starting in Bombay but mainly focused on the Kerala region, a South Indian state at the southernmost tip of India along the Malabar Coast off the Arabian Sea. Anjan had long wanted to dig deeper into Kerala's cuisine, and this seemed like a good excuse. With a few friends tagging along, they ate and cooked their way through Kerala, meeting up with local restaurant chefs and home cooks along the way. At Philipkutty's Farm, an old spice plantation run by Anu Mathew and her mother-in-law, Aniamma, they watched and then helped the two women make a Kerala chicken curry, sourcing not only the vegetables and fruits but also the spices from the lands around their home. With another chef in the town of Kumily, which sits in the Cardamom Hills by the Periyar Tiger Reserve, Gupta was shown the proper way to make the local Kerala *paratha*. In the village of Kumarakom, floating down the canals on a houseboat past the famous bird sanctuary, he learned the local technique for making fiery Kerala fried shrimp as Siberian storks flew by. Gupta would go off on his own and disappear into kitchens for a while, watching and then eventually cooking with the local chefs, who would all file out to wave good-bye when he left. Each new experience felt like some sort of Mr. Miyagi training exercise, wherein by the end Gupta had seen techniques, tasted dishes, and cooked enough to feel a renewed sense of confidence and excitement. At night, he and Anjan talked through how these things they were seeing and tasting could translate into a menu. On the plane ride back to California, Gupta sat the entire time working out a new Kerala tasting menu, working just off ideas he was keeping in his head.

AT HOME, EMILY AND ANJAN were also busy expanding the business side of the operation. They'd spent the last year working with the design and consulting firm IDEO to help build the brand for their product line. Most brands opt to test a product line with two or three different items, so naturally Emily and Anjan decided it made sense to do it with thirty-five. They'd noticed that if they didn't fill the shelves around their Dosateria café in Whole Foods with their own goods, Whole Foods would do it with other people's chips and drinks and snacks, so why not make sure you have enough items available to fill those shelves?

By 2018, the Lassi beverage line, and the other prepared foods were doing well enough that Whole Foods planned to offer them through most of their Northern California and Reno stores. Whole Foods had already introduced their samosas to those locations, and the commissary kitchen was now making fourteen thousand a week. Anjan and Emily also made a deal with Napa Farms, which put their products in the San Francisco airport. The delivery service Good Eggs had picked them up, as well as the other natural and high-end retailers in the Bay Area like Berkeley Bowl and The Market on Market, and they'd been tapped by Amazon Go to be one of the brands for their brick-and-mortar stores.

The counter service dosa by DOSA in Oakland was also taking off, with people spending an average of twenty-seven dollars per person, an incredible number in that space. They hoped to open another one in Mountain View by the second half of 2019. They had no plans to try opening anything else in San Francisco. If Dosateria was a model of a store within a store, and dosa by DOSA was their fast-casual stand-alone, the Valencia and Fillmore DOSAs were still the innovation lab, the flagships, the brand halo from which the rest gained their power and reputation.

Back in the DOSA kitchen, Chef Gupta, with help from the South Indian kitchen staff, re-created the chicken curry he'd tasted at Philipkutty's Farm and added it to the Kerala tasting menu, along with a crab *poori*, Lake Kochi grilled prawns with green garlic and coconut, and a smoked arctic char with *moilee* sauce that incorporated a smoking technique Gupta learned at Gramercy. He was excited, because this was just the beginning of what they could do as they continued to dig even deeper into specific regions of South India. There was so much to explore and introduce, and Gupta only hoped that people would get it, that they would understand that DOSA had been cooking South Indian food for twelve years, and if others were going to cook South Indian too, then it was time to evolve again, to go deeper into regionality and showcase the crazy versatility of flavors, from the Portuguese and Roman influences in Goa to the intensely spicy coastal Andhra cuisine along the Bay of Bengal. He'd witnessed this sort of evolution in Mexican cuisine, as chefs started to go deeper into Oaxaca and Jalisco.

But even as story after story came out praising the rise of spice levels in America as sriracha and other hot sauces took off, and every other trend piece began to expound on the rise of vegetable-focused meals, there were also stories warning that Americans weren't ready for this sort of thing from India, that they should go wide instead of deep, just as Tava Indian Kitchen did when it got rid of the "Indian" in its name and started incorporating other South Asian flavors, or how Saffron Fix packaged foods turned itself into Global Belly. But considering India was the size of Europe, Gupta was convinced there was plenty of room to go both wide and deep and still stay in the country.

In late spring 2018, Gupta unveiled his Kerala tasting menu to Anjan and Emily. Upon sampling it for the first time, they were ecstatic. This was why they'd brought Gupta along, they thought. There was technique, texture, and balance, but most of all, there was flavor.

CHAPTER 26

The Resistance, Sonja Finn, Pittsburgh, Pennsylvania

In October 2015, four months after Donald Trump announced his intention to run for president from Trump Tower in a speech that mentioned that Obama set up a five-billion-dollar website and is always out playing golf but not on Trump's courses, which are the best golf courses in the world, chef Sonja Finn went to Washington, DC, for the first time. She was there to lobby for the renewal of the Healthy, Hunger-Free Kids Act, a 2010 bill that provided more access to healthy food in schools for low-income children.

She'd assumed the bill wouldn't be controversial, because it was about taking care of kids, and all these senators and representatives had kids, so surely this wouldn't be a partisan issue. But of course it was, so she was there fighting over getting a half cup of fruit OR vegetables in the school lunch, and it left her feeling civically naive, but also upset at the Democrats, who'd meant well but came into negotiations as if they'd never bought a house before, timidly asking for the smallest things and then watching the Republicans whittle them down from there. Coming back from the trip, she felt angry but energized. Finn had always been civically minded, but now it was different. Her eyes felt open.

IN 2008, THE YEAR DONALD TRUMP said on his syndicated radio show *Trumped!* that Hillary Clinton would be a "very good president," Sonja Finn, at twenty-nine years old, opened her restaurant, Dinette, in Pittsburgh's East Liberty neighborhood, four blocks from the house she'd grown up in.

Finn had gone to Reizenstein Middle School across the street from the Nabisco factory, and Allderdice High School. She'd gotten heavily involved in both the feminist punk Riot Grrrl and local indie rock scenes, even hosting a radio show on 92.1 while still in high school. She'd gone to Columbia for college, and the Culinary Institute of America to train as a chef. She'd worked at Ben and Karen Barker's James Beard Award–winning Magnolia Grill in Durham, North Carolina, and Judy Rodgers's James Beard Award–winning Zuni Café in San Francisco. She'd run a kitchen staff of thirty-five people, and helped open a new restaurant on the Eastern shore of Maryland.

She'd moved back to Pittsburgh in early 2008 with her boyfriend, Jim, whom she'd met in San Francisco. While staying in her old bedroom in her parents' house, she wrote a business plan using a template she googled off the Internet to get a bank loan, scraped enough savings together to show she had equity, slowly increased the limits on two low-interest credit cards while staying debt free, still had to make personal guarantees to get a lease, offered her line cooks a dollar pay raise plus paid time off and health insurance (all of which were exceedingly rare at the time), was not allowed to put a sign on the outside of her restaurant's building, only used local seasonal ingredients despite the pains and increased costs, got a three-star review in the *Pittsburgh Post-Gazette* and a glowing write-up in *Pittsburgh Magazine* and two semifinalist nominations as a James Beard Rising Star Chef of the Year, and still got casually and repeatedly called the "rich bitch from Columbia" to her face by one of her purveyors, and still had to watch as everyone assumed her male bartender owned the place, and still was called out of the kitchen nightly to recite her résumé to older male patrons to prove why she should own a restaurant.

WHEN FINN OPENED DINETTE, in a new development built on a lot where taxis used to park at night, East Liberty was just beginning its redevelopment. The Nabisco plant had shut down a while back, and unlike, say, Walnut Street in Shadyside, there were no traditional shopping streets for pedestrians. Nonetheless, she'd chosen the space because, as she watched the development grow, with Whole Foods and a Borders and other slightly upscale but unremarkable large chains, there was no connection to the neighborhood. She thought if she put her spot there, as someone who grew up and went to school in the neighborhood and still lived close by, it might help connect it to families.

At the time, all her friends from high school were moving into the Lawrenceville neighborhood, where the rumor was you could buy homes for twenty thousand dollars and Butler Street was turning into something, but she didn't know that area well. East Liberty, she did.

By November 2016, the month Donald Trump won the election to become the forty-fifth president of the United States, East Liberty and Pittsburgh had changed. The old YMCA building had become an Ace Hotel, part of 2,800 new hotel rooms built in the city in the last five years. Hip restaurants had opened around Dinette, as had three yoga studios and a Pilates gym. The abandoned Highland Building, which had a tree growing out of it when Finn opened Dinette, was now luxury apartments. Her old middle school had been torn down; in its place were now townhomes starting in the mid-five hundreds. The Eastside Bond apartment complex opened up across the street, featuring stainless steel appliances and a resort-style saltwater pool. The old Nabisco plant was now a Google corporate campus in the new Bakery Square development alongside a West Elm and Anthropologie. *Zagat* had named Pittsburgh America's top food city of 2015. *The New York Times* wrote a Hot

New Food Town story shouting out the youth movement taking place in Pittsburgh, and mentioning Finn and Dinette. The article was supposed to be celebratory, but for Finn, things felt different.

She'd had a son, Miles, in 2012, and three years before had purchased a house a mile away from work, a straight shot up Penn that took her through the street she'd gone to school in, now nearly unrecognizable as the development careened forward unchecked. She worried that what everyone was considering progress was actually nearsighted. All of the luxury apartment buildings and complexes and tech campuses were catering to the single, young urban professionals and ignoring the families, which should be the lifeblood of any neighborhood. Instead, the city was enticing a transient population that would use the area for a brief time and then leave and go elsewhere when it was time to have kids.

Finn started attending a few political events and, through her new gig as the consulting chef for the Café Carnegie in the Carnegie Museum of Art, was able to gain more notoriety in the city. She paid attention when bids came in on the old armory building, and noticed that most developers wanted to make it a group office space with the requisite rock climbing wall, while Finn hoped it might become something that actually served the families in the community. These were quick money ideas, and everyone was so happy patting themselves on the back for Pittsburgh's resurgence, they weren't thinking about how to keep an engaged population for the long haul.

But it wasn't all bad. She'd gone to see her councilman, Dan Gilman, to talk through a restaurant issue, and he'd been incredibly nice and attentive, and she felt heard. As a small business owner with no real power and money, it was good to feel like someone was there for you, and she thought that might be a job she'd like to do in the future, maybe after she spent more time learning how to lobby for good in DC, and anyway, Gilman was never going to leave that seat. And then Dan Gilman announced he was going to leave that seat to become chief of staff for mayor Bill Peduto. The council spot representing Finn's own District Eight had just opened up.

ON DECEMBER 19, 2017, the day Disney World's Hall of Presidents added an animatronic president Donald Trump, Sonja Finn went to the public library, made a rudimentary campaign sign on the library computer, and then tweeted and Instagrammed said sign to announce her intention to run for Gilman's vacant seat. Of course, people from the restaurant industry had run for office before, as anyone watching Godfather's Pizza CEO Herman Cain's Icarus-like rise and fall during the 2012 presidential campaign could see, but they were usually wealthy restaurateurs and franchise owners. Chefs, on the other hand, basically never did it.

Finn was up against Erika Strassburger, Gilman's chief of staff and the heir apparent in a line of District Eight chief of staff successions. Mayor Bill Peduto had been chief of staff for District Eight councilman Dan Cohen, then served as councilman himself with Dan Gilman as his top aide, and once Peduto became mayor, Gilman took his seat, with Strassburger as his aide. So now, the thinking went, it was supposed to be Strassburger's time, the power baton seamlessly handed off during a quick special election only political insiders would pay attention to.

But Finn threw a wrench in that plan. She thought she could be good for the city—she was coming in from outside the slog of government, and as a restaurant owner who had to make something happen every day, no matter what the crisis, she felt she could offer up a sense of urgency and fiscal responsibility. And at the very least, she could learn a lot about the political process. She'd supported Gilman and the mayor, and was also a Democrat, and figured it would be good to get more local voices involved, so she went around and talked to people in the district, working off a speech she'd written late at night after Dinette closed, using her iPhone Notes while Miles slept:

> The joke is that if the end of the world is coming, you want to be in
> Pittsburgh bc then it will come ten years later. Well let's finally use that

to our advantage. We are not the first city to go through transition and innovation. Others have first and they made some good choices and they made some mistakes. We can learn from them and do it better, do it right. Let those other cities be the labs. We can be the success.

Let's stop giving money to corporations and developers to "entice" them to do what they were going to do anyway. Pittsburgh is a great city—world-class museums, parks, housing stock, sports teams, universities, hospitals and an über hot restaurant scene. People want to be here, they want to develop here. We don't have to pay them to do it.

Let's instead use money for things that improve the lives of all Pittsburghers: Things like universal pre-K or, immediately replacing water lines. Implement rent increase restrictions and tenants' rights. Increase the minimum wage.

I'm saying that we are on a precipice. We need to just stop and re-evaluate. Are we going about this in the right way? Just because this is what every other city did doesn't mean it was right.

And we also need to think about who we are. We are a city of unions, not $7.25 an hour. We are a city that built beautiful schools and the cathedral of learning, but we don't care about ensuring our children's education? We are the city where the polio vaccine was created, now we're poisoning our children with lead.

I'm a person who questions and who says there is a better way.

I did it in the restaurant industry. I questioned the status quo—I was told every restaurant does it this way, it's the only way. But I said it could be done better in a way that benefitted everyone. And I did it and it worked. I can do that for this city too.

ON JANUARY 14, 2018, as president Donald Trump accused *The Wall Street Journal* of misquoting him for saying he probably had a very good relationship with Kim Jong-un, the Democratic Committee for District Eight voted to decide who their candidate would be. It was three degrees out and a Steelers Sunday, which meant the Pittsburgh Steelers were on, which meant most people weren't leaving their house. Finn had written a letter to the Democratic Committee explaining who she was and then gone to the various wards in her district and given her speech, but now she just had to sit and watch as they counted up the votes. Forty-seven of the seventy-two Democrats in the committee made it out that day, and when all the votes were counted something remarkable happened. Finn won.

With Miles by her side, and her hand visibly shaking, she signed papers that day to become the chosen Democratic candidate for Pittsburgh City Council, District Eight. She was ecstatic. She'd never run for or won anything before in her life. It made her incredibly proud, and hopeful for the democratic process. Everyone she knew reached out. Her name began to trend on Twitter. Because the district was overwhelmingly Democratic, Finn's path to the council seat seemed like a lock. Except for one problem: it wasn't supposed to happen.

With the nomination in hand, Finn reached out to elected Democrats to ask if they would talk with her and support her. The mayor never returned any emails or phone calls. The county executive immediately returned her phone call, but told her he wouldn't be supporting her. "Look," he said, "we're a team. I support who Bill supports and Bill supports who Dan supports and Dan supports Erika."

Finn was shocked by his candor. These were three Democratic officials saying they would not support the Democratic candidate. But the political machine was only just getting started. After Strassburger got the necessary signatures to file her petition to run as an independent, Mayor Peduto retweeted Strassburger with the caption "I'm with Her!" Soon after that, the mayor sent out a three-page letter of support (paid for by Friends of Erika Strassburger) to District Eight voters.

It got uglier. "Fake news"–style comments started showing up on Twitter and Facebook, saying Finn charged forty dollars for pizzas, or wasn't actually

Jewish, or had singlehandedly gentrified East Liberty. When a local ice cream shop in District Eight's Shadyside neighborhood created a special "Sonja FTW" ice cream (pink peppercorn and lavender), the owner found a comment card that simply read "Fuck Sonja Finn." Dinette's business dwindled by 30 percent from that time the year before. The health inspector showed up separately from the standard yearly inspection after receiving an anonymous tip. And the city coincidentally audited her restaurant for the first time in its ten-year history.

Finn had even gotten a phone call at home from a man screaming at her, and as a single mother living alone with her son (she'd recently separated from her husband), she started to feel vulnerable, unsure where the line would be drawn.

Finn felt frustrated too—she'd heard people who'd been in Pittsburgh politics talk about some of the uglier things, but she'd always just assumed they were paranoid or exaggerating. She always tried to see the good in folks, and this all seemed so arbitrary. She was a Democrat, and her views were mostly in line with the mayor's. Finn had nothing against Strassburger—she thought she was competent and would make a good council person; she just didn't see why that should prevent her from running too. Wouldn't actually giving the voters a choice be good for everyone?

At first, the pundits didn't really give Finn a chance, especially with the city political machine against her, but over the next few months, she diligently campaigned, taking meetings all over the city, often with Miles in tow in his orange winter coat. She managed to secure support from the Pittsburgh Federation of Teachers and the Union of Operating Engineers and, in each debate, forced Strassburger to move further left and away from the mayor on issues like the city's secret bid for Amazon's new headquarters. The week before the election, the *Pittsburgh Post-Gazette* declined to pick a candidate in her race, saying both Finn and Strassburger would make good council people. She summed up the point in the caption of an Instagram picture of the editorial: "So, in just eight weeks, I've achieved parity with someone who has worked in the D8 council office for the last four years. Cool; imagine what I can get done in a four year term."

ON MARCH 6, 2018, as president Donald Trump met with Swedish business representatives and tweeted about the Academy Awards' poor ratings, the people of District Eight elected Erika Strassburger their new city council representative. Finn had expected around 2,500 people to show up that day, putting her "win number" somewhere around 1,400 votes. She got the number she needed; the only problem was that almost 5,000 people showed up.

That morning, she'd gone with Miles to the Catholic church by their house to vote (she let Miles push the button), and then she bought him a cinnamon bun and took him to school. Around eleven a.m., her sous chef called to say the freezer at Dinette was broken, so she told him to clean everything out and close the restaurant that day. She went home and placed some calls to the teachers' union to remind them to vote, and then visited her father at a polling place, and then went with her family back to the campaign office around seven p.m. when the polls were closing.

Watching the faces of the campaign volunteers, it became clear she was going to lose, and around seven forty-five p.m., the woman who had been helping her with the campaign pulled her into a small office and confirmed that fact. "So," she said, "you're going to lose."

Finn called Strassburger to congratulate her and concede, and then she went over to a pizza place close to Dinette where all of her supporters, volunteers, friends, the Dinette staff, and a few political reporters were waiting. She gave her concession speech and ate some pizza and thanked volunteers, and then went back to her house with a few close friends and drank a lot more wine. She was exhausted—she'd just spent three months campaigning, which meant three months of extra childcare and three months of people covering for her at Dinette, in addition to the emotional toll of facing constant attacks. But despite all that, there was so much to love.

Her best friend had worked for her campaign. Her father had gone door-to-door and volunteered in the campaign office, and both her parents worked the polls on Election Day. She knew Miles felt proud when they would pass a house with a "Finn for Council" sign in the yard, and she hoped that dragging him along to all of these events would help encourage him to be an engaged citizen and a super voter. Plus, she didn't think he'd ever forget voting for his mom. It was one of the most important things Finn had ever done.

She took a couple of weeks to put any lingering campaign stuff to rest and shake off the loss, and then Finn went back to Dinette and started making pizzas.

A FEW WEEKS AFTER THE ELECTION, while another one of president Donald Trump's lawyers resigned, Finn was picking up Miles at school when a guy on a bike passed them, looked over, then nearly fell over screeching to a clumsy stop. Miles was still in his orange winter coat, which had become something of a local icon thanks to campaign materials that showed Finn walking with him in the jacket. From thirty yards away, the man yelled, "Hey! Are you Sonja Finn?" When she nodded, he came over and shook her hand, and thanked her for running and for all she'd done for the city. These sorts of moments of recognition had been happening to her more and more all over Pittsburgh, sometimes because she had been on an episode of Anthony Bourdain's *Parts Unknown* but more because of the campaign.

Before he got back on his bike and pedaled away, Finn got his name and sent herself an email with his information. For the subject line, she wrote, only half-jokingly, "Part of the Resistance."

You never know, she reasoned, when you might need to start it all up again.

CHAPTER 27

The Plaza District, NW 16th Street from Blackwelder to Indiana, Oklahoma City, Oklahoma

It started with Saints. Before Saints, Sixteenth Street was mostly known as a phone booth alley, a place to score drugs, or merely a way to get from Penn to Classen without hitting Twenty-Third Street traffic. Scorecards had been there forever, a true dive, and the place for college kids to get cheap thrills, buying six-packs to go while getting yelled at by old-school Plaza smokers. But when a space across from Saint Anthony's in midtown fell through, Patrick Ireland and Carey Kirby, two local restaurant bartenders, opened up Saints at 1715 Northwest Sixteenth on May 13, 2011. The initial idea was sort of an upscale Irish pub, but that was only half-realized, mostly due to the fact that they didn't get a hood vent, and it's hard to be that upscale when the entire place smells of griddled burgers and fried fish.

The old-school locals didn't like the idea of a place where every beer was above three dollars, but the thing was, the live music was pretty good and the bar was open till two a.m., and most bars in Oklahoma City were not. Soon industry bartenders started to make it their final final. Biker James would come through on his Harley for a shot of Crown and a car bomb. Bike Mike would get the coldest amber they had and a shot of Jameson and end up asking the bartenders if they needed help closing. Crazy Jim would come in and threaten to kill everyone. And Ireland, whom everyone called the "patio manager," would just sit outside sipping a Jameson on the rocks and take it all in.

It was an arts district, after all, so the hipster industries were already in place. Amanda and Dylan Bradway had opened DNA Galleries, a space showcasing local artists, out of their house years before. Anyone getting tats knew to go to Viking Ashley at No Regrets, or hit up Tanner Frady for his custom signs. Michael Brown at RetrOKC sold 1950s televisions and tiki lamps and Eames chairs and velvet paintings he'd found in Goodwill stores. The stylists at Velvet Monkey Salon were dyeing hair pink and purple and green and advertising some of those DNA artists on their walls. Warpaint screenprinted T-shirts and blew the hell up when their "Thank You Seattle" T-shirt, celebrating the NBA's Seattle Supersonics' move to OKC, made News9. But everything changed with the Mule.

The owners, Joey Morris, John Harris, and Cody Rowan, all met up in college at Oklahoma State, and Joey and John worked in restaurants together after school, while Cody moved to Denver. They'd talked for a long time about opening something for themselves, but there was a problem: none were chefs. Then one day, after having an incredible BLT at the lobby bar at Will Rogers Theatre, they realized it didn't need to be complicated.

"Let's just do a bar with sandwiches," Joey said.

"Delicious sandwiches," said John.

"Wait, guys, I'm still in Denver," said Cody.

Cody came back and they found some former Section 8 housing off of Sixteenth in the Plaza that was being refurbished and needed a tenant for the first floor. The kitchen space was tiny—less than three hundred square feet—and the entire space only had room for seventy seats total, but that's what they wanted. They figured they'd start small, with Joey and John in the kitchen and Cody bartending, and hire a couple of servers and figure it out.

They opened their doors in September 2012, hoping they might have a couple of slow months to tweak and adjust. They did not get their wish.

The Mule was a phenomenon. People loved the comfort-food-heavy sandwiches, especially the Macaroni Pony—a combination of BBQ pulled pork, mac and cheese, and pickles on jalapeño cornbread. They loved the poutine, and the fried cheese curds, and the grilled cheese with a dipping cup of homemade tomato soup. Folks from Edmond—the nearest fancy, whitewashed suburb of OKC—who'd normally just come into the city to go to the Paseo or hit Cheever's for dinner, started gravitating toward the Mule. The hipsters who lived nearby dug the fact that they wouldn't bug you if you just got a beer and sat reading Teju Cole for a couple of hours.

By early 2013, the Mule's popularity altered the Plaza. With up to three-hour waits even on Wednesdays, the rest of the district became known as the Mule's waiting room. Bored Edmondites would put their name in at the Mule and then wander through DNA and RetrOKC looking for cool local art to put on their walls, or hip T-shirts, or really anything that might distinguish them from the other folks in Edmond. Second Friday art walks became a must-go event, with fire walkers and jugglers and the Velvet Monkey ladies serving boxed Franzia to folks shoulder to shoulder. Everyone talked about the energy, and the creativity, and the community. It felt cool and real and different.

The food kept coming. After an epiphany while sitting at Home Slice in Austin, Rachel Cope—a former coworker of Joey at the Mule and John at the Wedge—shipped herself off to San Francisco to learn everything she could about pizza making from legend Tony Gemignani's International School of Pizza, came back, teamed up with chef Avery Cannon, and launched Empire Slice House two blocks down from the Mule. Roxy's Ice Cream Social was there. And the Oak & Ore brewpub. And Pie Junkie. And Chiltepes Taco Joint. And Aurora. And the Pritchard. And Cope's next restaurant, Goro Ramen. And the Mule's follow-up space, the Press.

Folks called it "Little Austin." But by 2018, there were whispers and worries that the Plaza was over. That the energy from the past was gone. That homes in the area were now going for more than $150 per square foot, and more interesting things were happening in Classen Ten Penn, the neighborhood behind the Plaza, and over in Automobile Alley, where—across from the new-build Metropolitan Apartments filled with air traffic controllers, traveling nurses, and lower-level Oklahoma City Thunder staff—they were building 8th Street Market, OKC's "first urban market," featuring the Prairie Artisan Ales tasting room as its flagship tenant. In 2016, Oklahoma passed Senate Bill 424, which finally allowed craft breweries to start selling full-strength beer on their property, instead of the 3.2 percent beer that for so long dominated the landscape. Since the passing, several new breweries had popped up.

Three miles to the south, along the Oklahoma River, a large development plan projected to spend $576 million to build housing and restaurants and entertainment venues. To show intent, they'd already built a Ferris wheel. A few blocks north of what they were calling Oklahoma City's "Next Great Urban Neighborhood," the Jones Assembly, a combination restaurant and entertainment venue, was getting all sorts of buzz. Folks said it could be the connective tissue linking the rest of downtown with that Wheeler District. Folks said it could do for that neighborhood what the Mule did for the Plaza. It wasn't just local folks talking about OKC anymore either. In 2018, *Bon Appétit* named the small, experimental OKC restaurant Nonesuch as the Best New Restaurant in America. A week later, *The New York Times* penned a "Letter of Recommendation" for Oklahoma City. One more story, the locals said, and they'd officially be a Hot New Food Town.

Back in the Plaza, parking was a nightmare, especially on a weekend when the brunch crowd came through. OKC was not a walking town, so the two major landlords for the block, the Struble family and Steve Mason, continued making moves. A sign advertising one-dollar-an-hour parking in the

new parking lot built behind Sixteenth sat conspicuously close to the Mule. YogaLAB, across the street, offered six-dollar deals. The clothing store Jackson Dean + Co had a sign outside that read "No Trust Fund Needed."

At a dirt lot across from Blackwelder and Sixteenth, a small sign showcasing a fancy new brick mixed-retail building with the words "Now Pre-leasing" sat next to a tired brown-and-white house with wire-frame chairs on the porch. On the west side of the Plaza, at 1804 Northwest Sixteenth, a mixed-use building from Aimee and Jeff Struble was in the process of being built. Retail and office space was available.

CHAPTER 28

Phil Ward, New York City, New York, Part 3

Though it took a few years, by 2012, the Death & Co model of cocktail bar, as much as it could be replicated, was making its way into cities all over the country. As the ranks swelled with folks interested in creating cocktail programs incorporating fresh juice, good ice, and thoughtful menus, the originators began to look for ways to distinguish themselves from the proliferation of the original model. Taking the cue from Mayahuel, many saw opportunity in going deeper and more narrowly into certain niches.

DeRossi himself really leaned into this idea, opening both the self-explanatory Gin Palace and Amor y Amargo—an amaro-and-bitters-focused bar—right next to Cienfuegos. In Los Angeles, rum-focused speakeasy La Descarga, tequila-centric Las Perlas, and the vodka-themed Silo all opened within a year. DC featured an absinthe bar (Libertine) and a sherry bar from Derek Brown. Chicago anted up Scofflaw, a gin bar. The proto-tiki movement, elevating tiki drinks into the craft cocktail oeuvre, brought places like Martin Cate's Smuggler's Cove in San Francisco, Chicago's Three Dots and a Dash, and, in New Orleans, Neal Bodenheimer and his Cure crew's Cane & Table (the Cure crew also opened Bellocq, a bar serving Cobblers, a nineteenth-century cocktail filled with sherry, sugar, fruit, and crushed ice that was last popular in the 1890s).

With the market saturating, Mayahuel was no longer the national media darling it had once been. But there were other issues. Ward and DeRossi continued their awkward silence, only really communicating through Justin Shapiro, formerly an investor, who eventually came on as managing partner. Their landlord had built an extra two floors on top of Mayahuel to use as Airbnb properties and hadn't bothered to get the proper DOB licensing. Afterward, the shoddy plumbing and the influx of random out-of-towners taking showers and using the water closet caused nearly perpetual leaks into Mayahuel. On top of that, thanks to the extra floors, the hood vent for the kitchen stove no longer reached the top of the building, and so smoke would often pour back into the kitchen, making it a health hazard. They tried to replace the hood, but needed the landlord's go-ahead to do the work, and he refused to give it to them. With no more options available, they sued their landlord and spent years in court. As the lawsuits and counter lawsuits dragged on, it became clear that when the lease was up in September 2017, Mayahuel would no longer exist. Ward had no interest in doing another Mayahuel in a different place—he didn't like the idea of reopening the same bar, because it would either feel like a better or a worse version of the original, and either way that seemed disrespectful to its memory. Plus, you can't top a chandelier that looks like a tarantula.

Because of a rule preventing owners from sharing tips, Ward had stopped bartending at Mayahuel in its third year. He had no problem bartending for free at a place he owned, but it would be unfair to the bartenders who weren't working if he gave 100 percent of the tips to whomever worked alongside him. And anyway, he'd really grown to love his staff, and was happy to give them the work. He'd started picking up shifts elsewhere, at ZZ's Clam Bar, the Shanty in Williamsburg, and legendary bartender Toby Cecchini's Long Island Bar. He'd even done a second tour of Death & Co, working Saturdays there for a couple more years.

But in Mayahuel's last days, he got back behind the stick, bartending the final three nights. Those nights were magical for Ward. Old staff and friends, regulars, bartenders, servers, busboys, barbacks, cooks—they all came to pay their respects, even traveling in from out of state. The last night, the entire staff came in and they started passing out bottles of tequila and mezcal as parting gifts. Ward gave a toast and got ever-so-slightly choked up at the fact that this little piece-of-shit bar had provided twenty humans with a livelihood for eight years. They couldn't take that away.

As Del Maguey's Ron Cooper sat watching at the bar, slowly sipping a mezcal from his own private collection, people dug up tiles to keep as souvenirs. The next morning, Ward turned over in bed and, upon realizing it was Thursday, started thinking about what he needed for the liquor order when he suddenly stopped and realized he no longer had a bar to order liquor for. For so long, he'd been keeping track of things for Mayahuel, he felt like there was an empty spot in the center of his conscious. With nothing more to do, he turned over and went back to sleep.

By 2018, across the country, the cocktail bar industry seemed to be in its own state of reverie, but it was more like a *Groundhog Day*–style repeating dream. Each city seemed to follow a similar path. First came the pre-Prohibition speakeasy bar, the small, dark, reservation-only spot with rigid rules about hats, and bartenders with waxed mustaches who were slightly condescending to vodka drinkers. But, like army boot camp, the bars that practiced this sort of self-seriousness created bartenders with technique and knowledge and a base set of skills, and once they burnt out on sneering at folks who wanted Jack and Cokes and realized bars were supposed to be fun, they were free to leave and do their own thing, and that's when you started seeing the elevated pubs, the mezcalerias, the divey neighborhood bars with great cocktails, and the restaurants with the fantastic bar programs.

After that, the boutique hotel chains would usually come in with an outside consultant from a more established cocktail city and snatch up some of the top local talent, and so you'd see elevated cocktail programs at the local

Kimpton or Ace or Freehand or Andaz or Line or 21c Museum hotel. And when there were no longer new spaces to open, they could always follow the pop-up bar movement and create a short-lived theme bar based on the holidays (NYC's Mace bar's Miracle being the best example of that), or a current popular HBO show, or failing that, just do a seasonal themed menu with a stunt drink and lean into the fact that the rise of Instagram culture meant they would never have regulars, just a series of folks on a never-ending digital treasure hunt featuring an end game that involved being photographed pretending to drink a jet-black cocktail garnished with an edible flower on fire inside a drinking vessel made to look like an Edison lightbulb.

But not everyone was chasing the same thing. Twelve years after opening, Death & Co (now led by David Kaplan, Alex Day, and Ravi DeRossi) had morphed from just an East Village bar into so much more. In May 2018, they opened a second location in the Ramble Hotel in Denver and planned to open a third location in Los Angeles by summer 2019. Their 2014 cocktail book had sold over 120,000 copies. Their consulting business, Proprietors LLC, worked with Hilton, Pacific Theaters, and Bacardi. Using SeedInvest, a crowd-funding investment platform, they'd raised $2.1 million to help with expansion and growth. Kaplan talked of other "branded opportunities:" more books, other products, international licensing deals, etc. They were a full-on brand with fans around the world eager to give them money, not just for impeccably made cocktails, but also for the contact high that came with association.

While some of the legendary cocktail spots were expanding, others were following Mayahuel's lead and closing their doors. In late December 2018, Flatiron Lounge, the bar where Julie Reiner taught the masses about good cocktails and Phil Ward how to bartend, shut down. Reiner told *The New York Times* that rent had increased from $22,000 to over $30,000 a month, and paying $360,000 a year wasn't exactly in the business model they'd created fifteen years before.

A MONTH AFTER MAYAHUEL CLOSED, *New York Times* cocktail correspondent Robert Simonson wrote a profile for *Punch* magazine describing Ward as an oddity in the industry—not for his penchant for unpredictable hairstyles but because, unlike most famous bartenders who are "busy traveling the world, touring distilleries, entering cocktail competitions, judging cocktail competitions, consulting at bars not their own, writing books, collaborating on spirits and hosting pop-up bars in exotic locales," Ward was just bartending.

And he was, mainly over at Long Island Bar in Brooklyn. It was a beautiful little neighborhood spot, a place where you could get a great burger and a great cocktail without a lot of fuss. Every older cocktail bartender seemed to want to open a place like that, Ward thought. Once you got over your bullshit, fancy prima donna stage, you just wanted a place to make good drinks, interact with the regulars, and make fun of your coworkers. He had that at Long Island. He didn't think he was done opening bars though. He consulted on a cocktail menu revamp at Brooklyn bar Madre Mezcaleria, and was considering helping out on the menu at another place in Westchester County. But what he was most interested in was a tiny little bar in Brooklyn's Carroll Gardens/Red Hook neighborhood. Ward still had to feel out the guy and see if he was for real, but something about having a tiny little bar all to himself felt exactly right.

Even when he wasn't working, Ward still loved being in bars. His favorite thing to do was go down to Lucy's, the old Polish lady's place in the East Village. Ward loved playing pool—was kind of obsessed with it—and he loved going to Lucy's to play with buddies. He'd gotten to know her niece, Kasia, and on the best nights, after closing, Kasia would lock the door and they'd have the run of the place.

There was nothing better after a night of catering to everyone else, and playing the music that's mandated for your bar, picked by some ridiculous music consulting station, than to be in that bar with a couple friends, listening to the music you want to listen to, drinking what you want to drink, and shooting pool. You had to be careful, though—time flies in an empty bar after hours. More often than not, Ward would find himself thinking he'd been in the bar shooting pool for an hour, and come outside six hours later, squinting into the sunlight.

Hillary Dixler Canavan ✔ @hillarydixler · 15 Aug 2018
California has changed you, @davidchang. 🍇on a 🍴🍴

Momofuku Now Serves Fruit on a Plate
A dessert at LA's Majordomo features melon with salt, frozen grapes, but no figs (yet)
eater.com

💬 2   🔁 7   ♡ 34   ✉

Dave Chang ✔
@davidchang   Following

Replying to @hillarydixler

We at least cut it with a knife

12:57 PM · 15 Aug 2018

3 Retweets **46** Likes

CHAPTER 29

Freret Street, New Orleans, Louisiana, 2018, Part 3

The first thing people told you was they even made the Domino's Pizza nice. And it was true. The bulletproof glass was long gone, replaced by a fresh coat of bright blue and white paint, a new sign, and some new trees and shrubbery outside.

But it wasn't just Domino's. The entire street had that new car smell.

Upscale chains had come to Freret. Village Coffee was now a Starbucks. Halal Guys, once just a single New York street cart selling gyros, and now a franchise with "200 restaurants in development worldwide," opened in 2017, as did the LeBron James–backed Blaze Pizza chain, both in a new development with a peculiar puzzle-piece white-slatted metal exterior that brought to mind an impromptu postapocalyptic jail's makeshift security system. But the chains may have been a bridge too far. By fall 2018, Halal Guys had already shut down after barely a year, and Blaze was never in danger of being called crowded.

The Junior League's Bloomin' Deals shop was sold off, and the developer was in talks to put in a store from the beloved local grocery chain Rouses. The Publiq House music space was also looking to transform into a boutique grocery store with luxury condominiums on top.

Freret Street Poboy & Donut Shop had closed, and in its place, a young

LSU graduate from Houston had put in his third iteration of Kolache Kitchen, a breakfast/lunch joint he'd started in Baton Rouge, serving breakfast tacos, empanadas, and kolaches, a Czech pastry popular in Texas. Dat Dog had moved out of its tiny space and into a giant indoor-outdoor restaurant across the street. In its place was a small rotisserie chicken and sandwich shop called Good Bird.

Across the street, Freret Beer Room, opened by a young New Orleans native who'd recently returned from New York, offered craft beers and ambitious New American plates, with a bottle shop next door. A few blocks down, across from Sarita's Grill, there was now a natural wine bar next door to a gelato shop. The Company Burger planned to build a new patio. Across the street, Stan at Dennis' Barber Shop, one of the few pre-Katrina shops still open, kept cutting hair.

As the neighborhood went through yet another transformation, so did the narrative surrounding it. The piece most accurately capturing the zeitgeist came from an African-American novelist named Maurice Carlos Ruffin, who'd lived there since 2003. Published by the Southern Foodways Alliance, it was titled "The Taking of Freret Street" and detailed the author's complicated feelings about watching the street and surrounding areas change. One paragraph in particular stood out:

> Many post-Katrina restaurants have something in common: pretensions. They are well-capitalized, well-lit, and probably well-insured. When their owners went to the bank and asked for loans, they got the cash. When they called on parents and friends for investment capital, checks must have come in the mail. Dreams blossomed. Nothing was deferred.

As for the crew at Cure, in 2018, they won a national James Beard Award for Outstanding Bar Program. They'd been nominated many times before, with nothing to show for it, so the win came as a glorious shock, as did the influx of people who began pouring in. They decided to revitalize the space, refinish the front bar, replace the underbar, clean and repaint the space. When they wrapped up in early October, it felt new again for the first time in years. They were making other moves as well, with a deal to put a Cure in the new New Orleans airport, and a bar project up in Washington DC.

They'd also started to look around Freret for another project, something to serve as a home base for their talented chef Alfredo Nogueira and one of the original Cure bartenders, Turk Dietrich. Diagonally across from Cure, in between Bean's Formal Wear and the Humble Bagel shop, there was an empty grass lot where the old veterinarian office, long ago built with federal funds, had been razed in the years after Katrina. They'd made inroads to try to get something done there. A bar, they thought. Maybe something simple, with great tacos and cocktails.

CHAPTER 30

Gabriel Rucker, Portland, Oregon, Part 3

By 2018, Le Pigeon was a different restaurant. It wasn't the food, which still felt like exotic bar food dressed up in fine dining's fancier clothes and run through the creativity blender of Gabriel Rucker's mind. It was the kitchen. After he'd gotten sober in 2013, Rucker knew that he couldn't just come in the day after Halloween and say, "You guys can't do this!"

He knew that would be just as toxic, and also hypocritical, as he'd been operating the kitchen in a certain fiesta-oriented way since 2006, and it wouldn't be wrong for others in the kitchen to assume that's how it was always going to be. So he incorporated changes slowly, and found that, for the most part, the snake followed the head. If he wasn't drinking on shift, other cooks felt less and less like they should drink on shift, and those who had an issue getting over that either changed or faded away. Rucker expected this, and so all through 2014 and 2015 he'd watched the dynamics shift, eager to be sensitive to both sides of that coin.

In 2016, Rucker decided he wanted to spend the entire year avoiding events and the festival circuit and staying focused in the kitchen. He could feel himself growing up, and growing more and more into the role of a mentor chef, as opposed to people just coming along for the ride with him on his magic food bus. Though he'd always been outspoken and loud and eager to show others what he could do, he finally felt he was coaxing great food out of others, instead of just himself. Even his feelings about the whole "chef" moniker had changed. In his younger years, he'd dismissed the idea of being called "chef" as too formal and uncool, but now when he walked into a room and talked and heard "Yes, chef," he wore that status as a badge of pride.

The sobriety translated into other things. He and Kaufman had their third child, Freddie James, in 2017. Rucker stopped smoking cigarettes and started watching what he put in his body. He began to get serious about working out, and ran a half-marathon in Vancouver. He built a wood-fired pizza oven in his backyard and an Argentinian-type grill. He cycled through a variety of trendy food diets, like Paleo and the Whole 30. He recognized what was happening, that these sort of addictive behaviors around controlling diet and exercise were replacing the previous ones, but he figured that was fine as long as it continued to feel healthy.

IT STARTED WITH CHEESEBURGERS. Rucker had always wanted to replicate the little sliders at White Castle, so he started experimenting with his own steam burgers with pickles, onion, mustard, and American cheese. Passing them out to staff one day, everyone seemed to agree they would murder each other crab-in-a-barrel style for the chance to eat another one. Fortgang had always wanted to open a wine bar and had been talking about it forever—in fact, in 2013, they'd almost pulled the trigger around the corner, but Rucker was thankful they didn't, because opening a third restaurant at that point would've turned him into even more of a fucking nightmare.

Anyway, the idea started to coalesce: What if we opened a place that just served steam burgers, fresh oysters, and delicious wine? They'd always wanted to have their own sort of waiting area for Le Pigeon—over the last eleven years they'd sent thousands of people out to local establishments in the neighborhood—and so they decided that if the place next door opened up, they would go for it.

For the first decade that Le Pigeon was in business, the property next door was a *Karate Kid*–referencing waxing/grooming facility called Wax On, but in 2016, Wax On was … taken down (crane-kicked?) by a steampunk clothing store, which serviced the Burning Man Colonel Summers crowd with items like top hats with broken barometers glued on them, and flasks covered in extraneous pieces of leather. Though the store was owned by a fantastic and friendly lady named Panda, Rucker knew the rent, and also knew she'd have to sell a shit ton of esoteric leather vests to pay it, and that didn't seem like it was happening.

Panda somehow got word of their imminent interest and, being the kind woman she was, informed them she was going out of business in a couple of months, and told them the exact date she was going to close. On the day she sold her final extra-stretch men's harness, Rucker and Fortgang quickly swooped in to snag the space, which, in keeping with the fowl theme, they deemed Canard.

Canard opened on April 16, 2018. Six months before, Fortgang and Rucker had put a date on the calendar as the target soft open for the space. The actual opening date was only three days later. If Le Pigeon was essentially Rucker dressing up bar food for a fancy night out, Canard was taking that same bar food and telling it to take off a few layers. There were foie gras dumplings, and a Duck Stack, which was pancakes, duck gravy, Tabasco onions, and a duck egg. You could also get chicken wings and steam burgers and interesting wines from Fortgang. Plus, they had a soft serve machine, which fulfilled Rucker's true fantasy of owning and operating a Dairy Queen.

THE CITY OF PORTLAND IN 2018 was three worlds apart from the provincial, rainy timber town Rucker had moved to fifteen years earlier. In the last six years, Portland real estate prices had gone up 180 percent. Cranes ushering in new luxury condominium construction dotted the skyline. The scourge of the city, to the natives (or at least anyone who moved to the city before 2011), was an influx of people from Seattle, or worse, San Francisco, remote tech workers who were driving up real estate prices but still working outside the city. Cars with California license plates were getting defaced. Fred Armisen and Carrie Brownstein's show *Portlandia*, which gently mocked the stereotypically intense, low-stakes hipster lifestyles the city had become known for, had even run its course, ending after eight seasons in March 2018.

The City of Roses was no longer a cheap dream town surrounded by an unimaginable bounty. There were now start-up Portlands all over the country, cheaper facsimiles offering a version of the Portland experience at a quarter of the cost. Even the original Portland competitor, Austin, Texas, was now getting too expensive. Folks in Portland talked about going to Bend, Oregon, or Boise, Idaho.

And for the newer generations who actually could afford to move into Portland and work in the restaurant industry, talking about Greg Higgins, Cory Schreiber, Cathy Whims, or even Vitaly Paley seemed like grandfather-on-the-porch stuff. There was no memory of Ricker slinging martinis at Saucebox or Lucy Brennan's avocado daiquiris at Mint/820. No anecdotes about watching bike messenger polo or drinking PBR because it was actually cheap. To them, Rucker and Ricker and Pomeroy and Habetz were the old heads. Eventually, everyone became their parents.

Rucker didn't seem to mind. As he got older, he'd given up his quest for perfection. He'd come up with a rule of percentages he wanted to live by: 70-20-10.

Seventy percent of the time, he wanted to be really fucking happy.

Twenty percent of the time, he was okay with being blasé.

Ten percent of the time, he was going to allow himself to be in a bad mood or unhappy.

He'd started saying yes to more things. He was rollerblading again, and loved it, even filming a commercial for a collaboration he did with the local ice cream joint Salt & Straw while blading in spandex. At Feast Portland, one of the biggest food festivals in the country, Rucker came up with the idea of doing a "Zero Proof" dinner, featuring dishes cooked by sober chefs and paired with delicious nonalcoholic drinks. He brought in *Bizarre Foods* host Andrew Zimmern, and then other big names like Sean Brock and Michael Solomonov also got on board. When the tickets were released to the public, the event sold out in three minutes.

Rucker had a feeling it would work. The industry lifestyle was brutal and unforgiving, and for restaurant lifers, eventually something had to give, one way or another. Almost every time he traveled to a city, anywhere in the country, chefs or cooks would find out he was in recovery and would text him later asking how they could do it too.

Kaufman always talked about how things slowed down for Rucker. How he could see and react to things she hadn't even noticed. Like the time they were on Vancouver Lake and a baby fell out of a boat in front of them and the boat went over it, and before she'd even looked, Rucker had leaned over, plucked the baby from the water, and put it back on the stranger's boat, the entire episode maybe taking four or five seconds.

AT NOON ON A LATE-SUMMER WEDNESDAY, Rucker did many things. He checked with his fig guy about the supply of figs, he called the guy he rents the dishwasher from ("Never buy a dishwasher; that's restaurant 101") to tell him it was leaking pretty bad, he talked about discovering bubble trance music while watching a Sprint commercial ("And you know what? It's fucking good"), he chopped thirty-eight red peppers and deveined a baker's dozen foie gras, he talked about taking pigeon off the menu for the fall and doing a play on duck à l'orange with pepper and key lime, he met a purveyor to discuss six-inch gordita tortillas, he complimented the pastry chefs on how clean they'd kept the freezer, and he did a bad impression of a New York accent for his New York–born GM.

Around four p.m., two servers showed up and started taking down chairs and setting all the tables. As they did, Rucker kept tasting the beef cheek sauce for their classic dish Beef Cheek Bourguignon. In the last ten years they'd never started the sauce from scratch; they were always stretching the leftover sauce from nights before, adding the new braising liquids from the beef cheek to the old ones and straining it and tasting it and cooking it down again. So it was fair to say that elements of the actual, literal sauce in the pot went back nearly to the start of Le Pigeon.

At five p.m., they unlocked the door to let the folks lingering outside in. The crowd was typical, which is to say there were people in NASA T-shirts wearing sandals and people in suits who had expensive haircuts and status watches. A man in a professionally ironed shirt told Rucker he'd been to Le Pigeon "at least forty times." A skinny, sharply angled former Le Pigeon sous

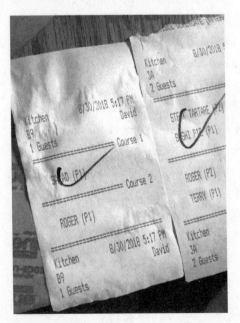

Order tickets from Le Pigeon

chef nicknamed Bones sat at the bar and silently crushed his way through foie gras fajitas with mescal-pepper jelly. A couple celebrating their thirty-eighth anniversary brought in the Le Pigeon cookbook for Rucker to autograph. His inscription to Lee and Jean was a paragraph long.

Two servers and a runner worked the room. By five thirty p.m., all the tables in the restaurant were full. The runner would call out an order—"Four tasting Terrys" or "Two Rogers, one Terry" or "Two Cancuns"—and it would be repeated back as an audible receipt. Most things were in code. "Terry" meant a fish dish, because at some point "steak" and "skate" had sounded too similar and were getting confused. "Roger" was any quail or chicken dish. "Cancun" meant the grilled shoyu pigeon, because it was served in the style of a crab rangoon, and somehow that got shortened to "Cancun." Pigeon legs were called "churros." The reserve pairing for the chef's tasting menu was called "fancy." Salad was called "salad."

Later that night, after cleaning his station, Rucker retreated down to his office to call in food orders on speakerphone while simultaneously discussing savings and retirement funds with his sauté cook. Then he went over to Canard to game-plan the fall menu with his head chef and talk through a port wine grape jelly. He took out the recycling and tidied up his garbage cans, which had been thoroughly shopped by some local homeless folks.

During his final walk-through, he kept thinking about a dish one of his young cooks had been working on. It was a watermelon barbecued black cod with black-eyed peas, green chorizo, fennel, and mustard. The day before, his cook had him try a version, and while he felt it was delicious, it had been too busy on the plate, and he needed him to streamline it down to the essential elements to really make it work. Rucker saw things in this kid, his curiosity, the way he pushed himself, the way he visualized dishes. The kid had the fire, and it was damn exciting to think about where he might go with it.

But he could think more about that tomorrow. It was nearly one a.m., and

Rucker was looking forward to getting home and being asleep by two, so he checked the oven to make sure the temperature was correct for the beef cheeks braising overnight, walked out the front door, locked it, and headed for his car. It was an unusually warm night, Rucker thought. The drive home would be nice.

CHAPTER 31

Kroger Marketplace, 9001 Old US Hwy 42, Union, Kentucky, Spring 2018

The town of Union, Kentucky, was seventeen miles south of Cincinnati, a straight shot down I-71 South. It was three square miles wide. It had roughly six thousand residents. The median home value, as of 2018, was $244,300.

In Union, on Old US Highway 42, across from the Villas of Fowler's Creek (off Fowlers Lane, but in front of Fowlers Fork), sat a giant Kroger Marketplace supermarket. Built into the massive brick structure housing the market, tucked next to Kroger Liquors, was a reclaimed wood box with a yellow-and-black sign that read "Kitchen 1883." Next to the sign was a banner that read "Come on in! We're open!"

Opened in November 2017, Kitchen 1883 (named for the year Barney Kroger launched his first grocery store) was the brainchild of Kroger Co.'s Culinary Development team, a pilot full-service "dining experience" serving "New American Comfort" food, which assimilates flavors from "the melting pot of traditional American cooking techniques mixed with international components" and "puts emphasis on local sourcing." This meant kale and Brussels sprouts salad tossed in a sweet chili ginger vinaigrette, honey-gochujang BBQ chicken wings, craft-beer-battered cod, chicken and waffles topped with pickled house slaw and cayenne-maple syrup, and a vegan Impossible Burger. The bar offered "hand-crafted cocktails" and, this being Kentucky, a bourbon list with thirty choices.

It was a "dining experience" because Kitchen 1883 still existed within the space of a grocery store. Kroger's CEO, Rodney McMullen, told Wall Street analysts it was an "opportunity to grow the business and create a new leg, a platform for growth." It could utilize Kroger's massive buying power to heavily subsidize food costs. It could offer thirty bourbons because it had access to Kroger's liquor store. In a way, Kitchen 1883 was just delivering Kroger's highest-end prepared food through the mechanism of something resembling a farm-to-table restaurant. And resemble a farm-to-table restaurant it did.

Kitchen 1883's ninety-four-seat interior featured avocado leather banquettes, a back photo wall with pictures of bourbon barrels, horses, fire, and other Kentucky-related things, one all-wood wall with Edison bulbs, and a semi-open kitchen in the back right-hand corner, across from a slate-black bar with outlets and hooks to hang your coat. A chalkboard sign advertising a "Winner Chicken Dinner" implored you to ask your server about Sunday supper. Said servers were all women in their fifties and sixties wearing black button-downs and black trousers with striped aprons. The restaurant was hiring, conducting open interviews from two to four p.m. on Mondays, Tuesdays, and Wednesdays.

Along the left-hand wall, above the avocado leather banquettes, were several frosted glass windows. If you looked through the stenciled "18 Kitchen 83" in the frosted glass, you could see into the eating area inside the Kroger supermarket. A mother fed her daughter coleslaw and soup, and a man with bandages from a broken nose attempted to drink whole milk through a straw. A teenage boy started to eat a clementine, then abandoned that effort.

In April 2018, Kroger Co. announced, based upon the success of their pilot dining experience, it planned to open a second Kitchen 1883 in the Anderson Township within Greater Cincinnati that fall. This Kitchen 1883 would offer new, local, made-from-scratch dishes inspired by American and international flavors. It would also have a patio.

As you exited, the host offered you a choice of mints.

CHAPTER 32

André Prince Jeffries, North Nashville, Tennessee, Part 3

On August 25, 2016, *Food Republic*'s George Embiricos posted an interview with chef John Lasater of Hattie B's, titled "Meet the Man Who Launched the Nashville Hot Chicken Craze." Lasater had been up in New York City at the James Beard House to do a "Hot Chicken in the City" dinner on August 11, and Embiricos, a diehard hot chicken fan who'd discovered the dish while attending Vanderbilt four years earlier and written several articles for *Food Republic* on its national rise, met with him beforehand to talk.

After the interview was over, Embiricos sat with the Bishop family to enjoy the meal of crispy hot chicken skins with Tennessee honey; Tennessee tomato gazpacho with fried chicken crunchies, fresh cheese, and pickled green tomatoes; Nashville-style hot chicken rillettes with three-bean salad and pickled watermelon rinds, ramps, and okra; and family-style Hattie B's hot chicken with Tennessee speckled butter beans, southern braised greens, raw corn salad, house-made chowchow, skillet cornbread, and bourbon barrel sorghum butter. Banana pudding with a torched meringue was served for dessert.

Two weeks later, the story published and Embiricos sent it over to Hattie B's head of PR, who lavished the story with praise and requested that the names of the owners also be included. On Friday, Embiricos added the owners' names and shared the story on his own Facebook page, and in the comments Chef Lasater complimented the story as well. Several hours after that, Hattie B's shared the story on their own Facebook page with the caption "So proud of our chef!" Everything appeared fine in the world of mutually beneficial food journalism and public relations. But quickly after Hattie B's shared the story, that all changed.

The story's headline, coupled with a few quotes from Lasater about Hattie B's having a lot to do with hot chicken turning into a national phenomenon and opening in a "good area," set off a perfect storm of Internet fury that rippled through Nashville, and then the country. A wound that had been quietly festering for a long time had suddenly been ripped open, and anger and frustration poured out. Within three days the story had five hundred thousand unique visitors. Hattie B's deleted it from their Facebook page. Lasater erased his comment, then unfriended and blocked Embiricos on Facebook. The Hattie B's team began demanding that *Food Republic* take down the story, but because there were no actual factual issues, the editors found no reason to do so.

The article's comments section quickly became a forum for debate about "Columbusization," appropriation, gentrification, and people on the Internet not reading an entire article. It mattered little that at the very end, Lasater had called Prince's the godfather of hot chicken. Most commenters, furious that the headline seemingly gave Lasater credit for introducing hot chicken to the country, did not make it past that point before unleashing their wrath. But the story acted as a starting point for a new, deeper round of journalistic inquiry into the complicated past and future of hot chicken. Dueling editorials appeared in *Nashville Scene* under the headline "Race, Credit, and Hot

Chicken." A long feature by Nashville native Zach Stafford mentioning the *Food Republic* drama was published in *Eater*, titled "Burned Out: Hot Chicken Was the Prince Family Legacy—Then Nashville Transformed It into an Icon, and Now Everybody Wants a Piece." The *Bitter Southerner's* Rachel Martin also went deep on the topic and Nashville history with African-American neighborhoods in "How Hot Chicken Really Happened."

Jeffries, through Semone and Mario and conversations with customers, heard about the hoopla going on. It was hard not to; it was all anyone was talking about. This sort of deal seemed the ultimate lack of respect, so they contacted their attorney and asked if there was something to be done. He looked through the story and the comments and the articles surrounding it and weighed in. "Do nothing," he said. "Your fans are taking care of it."

Though this mostly meant people in the community were sticking up publicly for Prince's, there was an uglier side as well. Embiricos began receiving death threats in private messages on Instagram and Facebook. Friends told him that in some closed East Nashville Facebook community pages, people were asking for his home address. His efforts to foster any sort of dialogue with the Hattie B's folks through both official and back channels were met with icy silence.

In the end, the story and the aftermath forced the hot chicken community in Nashville to retreat and retool. The positive side was that these tensions were at least out in the open now. But it was a small community, and all around, people were cautious and feeling wounded. The stakes had changed.

Pettier squabbles started cropping up. Jeffries got upset when Aqui Hines of 400 Degrees was being interviewed for a television show and told the story of Thornton Prince with a picture of her and Jeffries posing together, because it appeared like Hines was connected to her family. Isaac Beard was upset that Hines seemed to ignore him out in public and that he was being looped in with the hoopla surrounding Hattie B's, when he was just an older local fanboy who used to sell cars and work as a massage therapist.

Burned by the overwhelmingly negative public reaction, Hattie B's retreated into silence outside of their own tightly controlled social media. Writers seeking to talk to the Bishops or Lasater were asked to submit questions by email, to be vetted by their PR representatives, and those granted access would often have her seated at the table during the interviews.

Mayor Purcell's dream for the Hot Chicken Festival, of promoting and celebrating Nashville's only indigenous food, had, in some ways, worked out beyond his wildest dreams. The order in which the tents were placed was locked in, with Bolton's at the front, followed by 400 Degrees, Hattie B's, Party Fowl, Pepperfire, and Prince's always at the end. The wait-list to be a vendor ran several pages. The "Amateur Cooking Competition" had turned into a showcase for potential newcomers. No one lining up three hours before the festival started had to be told what hot chicken was. But it didn't always feel like a victory.

The night before the festival, local brewery Yazoo hosted a "Hot Chicken Kickoff" of sorts, where all the festival folks could get together and have a couple of beers and relax in the calm before the storm of the festival. At the 2017 kickoff, Nick Bishop Jr., Hines, and Jeffries posed for a picture together, each representing a different evolution of hot chicken in Nashville. After the kickoff, Bishop Jr. asked if he could get the photo. Hines didn't respond.

THERE WAS A TRAFFIC CONE OUTSIDE of Prince's Hot Chicken Shack. It sat in the parking spot closest to the entrance all day, even when the parking lot and satellite lot next door were both filled up, even when folks sat in their cars waiting, staring at the Prince's entrance, hoping someone was coming out. But sometime between four and five p.m. each day, that traffic cone would disappear, and soon after, Jeffries would come rolling up in her Honda Accord with the handicap tag around the rearview mirror.

As she pulled in, two of the younger Prince's employees came out. One took her big bag inside, and the other helped her out of her car. Though she used to be able to run like her mother, at seventy-two, she walked slowly with a cane now, each step thoughtful. Because everyone knew who she was, she frequently stopped to crack jokes with the men standing outside selling bottled water out of coolers, and the patrons who called out "Hi, Miss André!"

Most days, if she wasn't in the back, she would hold court in the booth closest to the ordering line, conducting interviews or talking to the old heads or keeping watch over some member of the family, sipping soda out of an oversize plastic cup from Jim 'N Nick's Community Bar-B-Q.

For years, Jeffries had turned down offers for expansion. She'd never advertised—her customers did that for her—and she'd never been interested in the offers she'd gotten. Folks had called her from all over the world; they'd wanted to put a Prince's in Harlem, and Miami, and even Dubai. She told them she was too old to relocate, too set in her ways to let someone else run

Longtime Prince's Hot Chicken employee Mario Hambrick had his bail bond business advertisement outside Hattie B's restaurant, downtown Nashville, Tennessee

it, and she feared mass production would mean the chicken would lose something.

She'd just wanted to keep the business in the family, and—like her mom did for her—leave them with something that might help pay some bills. But there was more family to provide for—she even had great-grandkids now— and despite the fact that her family had invented a dish all of America had fallen in love with, most people in her family were still working other jobs, just like Thornton and Will and the family back in the day. There was no clearer example than the fact that on the benches by the bus stop five hundred feet from Hattie B's original Midtown location, you could see an advertisement for Mario's bail bondsman business. He'd been working for Jeffries since he was eight and he still had a two-job hustle.

So now, as she got older and watched Hattie B's open three restaurants in Nashville, one in Birmingham, another in Memphis, another in Atlanta, and another in Las Vegas, with others planned for Los Angeles, Dallas, and New York City, she was finally questioning whether staying small was the right decision. She'd already become more amenable to some change.

In 2016, Mario had convinced her to open a second location in Nolensville. If this was the shack, she said, then the Nolensville spot was the mansion. It had beer, real silverware and plates, a POS system, all the trappings of a new restaurant. For the last few years, they also had a food truck to cater events and weddings and go all over the place. This year they were even going to do Bonnaroo. They'd also made a deal with Goldbelly, an online delivery service, to start shipping their hot chicken all over the country, and made a deal with a company to submit a proposal to try to get into the Nashville airport's $1.2 billion 2023 expansion.

But there were some things Jeffries didn't want to change. She'd turned down an offer to expand the shack into the business next door, because she still felt like people enjoyed an intimate mom-and-pop location. Plus, her blood and sweat and money built this place. Even in this day and age, you would think that getting a bank loan wouldn't be an issue, but the banks hadn't looked kindly on giving her money, and so she was forced to invest everything back into the business herself. America was two-faced, and if your face wasn't the right color, you were still being punished. But as her mother said, you had to keep it moving.

Jeffries had a few regrets. She'd always wanted to go back to school and finish her degree, but now her baby Semone was fifty years old, which meant she hadn't been to school in fifty years, and that seemed crazy. Every time she planned to go back, something had come up. She only had the one year left, and everyone was telling her that she could get that degree online now, but there was nothing like actually sitting in front of a professor and learning about plants and animals and everything else she loved. Plus, people were in front of screens way too much nowadays.

She still felt like her dreams told her things. Ever since she was little, she'd loved red birds. Semone and Yeae bought her pillows with red birds as gifts, and she kept them in her bedroom and bathroom. Red was her mother's favorite color—she looked stunning in red—and every spring and winter, her mother had taken her and her brother and sister to the concerts at Tennessee State in the chapel, and outside that chapel, you could always see red birds flying by.

At home in her bedroom, Jeffries had an oversize window. She loved looking out the window because her neighbors had lots of shrubbery on that side of their yard and you could see all sorts of animals: squirrels and birds and rabbits.

On a recent day, she'd been at her house alone—the kids were all gone when she got up, and asleep when she got home—and it was eerily quiet. As she sat by the window in her room, looking out at her neighbors' bushes, Jeffries found herself missing her mother. She started daydreaming that her mother sent her a beautiful red bird as a way of saying she was there and watching.

And sure enough, a few minutes later, a red bird flew by.

Epilogue

On June 7, 2018, I boarded a red-eye flight to South Carolina. I'd been writing what I intended to be a chapter for this book about Anthony Bourdain, a snapshot of a man at a crossroads, as he grappled with the legacy of his past in the wake of the #MeToo movement. No one, I'd felt, was more equipped to handle that responsibility than Bourdain, a man who'd spent college among progressive feminists in the first Vassar class to accept men, and his formative cooking years in the gay enclave of Provincetown. A man raised by two writers, who wasn't enveloped by fame's embrace until he was fully formed. I'd posited that, though the burden was tremendous, Bourdain was up to the task.

When I got off my flight and turned my phone back on, I had forty-two text messages, each essentially saying the same thing: Anthony Bourdain was dead. I knew nothing.

I tried to rewrite my Bourdain chapter. But it never felt satisfying or frankly very good, in comparison to the incredible elegies coming in from all over the food world and beyond. And then, just six weeks after Bourdain's death, as I grappled with just what to do, I found out, via an alert on my phone, that Los Angeles food legend Jonathan Gold had died too. The year

2018 was barely half over, and it felt like I might be sentenced to live inside it forever.

IF THE IMPACT OF THE LAST TWELVE YEARS in the food world has been a sort of rolling wave, the impact of this last year was more of a sonic boom. Bourdain's and Gold's deaths shocked, shook, and saddened a community that already felt raw and exposed. Immigrants, the lifeblood of any kitchen, felt constantly under attack from our government. The #MeToo movement exposed fissures in the foundations of the restaurant world, as women bravely stood up and publicly exposed the ugly side of an industry that, over the last decade, has seen its star chefs and bartenders enter the celebrity orbit, complete with the protective layers of satellite hangers-on and assistants intent on making sure that ride stayed smooth. Celebrity itself had such awesome and ugly power, and as was the case with John Besh, you could sometimes see those two forces simultaneously at play, as he did truly good things in the community while failing to hold himself to those same standards in his own world.

Relatedly, spending so much time with Gabriel Rucker opened my eyes to the very real addiction problems in those kitchens and behind those bars. Because, for so long, the restaurant kitchen was the place for people on the margins to work, because the job is a grind and takes place well into the night, and because everything is about showing how "hard-core" you are—how impervious you are to knife cuts and fire burns and insults—it creates a perfect storm for unhealthy behaviors around drugs and alcohol to be normalized and even encouraged in keeping up with said hard-core ethos. And it was easy to see how one particular problem fed (and continues to feed) into the other. These are struggles that aren't close to being "won," but at least they are finally being publicly addressed. In some capacities, publicity can be seen as the first step toward progress.

As I visited new cities and talked to more and more industry folks, and watched neighborhoods evolve, I couldn't help but feel like I was witnessing some sort of overarching new narrative: the mass professionalization of the restaurant/bar world. With respect to the #MeToo movement and substance abuse, this is a good thing, because professional industries hold themselves to a standard of decorum and traditionally offer help in ways the restaurant industry never has. I think of Mashama Bailey and what she told me about the fundamental change in the way people handled themselves when she worked in a big, corporate hotel kitchen as opposed to on the line at a small independent spot. It was night and day, she said. But from a business perspective, that professionalization means stories like what has happened with hot chicken in Nashville will become more and more the norm, if they're not already.

The Culinary Revolution I set out to capture is ending, the peace treaties are being ratified, and we've entered into what I might call the Era of the Operator, a time when the folks who come out of the gladiatorial culinary fighting grounds victorious are not necessarily the innovators or the true talents, but the folks with the capital, gumption, savvy, and marketing to do it best, or—perhaps fitting for our current times—loudest.

The operator doesn't create a trend, but sees it happening early, and figures out how to do it better than the people currently involved in it. I should say that this doesn't even need to have a negative connotation—people shouldn't be dinged for being good at what they do—but as markets saturate and rents and labor go up and ideas come faster and are put into the ether more quickly through social and traditional media outlets eager to fill virtual pages for "content" or "likes" or "follows" or grist for the algorithm mill, there is little space anymore to fuck up and figure it out and adapt. Restaurants and bars are now expected to come out fully formed and raring to go, because if they don't have their shit together, some other operator inevitably will.

If you're on your Ayn Rand ethical egoism capitalist grind, this might even be seen as a victory. But in squeezing inefficiencies from the restaurant industry, it loses its romance. Restaurants are deeply personal things, which explains why they're often kept going long after they've stopped making money, and the last twelve years saw that sort of romanticism and excitement spread all over the country, as the independent restaurant prospered.

I loved going to new cities that had only recently been taken by the spirit of food revolution, because the excitement in the air was nearly narcotic. There was a true sense of revolutionary zeal; that if you got creative chefs and bartenders and farmers together with a shared sense of mission, you could create remarkable things. But whereas in Portland in 2006 you saw maybe an eight-year gestation period, the timelines are stunted now. It was possible that Oklahoma City could be "discovered" and "over" in the very same year. World-weariness and cynicism set in more quickly now, with unabashed excitement seen as a weakness to be exploited or mocked online, and authenticity bandied about as another item on a checklist in a business plan.

And yet, I believe this is merely a symptom of a time, and not the malady itself. The legacies of Bourdain and Gold will live on. As the economic boom years fade out and we're faced with the cyclical inevitability of a recession, restaurants will close, the dispassionate will lose interest, the market will become less saturated, and we'll again see, as we did in 2008 with the Food Truck Insurrection, that in times of austerity, creativity reigns. And maybe during that time, a restaurant owner will be desperate to glean anything they can from a failing space, and so they will tap a new twenty-five-year-old to lead the kitchen. And that twenty-five-year-old will start to cook the food they want, not because it's been market tested or feels safe, but because they are young and creative and have nothing to lose. And in that moment, a fresh torch will be lit, and the fight will begin anew.

Afterword

On March 11, 2020, Gabriel Rucker cooked on the line at Le Pigeon in Portland, Oregon, as he'd done nearly every week for the last fourteen years. The thirty-four-seat restaurant was packed with folks who gathered to watch Rucker and his team serve Jamaican jerk foie gras in a red curry rum sauce and pork trotter croquettes with pickled pig tongue, and a choice mustard-crusted pork ribeye with bacon and cheese pierogis and hot horseradish cream.

It was a good night, but all people could talk about was the announcement by the NBA that it was suspending its season indefinitely after a player on the Utah Jazz had tested positive for a highly infectious disease. It was called the coronavirus. At the time, there had been plans in the works to put Rucker's signature Canard steam burgers in the Moda Center, where Portland's NBA team plays. Not anymore.

Over the next few days, as society skidded abruptly to a standstill, the discussion across the country turned to restaurants and bars. Rucker and his business partner Andy Fortgang gathered their staff and told them they would do everything in their power to stay open as long as they could. Rucker was determined to reassure their workers. But it didn't matter. Almost overnight, people stopped dining out entirely. By Sunday of that weekend—normally a difficult reservation to get—both of his restaurants were deserted.

On Monday, March 16, Rucker and his chef de cuisine, Taylor Daugherty, served three total customers. By 2:30 p.m., the writing was on the wall. He and Fortgang called a staff-wide meeting and told everyone to go into the walk-ins and take as much food home with them as they could. He kept their in-house HR staffer nearby to help with unemployment forms. And then, for the first time in fourteen years, Gabriel Rucker shut down Le Pigeon and Canard indefinitely and went home.

THE MUSIC MAY HAVE ALREADY BEEN SLOWING, but right then—not just at Canard, but in kitchens and restaurants across the country—it stopped. The American Culinary Revolution was over. The end point was not a moment of collective creative exhaustion or even a recession (although that will likely follow) but an uncontained coronavirus moving like wildfire through American cities and towns. At that moment, restaurants and bars didn't face a steady decline as much as a Gravitron-floor-dropping spiral. But for many of the industry people featured in this book, hard times had already arrived. On December 28, 2018, André Prince Jeffries's iconic Ewing Drive location of Prince's Hot Chicken in North Nashville suffered foundation damage after a car slammed into the building and started a fire. Their South Nashville location remained open during the pandemic for takeout and delivery, but the North Nashville spot, where so many of us had gone to pay homage to Miss André and hear her stories and eat her family's chicken, closed permanently.

In San Francisco, Anjan and Emily Mitra had closed DOSA on Valencia in 2019, and, while dealing with their own separation, they put their Fillmore restaurant into Chapter 11 bankruptcy protection. Then in mid-March, even before the Bay Area became the first region in the country to shut down essential businesses and order residents to shelter in place, they watched the business at Fillmore dwindle from 20 percent below average, to 50 percent, then 90 percent, leaving them little choice but to close the game changing-South Indian restaurant on March 15, likely for good.

By then everyone had begun making incredibly hard decisions, looking to find some sort of impossible balance between personal and employee safety and financial survival. In Pittsburgh, Sonja Finn's last night of service at Dinette was March 14. She wanted to close early so her employees could be among the first in line to send in unemployment applications. Along with her manager and her sous chef, she cooked off what she could, then Finn made twenty-five plain cheese pizzas for her son, Miles, and froze them in packs of three to ration out weekly. She stacked chairs and tables and tried to be all business, but when she turned the corner from the dining room to her office and saw eleven years' worth of framed write-ups and reviews on the wall, she began to cry.

Meanwhile in Oklahoma, Rachel Cope had been busy. She'd opened her sixth Oklahoma City restaurant, Burger Punk, and a branch of her pizza place, Empire, in her hometown of Tulsa, right by the legendary Cain's Ballroom. That Saturday, March 14, she sat in her newly built restaurant, which they'd funded entirely on their own, and watched as her dad, a partner in the business, stared uneasily out the window. Cope should've felt a sense of accomplishment, but she just felt waves of worry. The next day, she called an emergency meeting with all of her directors, and the next week, all seven of the restaurants shut down. They would pivot and do takeout and delivery and try to figure it out. Expansion was out the window, Cope thought. Now it was about survival.

By March 18, Mashama Bailey, who'd won the 2019 James Beard Award for Best Chef in the Southeast region, closed her now-famous restaurant The Grey in Savannah, Georgia, and focused her attention on creating grocery boxes to help feed the rest of the community. Neal Bodenheimer shut down his Freret Street cocktail bar Cure in New Orleans on March 16 with a short good-bye service that night for his regulars, then took to selling off rare bottles of liquor from his own personal stash to raise money for his staff.

And after years of strictly bartending and being ornery, the inimitable Phil Ward finally had been set to open another bar of his own, called Altar, in the Crown Heights neighborhood of Brooklyn. There had even been a February article in *The New York Times* by cocktail writer Robert Simonson, featuring Ward and the bar, titled "A Mezcal Master Turns to the Martini." The story cited a mid-March opening. It never came.

OF COURSE, THE RESTAURANT INDUSTRY WASN'T ALONE. At that moment, our entire economy was shaken up like a snow globe in the hands of a toddler and dropped on the floor. But the sheer scale of the destruction in the world of restaurants was unique. Most of the nearly half a million independent restaurants in America were forced to either shut down completely or make do with a skeleton crew serving takeout and delivery. The National Restaurant Association estimated that five to seven million restaurant workers would eventually be unemployed, and that up to 75 percent of restaurants would not survive the shutdown. This was an extinction-level event.

But independent restaurants, which for so long had been too fragmented and scattered and self-reliant to organize in any real way, quickly found their common voice. They were not going to go quietly. People were alarmed by the fact that President Trump had held a conference call with giant national restaurant chain CEOs but neglected to include any independent restaurant owners, and they were worried because he seemed to think that only three to ten percent of restaurants would close. Coalitions formed, almost overnight, with familiar faces leading the charge. The biggest of all, the Independent Restaurant Coalition (IRC), brought together more than three thousand independent chef/owners and restaurateurs, with Portland chef Naomi Pomeroy, *Top Chef*'s own Tom Colicchio, and Washington DC–based chef Kwame Onwuachi, as cofounders and spokespeople. They hired a top K-Street lobbying firm, which describes itself as both "elite" and "boutique," and a PR firm run by President Obama's former deputy campaign manager. They ran television commercials and radio spots and created Instagram and Twitter accounts and did interviews with any and all media. They were not, as we say, fucking around.

There was the passage of a $2.2 trillion "Coronavirus Aid, Relief, and Economic Security (CARE)" Act, but it was not heralded by the group as a salve that might actually heal the wound inflicted on the industry by the pandemic. There were various reasons. The Paycheck Protection Program within the CARE Act was set up to provide loans to small businesses like restaurants and then forgive those loans as long as pre-pandemic "employee and compensation levels are maintained." But because most restaurants were forced to close their dining rooms for safety reasons and lay off nearly all of their workers so they could apply for unemployment, this seemed all but impossible. On top of that, even getting that money from the banks was proving to be a Sisyphean task, as all small businesses applied at the same time, overwhelming banks and the all too often mismanaged federal agencies appointed to oversee the distribution.

The IRC's point, more or less, was that independent restaurants (and the eleven million people they employ) needed to be treated differently than other small businesses. They couldn't all fight for the same pieces of the pie. Independent restaurants were on life support and they needed a different pie. Something nutritious, with locally grown ingredients.

AS I WRITE, AT THE HEIGHT OF THE LOCKDOWN, the idea of eating at a restaurant seems far-fetched—risible, really. Going shopping for groceries is enough of an ordeal. But I am sure that soon enough (perhaps by the time you read these words), restaurants will be back and we, the eaters, will return, too, somehow immunized or vaccinated maybe, but certainly profoundly tired of cooking at home. But what seems less certain to me is if we'll soon see anything quite like the breakneck revolution of the last decade and a half. It's very possible we have just come out of the food version of the Roaring

Twenties, obliviously eating our plant-based burgers and ube cupcakes with watermelon seed buttercream frosting, sipping our collagen and adaptogenic-infused cheese teas (all delivered to us by drones from zero-waste ghost kitchens) without ever stopping to appreciate the fact that we may never have it this good again.

The underbrush of issues I tried to track in this book—exorbitant rents pushing independent restaurants and the labor they employ out of cities; 100,000 new restaurants in America over the past decade saturating the market and causing a back-of-the-house labor crisis; the universality of delivery app dining by younger generations cutting deeper into profits, thanks to the loan shark-like percentages these companies charge, etc.—have acted as accelerants to the crisis inflicted by the pandemic. The entire restaurant industry has been skating on thin ice for years now, somehow still managing to stick triple-axel landings and dazzle the crowds. But we've all been watching the moves, when we should've been watching the ice. Because when the pandemic broke, and all the structural weaknesses that had been accumulating were revealed, everyone fell in.

I've tried to be objective in these pages about the people in this industry and to show you their flaws as well as their incredible strengths and talents. But after all the time I've spent with some of them, witnessing the care they put into their work and the food they make for us, any principles of journalistic objectivity don't really apply here. It is tragic what's happening, and it breaks my heart.

Independent restaurants are never rational. They are fiery cauldrons of emotion, hope, anguish, adrenaline, joy, gratitude, hurt, and toil, all fronted by a host stand. People talk about restaurants like their children because they pour comparable amounts of time and money into them, even when it seems like a lost cause, because they are you, and you are them. This work defines people.

But this shouldn't paper over the very real problems. Changes need to happen in the restaurant industry to make it more sustainable. Today, few restaurants give their employees health care coverage or paid leave. Wages remain low (case in point: the tipped minimum wage is $2.13, and has remained at that number since 1991) and job security, on the whole, doesn't exist. Recently, Tunde Wey, ever the voice of public dissent, wrote an essay, which, naturally, he published in ten parts on Instagram, essentially arguing *against* saving the restaurant industry. Instead, he advocated for supporting "radical and comprehensive economic legislation that is industry agnostic" like the Green New Deal.

I don't know what's going to happen next, and I doubt many people would say they do, either. We don't know how long our economy will keep hitting the sleep button, or just what people's behaviors will be like when they emerge unshorn and pale from their homes. But I have hope.

I have hope that the restaurants that do survive will be scrappy and adaptive, bringing with them a little bit of the "austerity breeds creativity" ethos that defined the events described at the start of this book. Even now, chefs are bending the ideas of strict takeout and delivery. Chicago's three-Michelin-starred bastion of fine dining, Alinea, which normally charges diners around $300 a person, began offering $35 to-go meals reserved through their Tock reservation site, with appointed pickup times and curbside delivery. The first offering sold out in five hours. In Portland the newest darling of the food scene there, Eem, a Thai/Texas BBQ mashup (tell the early 2000s that although *fusion* became a dirty word, now their playbook is back, baby!), relaunched with a similar set up and sold out in minutes.

But, most important, I hope that this crisis will fundamentally change the attitudes of American restaurant customers, shifting us away from viewing restaurants as hip food-based Instagram hashtag scavenger hunt checklists and delivery app commissaries, to thinking about them as integral employers and pillars within a community. For some people food is about lifestyle, but for many it is just life. A way of getting by. One of the few silver linings of the pandemic has been, if not straight-up appreciation, some acknowledgement of the plight of people who work in all aspects of food service, from the cooks preparing the food in the kitchen, to the people in some cases quite literally risking their lives to deliver meals to our doors. Perhaps all of this time isolated will give people a different view of what it even means to eat out, and how vital and nourishing being surrounded by that community is to a healthy life. Maybe after months of enforced sheltering, staring at screens, we'll recognize that our phones should be the last thing we want to look at when we're out with friends and family. Maybe, instead of wooing a few megarich investors, restaurants will start being funded by and within their communities, almost like co-ops, giving everyone there an investment in keeping them around and making them work.

For nearly fourteen years, we got to witness a Culinary Revolution transform the way Americans eat, think, and talk about food. And now it's over. People are scared and unsure of where things will go from here, and they're looking for leadership and direction. In other words, it seems like a pretty damn good time to start another Revolution.

ACKNOWLEDGMENTS

One January afternoon early in 2017, David Granger called me. This made me nervous. During his twenty years editing *Esquire* magazine, Granger was my hero, so my mission became simple: don't embarrass myself. But once on the phone, Granger proved to be incredibly disarming. He told me he'd read some of my stories, and wondered if I hadn't thought about a book. For the next two and a half hours we talked about what we'd seen in the restaurant world over the past decade and shared some sort of incredible mind-meld, and by the end, the seed of a book idea took form. Over the next few months Granger helped me shape that into a proposal, and that proposal became this book you've likely just skimmed. Since that January afternoon, Granger has become a mentor, adviser, editor, and incredible friend. Without him, there would be no book.

In a more tangible way, this book wouldn't exist without the nearly one hundred people in the restaurant and bar industries who opened up to me in exceedingly intimate and honest ways. The first person I reached out to was Gabriel Rucker. Sweat poured down my back as I rambled on, explaining the rough idea, desperately hoping he might be interested. If he hadn't said yes that day to this nervous stranger, this book might never have come together. But I could probably say that about at least twenty more interactions. If

André Prince Jeffries and her incredible daughter Semone hadn't patiently sat with me and answered my questions as I returned to Prince's in North Nashville over and over again; if Anjan and Emily Mitra hadn't let me repeatedly intrude into their Bay Area lives; if Phil Ward hadn't begrudgingly agreed to meet me for lunch one day in Brooklyn; if Tunde Wey hadn't stopped responding to my non-soccer-related texts; if Mashama Bailey hadn't sat with me for three hours one Savannah morning; if Sonja Finn hadn't finally agreed to let me tell her story; if Rodney Scott hadn't fed me and told me stories on a rainy Charleston day; if Neal Bodenheimer hadn't repeatedly walked me around New Orleans; none of this could've happened. This book is entirely built on the generosity of folks far more important and intelligent and interesting than me, and for those conversations I am and will always be eternally grateful.

Others played large roles in the background. In Nashville, my dear friend Jennifer Justus introduced me to countless helpful folks, especially Tim Davis. From his perch in Wyoming, David Kaplan did the same in the bar industry. David Wondrich, Joaquín Simó, William Grimes, Julie Reiner, and Robert Simonson all helped shape my understanding of the cocktail world during different eras. Ruth Reichl humored me as I emailed her question after question on wide-ranging topics, and embarrassingly sent her photos of her old *New West* magazine stories I'd found in the San Francisco Public Library archives. John T. Edge stayed on the phone correcting my misconceptions even as the plane he was on took off. Maneet Chauhan relayed her first experiences with Indian food in America as she made a birthday cake for a friend. Sue Chan spoke on the food world trends of the last decade with a clarity and intelligence that made me jealous.

Outside the food world, my editor, Will Heyward, managed to somehow wrangle my digressive prose, bad ideas, and remarkable ability to keep talking long after I'd stopped having anything to say, and made me sound much smarter and more coherent than I am. He also at least pretended to take it in stride when, at four a.m. one morning, I began excitedly sending him *New*

Republic stories I'd written years earlier on the Australian World Cup soccer team. He's an incredible editor, a fine gentleman, and now, whether he likes it or not, a friend. Ann Godoff and Scott Moyers were also immensely helpful in providing edits, insights, and deft suggestions as we neared the final stages. Glyn Peterson and Tom Colligan provided crucial fact-checking help.

Joe Keohane kept me sane and grounded by texting me daily to ask how my "history of the hot dog" book was coming along. Though I would never admit it to his face, Keohane deserves much of the credit for getting this book off the ground, both by introducing me to Granger and by editing and significantly improving all of my best feature stories. He's a fantastic editor and, infuriatingly, an even better writer.

Liz Childers-Gay was an important sounding board for my mostly bad ideas, Alessandra Lusardi crucially explained to me how people actually make books, Ben Robinson encouraged me to go back to writing in the first place, Casey Hurley called me every three months to ask if I was okay, and my sister-in-law, Kerry Hoeveler, helped me transcribe interviews and definitely deserved more than one pitiful meal as compensation.

I want to thank the San Francisco Public Library for allowing me to spend months going through every food magazine in their archives from the last twelve years. I'd also like to thank George Packer, whose excellent book *The Unwinding* served as a sort of North Star for my own work. When I couldn't figure out where to go next or needed a literary kick in the pants, I always went back to Packer's work and read it as if it were a religious tome. Honestly, it just might be. It means that much.

I wrote almost the entire book at a café called M.H. Bread and Butter, which is not typically a place where someone spends eight straight hours day after day, and so I would like to thank everyone there, both for putting up with me and making the best damn soft scrambled eggs in Northern California. I'd also like to thank Nany Topanotti for her incredible help at home and keen sense of humor, especially after witnessing me attempting to parent after staying up all night on a deadline.

And before the house band begins playing me off my own Acknowledgments page, I want to, of course, thank my family. My mother, Christine, for instilling in me a curiosity about all things, and encouraging me to go out and talk to people and hear their stories. My father, Rand, for giving me his deep love of books and prose. My stepmom, Cheryl, for her intelligence and insights. My grandfather, Raymond, for his unabashed love of food, drink, and argument. My siblings, Kathryn, Brian, and Lauren, for their weird, shared senses of humor and encouragement. My daughter, Annie, for her genuine enthusiasm when helping me cook ("You and I are the chefs in the family," she told me the other day, holding her rainbow whisk up to give me a hug as we scrambled eggs together, and my heart swelled until it nearly burst). My son, Peter, for his genuine enthusiasm about life, pancakes, and imitating Cookie Monster. And finally my wife, Wendy, who has somehow managed to be an incredible mother to two children under four, maintain an involved and important full-time job to pay our bills, and skillfully deal with an insecure, doubt-riddled, embarrassingly dramatic husband clumsily attempting to figure out how to write his first book without a full-scale anxiety attack. At different moments, she's had to play the part of therapist, motivator, managing editor, disciplinarian, and public relations professional, and in each role, she's excelled. Without her, this book (and everything else in my life) would fall apart.

A NOTE ON SOURCES

B etween June 2017 and January 2019, the author conducted hundreds of hours of interviews for this book. Many of the main characters featured were interviewed dozens of times, supplemented by contextual and informational interviews with others in their periphery. Information not gleaned from direct interviews and acquired through secondary sources can be found in the Notes section. Profiles of well-known people in the book who declined to participate or didn't respond to interview requests were constructed exclusively using secondary sources: books, magazine profiles, interviews, social media, and, most helpfully, podcast interviews (the author believes the explosion of podcasts over the last few years has created an amazing, essentially untapped research resource, basically a library of long, intimate, transcribed interviews). For the year cover pages, the author sourced headlines and phrases exclusively from popular food and general interest magazines (*Bon Appétit*, *Esquire*, *Food & Wine*, *Gourmet*, *GQ*, *Saveur*, etc.), newspapers, and blogs from the year indicated.

List of Interviews

Bill Addison

Brett Anderson

Anonymous

Chip Apperson

Mashama Bailey

Scott Baird

Jason Barwikowski

Isaac Beard

Greg Best

Adam Biderman

Neal Bodenheimer

Eliza Borné

Philipe Boulot

Karen Brooks

Chris Chamberlain

Sue Chan

Maneet Chauhan

Rachel Cope

Timothy Davis

Alex Day

Ravi DeRossi

Michael Dorio

John T. Edge

George Embiricos

Sonja Finn

Samantha Fore

Amanda Fortini

Ken Forkish

Andy Fortgang

Kelly Gaston

Jessica Gonzalez

John Gorham

William Grimes

Arun Gupta

Tommy Habetz

John Harris

Aqui Hines

Linton Hopkins

André Prince Jeffries

Semone Jeffries

Michael Jordan

Maura Judkis

David Kaplan

Andy Kryza

Caitlin Laman

Geoff Latham

Jane Lear

John Lewis

Troy MacLarty

Manish Mehrotra

Brian Miller

Anjan Mitra

Emily Mitra

Jeffrey Morgenthaler

Joey Morris

John Navarre

Vitaly Paley

Naomi Pomeroy

Roger Porter

Dr. Krishnendu Ray

Ruth Reichl
  (email correspondence)

Julie Reiner

Andy Ricker

Cody Rowan

Gabriel Rucker

Hana Kaufman Rucker

Maurice Carlos Ruffin

Michael Russell

Cory Schreiber

Rodney Scott

Matt Semmelhack

Joaquín Simó

Robert Simonson

Austin Smith

Arvinder Vilkhu

Phil Ward

Tunde Wey

Cathy Whims

Cody Wilson

Heidi Yorkshire

Dushan Zaric

Jennifer Zyman

NOTES

Introduction

1 **that changed along with the food:** Bauer, M. (2012, December 27). Changing with the Seasons. *San Francisco Chronicle.* Retrieved from https://www.sfgate .com/restaurants/diningout/article/AQ-restaurant-review-changing-with-the -seasons-2516622.php

2 **three and a half stars:** Bauer.

2 **They were James Beard Foundation finalists:** 2012 JBF Award Nominees [Web log post]. (n.d.). James Beard Foundation. Retrieved from https://www .jamesbeard.org/awards/2012-jbf-award-nominees

2 *Esquire*'s **2012 Best New Restaurant list:** Mariani, J. (2012, October 5). The Best New Restaurants 2012 [Web log post]. *Esquire.* Retrieved from https://www .esquire.com/food-drink/g1296/best-new-restaurants-2012/

3 **Meyer's restaurants had won several awards:** 2012 JBF Award Winners [Web log post]. (n.d.). James Beard Foundation. Retrieved from https://www.jamesbeard .org/blog/2012-jbf-award-winners

5 **small hot sauce company:** Alexander, K. (2016, February 11). Who Killed Sriracha? [Web log post]. *Thrillist.* Retrieved from https://www.thrillist.com/eat/nation /the-rise-and-fall-of-sriracha

5 **regional pizza styles (Detroit!):** Dawson, G. (2018, April 24). Detroit-Style Pizza Finds Its Niche Outside Motor City [Web log post]. *Restaurant Hospitality.* Retrieved from https://www.restaurant-hospitality.com/food-trends/detroit-style-pizza-finds -its-niche-outside-motor-city

5 **European-style food halls flourishing:** Lewis, L. (2018, April 8). Food Halls Are the Next Step in the Evolution of Retail [Web log post]. *Stores.* Retrieved from https://stores.org/2018/04/02/a-taste-for-success/

5 **bakers merging together croissants *and* donuts:** Dominique Ansel Bakery website. https://dominiqueansel.com/

5 **stretching back to the original Delmonico's:** Freedman, P. (2016). *Ten Restaurants That Changed America.* New York: Liveright Publishing Corporation.

5 **but chefs at the best restaurants:** Friedman, A. (2018). *Chefs, Drugs, and Rock and Roll: How Food Lovers, Free Spirits, Misfits, and Wanderers Created a New American Profession.* New York: HarperCollins Publishers.

6 **"for seasonal foods":** Sheraton, M. (1999, August). Seasons in the Sun. *Vanity Fair.* Retrieved from https://www.vanityfair.com/news/1999/08/four-seasons-199908

6 **when Larry Forgione took over:** Friedman, *Chefs, Drugs, and Rock and Roll.*

6 **Alice Waters, who opened Chez Panisse:** Wells, P. (2017, September 20). Alice Waters Retraces the Path That Led Her to Chez Panisse. *The New York Times.* Retrieved from https://www.nytimes.com/2017/09/20/books/review/alice-waters-coming-to-my-senses-autobiography.html

6 **Jeremiah Tower as chef:** Goodyear, D. (2017, May 1). Jeremiah Tower, a Forgotten Father of the American Food Revolution. *The New Yorker.* Retrieved from https://www.newyorker.com/culture/cultural-comment/jeremiah-tower-a-forgotten-father-of-the-american-food-revolution

6 **Bruce Marder's West Beach Café:** Friedman, *Chefs, Drugs, and Rock and Roll.*

7 **One dish in particular:** Pope, J. (2015, October 8). Internationally Known Chef Paul Prudhomme Dies at Age 75. *The Times-Picayune.* Retrieved from https://www.nola.com/dining/index.ssf/2015/10/paul_prudhomme_dies.html

7 **a Dallas culinary consultant:** Sharpe, P. (1996, February). Texas Food Conquers the World! *Texas Monthly.* Retrieved from https://www.texasmonthly.com/food/texas-food-conquers-the-world/

9 **"name itself is a nod":** Levy, M. (2013, January 23). Alden & Harlow Will Replace Casablanca, with Focus on Food, Nod to History. *Cambridge Day.* Retrieved from http://www.cambridgeday.com/2013/01/23/alden-harlow-will-replace-casablanca-with-focus-on-food-nod-to-history/

10 **Sean Brock was bringing back:** Sifton, S. (2011, February 8). A Southern Chef Doesn't Stray Far. *The New York Times.* Retrieved from https://www.nytimes.com/2011/02/09/dining/09notebook.html?mtrref=www.google.com

11 **incredible increase in culinary school applications:** Forbes, P. (2011, July 27). Culinary School Enrollment Keeps Increasing for Some Reason [Web log post]. *Eater.* Retrieved from https://www.eater.com/2011/7/27/6666745/culinary-school-enrollment-keeps-increasing-for-some-reason

11 **people writing celebrity profiles:** Grigoriadis, V. (2007, October 14). Everybody Sucks: Gawker and the Rage of the Creative Underclass. *New York Magazine.* Retrieved from http://nymag.com/news/features/39319/

16 **there'd been a 211 percent increase:** Alexander, K. (2016, December 30). There's a Massive Restaurant Industry Bubble, and It's About to Burst [Web log post]. *Thrillist.* Retrieved from https://www.thrillist.com/eat/nation/american-restaurant-industry-bubble-burst

2006

20 **"The Restaurant Rat Pack?":** (2006, August). *Bon Appétit.*

20 **"Year-old Eater (eater.com)":** Krader, K., & Tep, R. (2006, November 1). '06 Taste-maker Awards [Web log post]. *Food & Wine.* Retrieved from https://www.foodand wine.com/articles/06-tastemaker-awards

20 **"'When you have the Internet'":** Moskin, J. (2006, December 27). Food for the People, Whipped Up by the People. *The New York Times.* Retrieved from https://www.nytimes.com/2006/12/27/dining/27cook.html

20 **"The next day, though":** Early Frustrations and Late Saves. (2006, February 14). *The New York Times.* Retrieved from https://dinersjournal.blogs.nytimes.com/2006 /02/14/an-introduction-to-diners-journal/

20 **"I had some terrific times":** Bruni, F. (2006, December 27). To Construct the Perfect Meal, Imagine a Restaurant Crawl. *The New York Times.* Retrieved from https://www.nytimes.com/2006/12/27/dining/27year.html

20 **"Sous-Vide (soo-VEED)—literally 'under vacuum'":** Vocabulary. (2006, September). *Bon Appétit.*

20 **"The $40 entree":** Kantor, J. (2006, October 21). Entrees Reach $40, and, Sorry, the Sides Are Extra. *The New York Times.* Retrieved from https://www.nytimes .com/2006/10/21/dining/21plate.html

20 **"There's pork fat":** (2006, July). *Food & Wine.*

20 **"Popping a few CDs":** Druckman, C. (2006, December). The Greatest Party Play-lists. *Food & Wine.* Retrieved from https://www.foodandwine.com/articles/the -greatest-party-playlists

20 **"These gastronauts, who have fallen":** (2006, May). *Gourmet.*

Chapter 1: Gabriel Rucker, Portland, Oregon, Part 1

29 **Digger O'Dell's Oyster Bar:** *Oregonian* Staff. (2016, December 31). Tasty Memories: 97 Long-Gone Portland Restaurants We Wish Were Still Around. *The Oregonian.* Retrieved from https://www.oregonlive.com/dining/index.ssf/2016/12/tasty _memories_97_long-gone_po.html

29 **Vietnamese at Mai or Thanh Truc:** Anderson, H. A. (2014). *Portland: A Food Biography.* Lanham, MD: Rowman & Littlefield.

29 **Fellow co-owner Monique Siu:** Brooks, K. (2016, August 15). How Zefiro Changed Everything for Portland's Food Scene. *Portland Monthly.* Retrieved from https://www.pdxmonthly.com/articles/2016/8/15/how-zefiro-changed-everything -for-portland-s-food-scene

30 **"the culinary version":** Author interview with Karen Brooks.

30 **Oregon's strict urban growth boundary law:** *Metro* Staff. (2018, May 30). Urban Growth Boundary. *Metro.* Retrieved from https://www.oregonmetro.gov /urban-growth-boundary

35 **the list soon grew:** Rommelmann, N. (2009, May 19). Last Supper. *Portland Monthly.* Retrieved from https://www.pdxmonthly.com/articles/2009/5/19/last-supper

42 **transitioning the menu:** Gotham Building Tavern press release, as quoted in *Portland Food & Drink*. (2006, April 28). Retrieved from https://portlandfoodand drink.com/gotham-building-tavern/

43 **"dude in the cage":** Author interview with Andy Ricker.

46 **"I think you've got":** Author interview with Tommy Habetz.

48 **"25-year-old chef Gabriel Rucker":** Davis, C. (2006, August). *Portland Monthly.*

48 ***Portland Monthly* named Rucker:** Davis, C. (2006, November). Best Restaurants. *Portland Monthly.*

48 **Andrew Knowlton called Rucker:** Knowlton, A. (2007, February). *Bon Appétit.*

48 **He was named one:** Cowin, D. (2007, April). *Food & Wine* Magazine Names 19th Annual Best New Chefs. *Food & Wine*. Retrieved from https://www.foodandwine .com/articles/2007-best-new-chefs

48 **"In Portland, a Golden Age":** Asimov, E. (2007, September 26). In Portland, a Golden Age of Dining and Drinking. *The New York Times*. Retrieved from https:// www.nytimes.com/2007/09/26/dining/26port.html

48 **"Hot New Food Town":** Alexander, K. (2016, May 12). Why the Hot New Food Town Must Die [Web log post]. *Thrillist*. Retrieved from https://www.thrillist.com /eat/nation/why-the-hot-new-food-town-must-die

Chapter 2: TV Dad, Tom Colicchio, New York City, New York

53 **Thomas Colicchio, a former barber:** Maron, M. (2017, September 28). Tom Colicchio. *WTF with Marc Maron* [Audio podcast]. Retrieved from http://www.wtfpod .com/podcast/episode-850-tom-colicchio

54 **And he knew a guy:** Black, M. I. (2015, October 13). #14 Tom Colicchio. *How to Be Amazing with Michael Ian Black* [Audio podcast]. Retrieved from https://player .fm/series/how-to-be-amazing-with-michael-ian-black/14-tom-colicchio

55 **the audacity to start closing:** Fabricant, F. (1998, May 6). The Quilted Giraffe Cooks Again. *The New York Times*. Retrieved from https://www.nytimes.com/1998 /05/06/dining/the-quilted-giraffe-cooks-again.html

56 **A mutual friend had told Meyer:** Maron, M. [Audio podcast].

57 **"Mr. Colicchio's cooking":** Reichl, R. (1994, October 14). Restaurants. *The New York Times*. Retrieved from https://www.nytimes.com/1994/10/14/arts/restau rants-527327.html

57 **What if we just serve:** Cheshes, J. (2016, September 1). The Oral History of Tom Colicchio's Craft [Web log post]. *The Daily Beast*. Retrieved from https://www .thedailybeast.com/the-oral-history-of-tom-colicchios-craft

57 **They left for their wedding:** Allen, J. (2001, September 30). WEDDINGS: VOWS; Lori Silverbush, Tom Colicchio. *The New York Times*. Retrieved from https://www .nytimes.com/2001/09/30/style/weddings-vows-lori-silverbush-tom -colicchio.html

58 **The fourth time, he said maybe:** Black, M. I. [Audio podcast].

61 **saw enrollment increase:** Forbes, P. (2011, July 27) Culinary School Enrollment Keeps Increasing For Some Reason [Web log post]. Retrieved from https://www

.eater.com/2011/7/27/6666745/culinary-school-enrollment-keeps-increasing
-for-some-reason

Chapter 3: Anjan and Emily Mitra, San Francisco, California, Part 1

67 **Thanks to the Chinese Exclusion Act:** Bald, V. (2015). *Bengali Harlem and the Lost Histories of South Asian America*. Cambridge, MA: Harvard University Press.

68 **Sarah Lohman details:** Lohman, S. (2016). *Eight Flavors: The Untold Story of American Cuisine*. New York: Simon & Schuster.

69 **"eat crystallized Calcutta sugar":** Prashad, V. (2001). *The Karma of Brown Folk*. Minneapolis: University of Minnesota Press.

69 **first Indian restaurant in America:** Sietsema, R. (2016, May 26). 10 Old-Fashioned Indian Restaurants to Try in New York City [Web log post]. *Eater*. Retrieved from https://ny.eater.com/2016/5/26/11789126/NYC-best-indian-restaurants -curry-sixth-street-jackson-heights

69 **British India was split:** The World; A Legacy of Conflict. (1990, April 22). *The New York Times*. Retrieved from https://www.nytimes.com/1990/04/22/weekinreview /the-world-a-legacy-of-conflict.html

69 **"early movers," and their ranks:** Chakravorty, S., Kapur, D., & Nirvikar, S. (2016). *The Other One Percent: Indians in America*. London: Oxford University Press.

70 **Manir Ahmed and his five brothers:** Lam, F. (2015, April 29). The Mysteries of Manhattan's Curry Row. *The New York Times Magazine*. Retrieved from https:// www.nytimes.com/2015/05/03/magazine/the-mysteries-of-manhattans-curry -row.html

75 **"rapidly growing roster":** Sheraton, M. (1977, February 18). Restaurants. *The New York Times*. Retrieved from https://www.nytimes.com/1977/02/18/archives/new -jersey-weekly-restaurants-it-started-with-the-moguls.html

75 **"It is easy to understand":** Sheraton, M. (1979, October 5). Restaurants. *The New York Times*. Retrieved from https://www.nytimes.com/1979/10/05/archives/restau rants-bombay-palace-upstream.html

75 **Paul Bhalla's Cuisine of India:** Rushdie, S. (2018). *Indian Cookery*. New York: Picador Cookstr Classics.

75 **"American Palates Awaken":** Fabricant, F. (1998, March 25). American Palates Awaken to the Bold Tastes of India. *The New York Times*. Retrieved from https:// www.nytimes.com/1998/03/25/dining/american-palates-awaken-bold-tastes -india-latest-fusion-star-creative-indian.html

76 **three stars from *Times* critic:** Reichl, R. (1999, February 24). Restaurants; American Food, Indian Spices. *The New York Times*. Retrieved from https://www.nytimes .com/1999/02/24/dining/restaurants-american-food-indian-spices.html

76 **Anita Jaisinghani's 2001 Houston stunner:** Walsh, R. (2001, September 13). Postmodern Punjabi. *Houston Press*. Retrieved from https://www.houstonpress .com/restaurants/postmodern-punjabi-6560832

83 **The review, titled:** Bauer, M. (2006, February 19). Fire and Spice: Dosa Offers a Contemporary, Hip Taste of South Indian Cuisine. *San Francisco Chronicle*.

Retrieved from https://www.sfgate.com/restaurants/diningout/article/Fire-and
-Spice-Dosa-offers-a-contemporary-hip-2300744.php

Chapter 4: King of Trucks, Roy Choi, Los Angeles, California

86 **with Choi being born:** Choi, R., Nguyen, T., and Phan, N. (2013). *L.A. Son: My Life, My City, My Food*. New York: Ecco.

87 **hide them on Roy:** Choi, Nguyen, and Phan.

87 **They bought a Cadillac Fleetwood Brougham:** Kang, J. C. (2014, December 7). Roy Choi's Master Plan. *The California Sunday Magazine*. Retrieved from https:// story.californiasunday.com/roy-choi-food-revolution

88 **Choi was a damn good gambler:** Choi, Nguyen, and Phan, *L.A. Son*.

88 **it all bottomed out:** Choi, Nguyen, and Phan.

89 **making Kit Fox salads:** Choi, Nguyen, and Phan.

89 **Choi went to his car:** Choi, Nguyen, and Phan.

90 **His buddy Mark Manguera:** Gross, T. (2013, November 7). Roy Choi's Tacos Channel LA and the Immigrant Experience. *NPR Fresh Air* [Audio podcast]. Retrieved from https://www.npr.org/2013/11/07/243527051/roy-chois-tacos-channel -la-and-the-immigrant-experience

91 **"Followers keep track of Kogi's whereabouts":** Gold, J. (2009, January 28). The Korean Taco Justice League: Kogi Rolls into LA. *LA Weekly*. Retrieved from https:// www.laweekly.com/restaurants/the-korean-taco-justice-league-kogi-rolls -into-la-2158048

Chapter 5: André Prince Jeffries, North Nashville, Tennessee, Part 1

94 **The origin story of Thornton's:** Davis, T. C. (2015). *The Hot Chicken Cookbook: The Fiery History and Red-Hot Recipes of Nashville's Beloved Bird*. Nashville: Spring House Press.

95 **Jefferson was the road:** Martin, R. (2015, July). How Hot Chicken Really Happened [Web log post]. *The Bitter Southerner*. Retrieved from http://bittersoutherner.com /how-hot-chicken-really-happened/

96 **"This," he told her:** Author interview with André Prince Jeffries.

97 **When she finally hit that age:** Author interview with Jeffries.

105 **they started construction:** Martin, R. *The Bitter Southerner*.

106 **most famous example was Hotchickens.com:** Edge, J. T. (2007). *Southern Belly: A Food Lover's Companion*. Chapel Hill: Algonquin Books.

106 **he'd worked to have the area:** Stafford, Z. (2017, September 21). Burned Out [Web log post]. *Eater*. Retrieved from https://www.eater.com/2017/9/21/16343192 /princes-hot-chicken-profile-nashville

Chapter 6: Freret Street, New Orleans, Louisiana, 2008, Part 1

108 **Coupled with the Canal Villere:** Warner, C. (2001). Freret's Century: Growth, Identity, and Loss in a New Orleans Neighborhood. *Journal of Louisiana Historical Association.*

109 **"public perception of lawlessness in Freret":** Warner, C. *Louisiana History: The Journal of the Louisiana Historical Association.*

Chapter 7: Phil Ward, New York City, New York, Part 1

112 **ostensibly because having ferns:** Twilley, N. (2015, July 2). How T.G.I. Friday's Helped Invent the Singles Bar. *The New Yorker.* Retrieved from https://www.new yorker.com/culture/culture-desk/how-t-g-i-fridays-helped-invent-the-singles-bar

113 **by 1988, there were more:** Grimes, W. (1988, March). Impeachable Offenses. *Esquire.* Retrieved from https://archive.esquire.com/issue/19880301/#!&pid=36

113 **including Four Seasons:** Grimes, W. (1998, October 6). Joseph Baum, American Dining's High Stylist, Dies at 78. *The New York Times.* Retrieved from https://www.nytimes.com/1998/10/06/us/joseph-baum-american-dining-s-high-stylist-dies-at-78.html

115 **He also actively banned:** Simonson, R. (2016). *A Proper Drink.* Berkeley: Ten Speed Press.

115 **"Wurlitzer organ, cranking out":** Author interview with William Grimes.

116 **a brasserie whose deco-style bar:** DiGiacomo, F. (2005, November). Live, from Tribeca! *Vanity Fair.* Retrieved from https://www.vanityfair.com/style/2005/11/odeon200511

116 **the surprise indie hit *Swingers*:** Gallagher, B. (2018, April 18). "Swingers" and the Fashion Faux Pas That Swept America [Web log post]. *Grailed.* Retrieved from https://www.grailed.com/drycleanonly/swingers-fashion-faux-pas

116 **Fred McKibbin's Grace . . . Grange Hall:** Simonson, R. *A Proper Drink.*

117 **On New Year's Eve:** Simonson, R. (2015, August 21). Sasha Petraske, 42, Dies; Bar Owner Restored Luster to Cocktail Culture. *The New York Times.* Retrieved from https://www.nytimes.com/2015/08/22/nyregion/sasha-petraske-bar-owner-who-revived-luster-to-cocktail-culture-around-the-world-dies-at-42.html?_r=0

128 **"rely on techniques":** Williams, A. (2007, January 14). Come to Our Club. Or Not. Whatever. *The New York Times.* Retrieved from https://www.nytimes.com/2007/01/14/fashion/14secret.html

130 **Like the Ramble, and the Rigadoon:** All cocktails included in Kaplan, D., Fauchald, N., & Day, A. (2014). *Death & Co: Modern Classic Cocktails.* Berkeley: Ten Speed Press.

132 **Marco Dionysos's Absinthe:** Simonson, R. *A Proper Drink.*

132 **first dog-whistling the cocktail nerds:** Shilcutt, K. (2009, March 30). Crafty Cocktails at Anvil Bar & Refuge. *Houston Press.* Retrieved from https://www.houstonpress.com/restaurants/crafty-cocktails-at-anvil-bar-and-refuge-6433811

2009

134 **"Only these days, in Williamsburg":** Martin, B. (2009, May). A Scene Grows in Brooklyn. *Bon Appétit.* Retrieved from https://www.bonappetit.com/entertaining -style/gift-guides/article/a-scene-grows-in-brooklyn

134 **"For nearly twenty-five years":** Goodyear, D. (2009, November 9). The Scavenger. *The New Yorker.* Retrieved from https://www.newyorker.com/magazine/2009/11 /09/the-scavenger

134 **"Light bulbs have been popping":** Simonson, R. (2009, December 29). A Decade of Invention, and Reinvention. *The New York Times.* Retrieved from https://www .nytimes.com/2009/12/30/dining/30cocktail.html

134 **"Avocados: 'Poor Man's Butter'":** Shulman, M. (2009, May 4). Avocados: "Poor Man's Butter" No More. *The New York Times.* Retrieved from https://www.nytimes .com/2009/05/04/health/nutrition/04recipehealth.html

134 **"Tablecloths, Asian fusion":** Moskin, J. (2009, September 15). In Portland's Restaurants, a Down East Banquet. *The New York Times.* Retrieved from https://www .nytimes.com/2009/09/16/dining/16chefs.html

134 **"So, obviously 'food blogging'":** Boyle, C. (2009, May 28). The Good, the Bad, and the Ugly of Food Blogs [Web log post]. *Healthy Tipping Point.* Retrieved from http://www.healthytippingpoint.com/2009/05/the-good-the-bad-the-ugly-of -food-blogs.html

134 **"On a day when the Nasdaq":** Schonfeld, E. (2009, May 21). OpenTable Has a Healthy IPO [Web log post]. *TechCrunch.* Retrieved from https://techcrunch.com /2009/05/21/opentable-has-a-healthy-ipo-shares-shoot-up-40-percent-market -cap-hits-600-million/

134 **"These new culinary entrepreneurs":** Moskin, J. (2009, June 30). Turf War at the Hot Dog Cart. *The New York Times.* Retrieved from https://www.nytimes.com /2009/07/01/dining/01truck.html

Chapter 8: Holeman & Finch, Atlanta, Georgia, January 2009, Ten p.m.

139 **resulting in co-owners Greg Best:** Addison, B. (2013, August 30). Greg Best and Regan Smith Are Leaving Holeman & Finch. *Atlanta.* Retrieved from https://www .atlantamagazine.com/dining-news/greg-best-and-regan-smith-are-leaving -holeman-and-finch/

139 **The 50,000-square-foot facility:** Zyman, J. (2018, March 1). For Its 10 Year Anniversary, H&F Bread Co. Is Undergoing a Massive Expansion. *Atlanta.* Retrieved from https://www.atlantamagazine.com/dining-news/for-10-year-anniversary-hf -bread-co-undergoing-massive-expansion/

Chapter 9: Barbecue Man, Rodney Scott, Hemingway, South Carolina

145 **John T. Edge's story:** Edge, J. T. (2009, June 9). Pig, Smoke, Pit: This Food Is Seriously Slow. *The New York Times*. Retrieved from https://www.nytimes.com/2009/06/10/dining/10United.html

145 **"tin-roofed and time-worn":** Edge.

145 *Texas Monthly,* **as a quinquennial event:** Lexington: Snow's BBQ. (2008, June). *Texas Monthly*. Retrieved from https://www.texasmonthly.com/food/lexington-snows-bbq/

146 **Lewis left—ironically:** Vine, K. (2012, February). Of Meat and Men. *Texas Monthly*. Retrieved from https://www.texasmonthly.com/food/of-meat-and-men/

148 **they showcased a documentary:** York, J. (2010, March 4). *CUT/CHOP/COOK* [Video]. Southern Foodways Alliance. Retrieved from https://www.southernfoodways.org/film/cut-chop-cook/

149 *Food & Wine* **put his joint:** Yagoda, M. (2018, August 10). The Most Important 40 Restaurants of the Past 40 Years. *Food & Wine*. Retrieved from https://www.foodandwine.com/lifestyle/40-most-important-restaurants-past-40-years

149 **a subject that had simmered:** Carman, T. (2018, July 16). How a Small-Town Pitmaster Turned a Dying Cuisine into the Stuff of Celebrity. *Washington Post*. Retrieved from https://www.washingtonpost.com/lifestyle/food/how-a-small-town-pitmaster-turned-a-dying-cuisine-into-the-stuff-of-celebrity/2018/07/16/e525e244-8135-11e8-b658-4f4d2a1aeef1_story.html?utm_term=.c881a36593d4

Chapter 10: Not an Activist, Tunde Wey, Detroit, Michigan, Part 1

160 **she didn't write "about pop-ups":** Author interview with Tunde Wey.

161 **"was trying to get white folks":** Author interview with Wey.

163 **food writer Maura Judkis:** Judkis, M. (2014, December 2). Bold Nigerian Flavors Coming to Northeast for Two Pop-Ups. *Washington Post*.

Chapter 11: Pioneer Woman, Ree Drummond, Pawhuska, Oklahoma

165 **Ree was obsessed with ballet:** Drummond, R. (2011). *The Pioneer Woman: Black Heels to Tractor Wheels*. New York: William Morrow.

166 **"wrangle celebrity guests":** Fortini, A. (2011, May 9). O Pioneer Woman! *The New Yorker*.

167 *Modern Farmer's* **"Land Report":** Brasch, S. (2013, October 16). America's Top 100 Land Owners. *Modern Farmer*. Retrieved from https://modernfarmer.com/2013/10/americas-top-100-land-owners/

167 **quickly got savvy with the technology:** Fortini, A. (2011, May 9). O Pioneer Woman! *The New Yorker*.

168 **More than four million unique visitors:** Fortini, A. O Pioneer Woman!

168 **"comes off as nervous":** Fortini, A. (2012, February 3). The Pioneer Woman Gets Lost on the Range. *The New Yorker*.

169 **On October 31, 2016:** Ree Drummond's New Pioneer Woman Mercantile Opens in Pawhuska. (2016, October 31). *Tulsa World*. Retrieved from https://www.tulsaworld .com/photovideo/slideshows/photo-gallery-ree-drummond-s-new-pioneer -woman-mercantile-opens/collection_57665f6f-7a78-5914-a873-c44187b3a82a .html

170 **How they'd created:** Morgan, R. (2017, October 22). Prairie Companions: Year-Old Pioneer Woman Mercantile Spawns New Businesses in Pawhuska. *Tulsa World*.

171 **serving wood-fired pizzas:** Watts, J. (2018, June 11). Pioneer Woman's P-town Pizza to Open in Pawhuska Next Week. *Tulsa World*.

Chapter 12: Freret Street, New Orleans, Louisiana, 2011, Part 2

173 **By 2011, *Esquire*'s David Wondrich:** Wondrich, D. (2011, May 22). *Esquire* Best Bars 2011: Cure, New Orleans. *Esquire*. Retrieved from https://www.esquire.com /food-drink/bars/reviews/a9978/cure-bar-0611/

174 **"The Rebirth of Freret Street":** McNulty, I. (2011, August 8). The Rebirth of Freret Street. *Gambit*. Retrieved from https://www.theadvocate.com/gambit/new _orleans/news/article_03b879df-1de1-5a3a-8a76-26e3f9b96d97.html

Chapter 13: Gabriel Rucker, Portland, Oregon, Part 2

176 **"Hey, Andy," he said:** Author interview with Andy Fortgang.

183 **"That's you, buddy":** Author interview with Hana Kaufman Rucker.

185 **The *Oregonian* had even named:** Russell, M. (2012, January 21). Portland's 2012 Restaurant of the Year: Little Bird. *The Oregonian*. Retrieved from https:// www.oregonlive.com/diner-2012/index.ssf/2012/06/2012_restaurant_of_the _year_li.html

186 **"That's me—let me just see":** Author interview with Gabriel Rucker.

Chapter 15: Anjan and Emily Mitra, San Francisco, California, Part 2

201 **"The Craziest New Cocktail Menu":** English, C. (2008, November). The Craziest New Cocktail Menu in San Francisco [Web log post]. *Alcademics*. Retrieved by http://www.alcademics.com/2008/11/the-craziest-new-cocktail-menu-in-san -francisco.html

201 **"Bay Area's Power Couples":** Mason, L. (2010, September 17). Bay Area Power Couples: Dosa's Anjan & Emily Mitra. *7x7*. Retrieved from http://www.7x7.com /bay-area-power-couples-dosas-anjan-emily-mitra-1779489083.html#

Chapter 16: Mayor, Flavortown, Guy Fieri, Santa Rosa, California

207 **Or that his younger sister:** Patches, M. (2017, June 26). Guy Fieri Just Wants You to Eat Healthy, Donkey Sauce Be Damned. *Thrillist*. Retrieved from https://www .thrillist.com/eat/nation/guy-fieri-diners-drive-ins-and-dives-interview

208 **cart became a fixture:** Tam, D. (2009, August 15). Off the Hook. *Times Standard*. Retrieved from https://www.times-standard.com/2009/08/15/off-the-hook-food -network-to-premiere-ldquochefographyrdquo-on-ferndale-native-guy-fieri/

208 **gone to a junior college:** Moskin, J. (2010, August 10). Guy Fieri, Chef-Dude, Is in the House. *The New York Times*.

209 **famous 2012 disemboweling:** Wells, P. (2012, November 13). As Not Seen on TV. *The New York Times*. Retrieved from https://www.nytimes.com/2012/11/14/dining /reviews/restaurant-review-guys-american-kitchen-bar-in-times-square.html

209 **Fieri believes Wells knew:** Oldenburg, A. (2012, November 15). Guy Fieri Fires Back at Searing "NYT" Restaurant Review. *USA Today*. Retrieved from https:// www.usatoday.com/story/life/people/2012/11/15/guy-fieri-new-york-times -restaurant-review-defends-fires-back/1706207/

209 **Fieri believes it wasn't:** Baker, K. (2012, November 16). Guy Fieri Battles Scath-ing *New York Times* Review by Pete Wells [Web log post]. *The Daily Beast*. Retrieved from https://www.thedailybeast.com/guy-fieri-battles-scathing-new-york-times -review-by-pete-wells

210 **Anthony Bourdain also weighed in:** Forbes, P. (2012, September 28). Watch Bourdain Rip into Guy Fieri's NYC "Terror-Dome" [Web log post]. *Eater*. Retrieved from https://www.eater.com/2012/9/28/6540469/watch-bourdain-rip-into-guy -fieris-nyc-terror-dome

210 **British comedian John Oliver:** Oliver, J. (2015, August 24). *Last Week Tonight* [Video]. HBO.

211 **Fieri officiated more than a hundred:** Hollyman, H. (2017, February 15). Who Is Guy Fieri? [Web log post]. *Munchies*. Retrieved from https://munchies.vice.com /en_us/article/bm3xeq/who-is-guy-fieri

Chapter 17: André Prince Jeffries, North Nashville, Tennessee, Part 2

213 **"Mom, you better make some more":** Author interview with Semone Jeffries.

214 **an entertaining ten-minute documentary:** York, J. (2008, July 28). *Prince's Hot Chicken* [Video]. Southern Foodways Alliance. Retrieved from https://www .southernfoodways.org/film/hot-chicken/

214 **"Hey," Jeffries said:** York.

216 **What followed established André Prince Jeffries:** Jeffries, A. P. (2009). Speech at Hoodie Awards. Retrieved from https://www.youtube.com/watch?v=_C0VWm Tr7B8

219 **"perfectly golden and crispy":** Chamberlain, C. (2010, November 19). Fire in the Hole! Pepperfire Spiced Chicken Opens on Gallatin Pike. *Nashville Scene*. Retrieved

from https://www.nashvillescene.com/food-drink/article/13036257/fire-in-the-hole
-pepperfire-spiced-chicken-opens-on-gallatin-pike

220 **chef Thomas Keller:** Sietsema, T. (2011, January 28). Postcard from Tom: At This
Nashville Joint, the Chicken's Really Hot. *The Washington Post.* Retrieved from
https://www.washingtonpost.com/opinions/postcard-from-tom-at-this
-nashville-joint-the-chickens-really-hot/2011/01/28/ABErU5Q_story.html?nore
direct=on&utm_term=.ca569f1a8a8d

223 **KFC had been quietly testing:** Shah, K. (2015, October 2). KFC Rips Off Nashville
and Adds Hot Chicken to Its Menu [Web log post]. *Eater.* Retrieved from https://
www.eater.com/2015/10/2/9439433/kfc-nashville-hot-chicken

223 **"The Year of Hot Chicken":** Embiricos, G. (2015, December). The United States
of Hot Chicken. *Food Republic.* Retrieved from http://www.foodrepublic.com/2015
/12/17/the-united-states-of-hot-chicken/

223 **James Beard America's Classics Award:** America's Classic: Prince's Hot
Chicken Shack. (2013, May 6). James Beard Foundation. Retrieved from https://
www.jamesbeard.org/blog/americas-classic-princes-hot-chicken-shack

Chapter 18: Phil Ward, New York City, New York, Part 2

229 **a Dan Saltzstein piece:** Saltzstein, D. (2009, April 21). Hoping Mezcal Can Turn
the Worm. *The New York Times.* Retrieved from https://www.nytimes.com/2009
/04/22/dining/22mezcal.html

229 **Eric Asimov–introduced Q and A:** Asimov, E. (2009, April 22). Mezcal's Moment. *The New York Times.* Retrieved from https://dinersjournal.blogs.nytimes.com
/2009/04/22/mezcals-moment/

232 **The *Times* critic Pete Wells:** Wells, P. (2009, June 16). Checking Out Mayahuel and
Revisiting Benoit. *The New York Times.* Retrieved from https://www.nytimes.com
/2009/06/17/dining/reviews/17brief-001.html

233 **Death & Co won:** 2010 Spirited Award Winners. (n.d.). Tales of the Cocktail Foundation. Retrieved from https://talesofthecocktail.com/events/spirited-awards
-ceremony/ArchiveByYear/2010Archive/

2013

234 **"Restaurants are putting":** Knowlton, A. (2013, August). The Foodist's Top 25
Food Trends of 2013. *Bon Appétit.*

234 **"Nduja (en-DOO-yah), the fiery pork paste":** Knowlton, The Foodist's Top 25.

234 **"Sorry, Instagrammers, but you":** Wells, P. (2013, May 21). The View from West
12th. *The New York Times.*

234 **"No more chasing your lunch":** Duckor, M. (2013, May 30). The 5 Best Food
Halls in America. *Bon Appétit.*

234 **"I was an early supporter":** Knowlton, A. (2013, March 11). Fatty Food. *Bon
Appétit.*

234 **"'In 5 years'":** Top 10 Food Trends of 2013. (2013). *Forbes*. Retrieved from https:// www.forbes.com/pictures/ehlk45jhll/octopus/#5cb01c964b71

234 **"Starting tomorrow, this round":** Merwin, H. (2013, May 9). Introducing the Cronut, a Doughnut-Croissant Hybrid That May Very Well Change Your Life. *Grub Street*. Retrieved from http://www.grubstreet.com/2013/05/dominique-ansel-cronut.html

234 **"Things are getting confusing":** Canavan, H. D. (2013, May 16). Cooper's Chef Sends Cease-and-Desist to Favreau's Chef. *Eater*. Retrieved from https://www.eater .com/2013/5/16/6433713/coopers-chef-sends-cease-and-desist-to-favreaus-chef

Chapter 19: South Again, Mashama Bailey, Savannah, Georgia

244 **During his drives back and forth:** Gordinier, J. (2015, July 27). At The Grey in Savannah, History Takes Another Turn. *The New York Times*. Retrieved from https://www.nytimes.com/2015/07/29/dining/the-grey-savannah-history-takes -another-turn.html

245 **Howie Kahn mentioned The Grey:** Kahn, H. (2014, October). Southern Hospitality. *The Wall Street Journal Magazine*.

245 **In *Elle* magazine's February 2015 issue:** Restaurants Where Women Call the Shots. (2015, January 21). *Elle*. Retrieved from https://www.elle.com/culture/travel -food/a26106/the-tastemakers/

245 **Jeff Gordinier from . . . *Times*:** Gordinier, J. *The New York Times*.

247 **He'd named The Grey Best Restaurant:** Addison, B. (2017, November 8). The Triumph of The Grey. *Eater*. Retrieved from https://www.eater.com/2017/11/8/16620892 /the-grey-restaurant-of-the-year

Chapter 20: Souvla, 517 Hayes Street, San Francisco, California, Winter 2014

249 ***New York Times*** **wrote a story:** Badger, E. (2018, June 25). San Francisco Restaurants Can't Afford Waiters. So They're Putting the Diners to Work. *The New York Times*. Retrieved from https://www.nytimes.com/2018/06/25/dining/san-francisco -restaurants-service.html

Chapter 21: A Story About Rosé, aka The Fat Jew Interlude

250 **described on MTV:** Anitai, T. (2007, August 6). Meet Team Facelift. MTV News. Retrieved from http://www.mtv.com/news/2291302/meet-team-facelift/

251 **his rhetorical response:** Shapiro, B. (2014, September 17). A Shortcut to Comic Celebrity. *The New York Times*.

252 **Sutter Home white zin:** Prial, F. (1998, October 28). Wine Talk; the House Built on White Zinfandel. *The New York Times*.

253 **Page Six reported:** Siegler, M. (2015, July 13). "Fat Jew" Gets Naked at White Girl Rosé Launch Party. *Page Six*. Retrieved from https://pagesix.com/2015/07/13 /fat-jew-gets-naked-at-white-girl-rose-launch-party/

253 **The wine, they'd report:** Mobley, E. (2015, September 2). Rosé Goes Viral. Is That a Bad Thing? *San Francisco Chronicle.*

Chapter 22: Not an Activist, Tunde Wey, Detroit, Michigan, Part 2

256 **Hillary Dixler wrote a story:** Canavan, H. D. (2016, May 22). How Gullah Cuisine Has Transformed Charleston Dining. *Eater.* Retrieved from https://www.eater.com/2016/3/22/11264104/gullah-food-charleston

257 *Oxford American* **put the piece online:** Wey, T. (2016, June 3). Who Owns Southern Food? *Oxford American.* Retrieved from https://www.oxfordamerican.org/magazine/item/870-who-owns-southern-food

Chapter 24: Downfall, John Besh, New Orleans, Louisiana

263 **The restaurant they opened together:** Price, T. (2014, September 3). August "Duke" Robin, Founder of Restaurant August, Dies at 72. *The Times-Picayune.*

264 **Using propane burners:** McCausland, P. (2015, August 27). How New Orleans' Restaurant Industry Helped Revive the City After Katrina. *Munchies.* Retrieved from https://munchies.vice.com/en_us/article/kbxxga/how-new-orleans-restaurant-industry-helped-revive-the-city-after-katrina

265 **He embarked on an exhausting tour:** Severson, K. (2007, October 31). From Disaster, a Chef Forges an Empire. *The New York Times.*

265 **The publisher of the** *Times-Picayune***:** Price, T. (2016, July 9). Chef John Besh Wins First T.G. Solomon Excellence in Innovation Award. *The Times-Picayune.*

266 **story he'd spent eight months investigating:** Anderson, B. (2017, October 21). John Besh Restaurants Fostered Culture of Sexual Harassment, 25 Women Say. *The Times-Picayune.*

267 **a public and ugly trademark dispute:** Carter, S. (2018, January 25). Besh Says Shaya Took "Lavish Vacations" on the Company Credit Card. *Eater.* Retrieved from https://nola.eater.com/2018/1/25/16932084/besh-shaya-relationship-lawsuit-new-orleans-nola

267 **Besh stepped down as CEO:** Chokshi, N. (2017, October 23). Chef John Besh Steps Down amid Sexual Harrassment Scandal. *The New York Times.*

267 **promoting the first event:** MiNO (Made in New Orleans) Foundation Rebirth Event page. Retrieved from https://www.eventbrite.com/e/mino-made-in-new-orleans-foundation-re-birth-event-tickets-50175211408

2017

268 **"John Besh restaurants":** Anderson.

268 **"Mario Batali Steps Away":** Hauser, C. (2017, December 11). Mario Batali Steps Away from Restaurants amid Sexual Misconduct Allegations. *The New York Times.*

268 **"Ken Friedman, Power Restaurateur":** Moskin, J. (2017, December 12). Ken Friedman, Power Restaurateur, Is Accused of Sexual Harassment. *The New York Times.*

268 **"Oakland chef Charlie Hallowell":** Duggan, T. (2017, December 27). Oakland Chef Charlie Hallowell Steps Away from Restaurants as 17 Women Accuse Him of Sexual Harassment. *San Francisco Chronicle.*

268 **"Lawsuit accuses celebrity chef":** Paquette, D. (2018, March 19). Lawsuit Accuses Celebrity Chef Mike Isabella of "Extraordinary" Sexual Harassment. *The Washington Post.*

268 **"4 former employees":** Paley, R. T. (2017, November 29). 4 Former Employees Accuse Celebrity Chef Johnny Iuzzini of Sexual Harassment and Abuse. *Mic.*

Chapter 25: Anjan and Emily Mitra, San Francisco, California, Part 3

274 **"Why Indian Cuisine":** Ramachandran, V. (2016, October 5). Why Indian Cuisine Is Having a Fast-Casual Moment Right Now [Web log post]. *Eater.* Retrieved from https://www.eater.com/2016/10/5/13156412/indian-restaurant-fast-casual

274 **"South Indian Food Is Having":** Suri, C. (2017, November 13). South Indian Food is Having a Major Moment in America. *Food & Wine.*

276 **"traditional Indian flavors":** Fort, E. (2016, November 17). Babu Ji's Menu Offers Amped Up Indian Cuisine and a Party Spirit in the Mission [Web log post]. *Eater.* Retrieved from https://sf.eater.com/2016/11/17/13671676/babu-ji-mission-san -francisco-menu

276 **"California-influenced Indian flavors":** Fort, E. (2016, November 11). Enter August 1 Five's World of Bright Colors and Bold Indian Flavors in Civic Center [Web log post]. *Eater.* Retrieved from https://sf.eater.com/2016/11/11/13571776/august -1-five-indian-open-menu-photos-san-francisco#0

276 **"progressive versions of Indian dishes":** Fort, E. (2017, February 9). Rooh's Splashy Interior Heralds the Rise of Progressive Indian Cuisine in SF [Web log post]. *Eater.* Retrieved from https://sf.eater.com/2017/2/9/14562172/rooh-indian-soma-san -francisco-photos

Chapter 26: The Resistance, Sonja Finn, Pittsburgh, Pennsylvania

284 **America's top food city:** Majors, D. (2015, December 15). Zagat: Pittsburgh Restaurant Scene Is No. 1. *Pittsburgh Post-Gazette.*

284 **a Hot New Food Town story:** Gordinier, J. (2016, March 15). Pittsburgh's Youth-Driven Food Boom. *The New York Times.*

286 **"The joke is that":** Finn, S. (2018). Campaign Speech.

288 **Forty-seven of the seventy-two:** Potter, C. (2018, January 14). Sonja Finn Wins Democratic Nod for City Council's District 8 Seat. *Pittsburgh Post-Gazette.* Retrieved from http://www.post-gazette.com/local/city/2018/01/14/Sonja-Finn-wins -Democratic-nomination-Pittsburgh-City-Council-District-8-Dan-Gilman /stories/201801140181

289 **declined to pick a candidate:** The Editorial Board (2018, March 3). District 8 Dilemma: Both Finn and Strassburger Would Serve City Well. *Pittsburgh Post-Gazette.*

Chapter 27: The Plaza District, NW 16th Street from Blackwelder to Indiana, Oklahoma City, Oklahoma

292 **Patrick Ireland and Carey Kirby:** "Saints" Alive: Irish Restaurant and Bar to Open in Plaza District. (2011, May 9). *The Oklahoman.* Retrieved from https://newsok .com/article/3566328/saints-alive-divirish-restaurant-and-bar-to-open-in-plaza -districtdiv

295 **In 2018, *Bon Appétit* named:** Knowlton, A. (2018, August 14). America's Best New Restaurants 2018. *Bon Appétit.* Retrieved from http://projects.bonappetit.com /hot10/p/2

295 **penned a "Letter of Recommendation":** Anderson, S. (2008, August 21). Letter of Recommendation: Oklahoma City. *The New York Times.*

Chapter 28: Phil Ward, New York City, New York, Part 3

300 **other "branded opportunities":** Ramirez, E. (2018, July 31). Death and Co.'s David Kaplan on Turning Cocktail Fans into Investors. *Forbes.* Retrieved from https:// www.forbes.com/sites/elvaramirez/2018/07/31/death-co-s-david-kaplan-on -turning-cocktail-fans-into-investors/#12df9172352d

300 **Reiner told *The New York Times*:** Simonson, R. (2018, December 7). Flatiron Lounge, a Craft Cocktail Pioneer, Will Close. *The New York Times.* Retrieved from https://www.nytimes.com/2018/12/07/dining/flatiron-lounge-closing.html

301 **describing Ward as an oddity:** Simonson, R. (2017, September 21). Phil Ward Just Wants to Bartend. *Punch.* Retrieved from https://punchdrink.com/articles /phil-ward-bartender-nyc-mayahuel-long-island-bar/

Chapter 29: Freret Street, New Orleans, Louisiana, 2018, Part 3

305 **"Many post-Katrina restaurants":** Ruffin, M. C. (2018, August 21). The Taking of Freret Street. *Gravy.* Retrieved from https://www.southernfoodways.org/the-taking -of-freret-street/

Chapter 30: Gabriel Rucker, Portland, Oregon, Part 3

309 **Portland real estate prices:** Real Estate Data for Portland. Trulia.com. Retrieved from https://www.trulia.com/real_estate/Portland-Oregon/market-trends/

310 **Cars with California license plates:** Perry, D. (2017, July 2). "Go Back to California!" Graffiti on Car, House, Stuns New Arrivals, Highlights Old Tensions in Portland. *The Oregonian.* Retrieved from https://www.oregonlive.com/portland/index .ssf/2017/07/go_back_to_california_vandalis.html

Chapter 31: Kroger Marketplace, 9001 Old US Hwy 42, Union, Kentucky, Spring 2018

315 **Kitchen 1883 . . . Development team:** Kroger Co. press release. (2017, September). Retrieved from https://www.prnewswire.com/news-releases/the-kroger-co -introduces-restaurant-concept-kitchen-1883-300519678.html

316 **In April 2018, Kroger Co. announced:** Redman, R. (2018, April 5). Kroger Readies Second Kitchen 1883 Restaurant. *Supermarket News.* Retrieved from https:// www.supermarketnews.com/prepared-foods/kroger-readies-second-kitchen -1883-restaurant

Chapter 32: André Prince Jeffries, North Nashville, Tennessee, Part 3

318 **George Embiricos posted an interview:** Embiricos, G. (2016, August 25). Meet the Man Who Launched the Nashville Hot Chicken Craze. *Food Republic.* Retrieved from http://www.foodrepublic.com/2016/08/25/meet-the-man-who-launched-the -nashville-hot-chicken-craze/

319 **Dueling editorials appeared in *Nashville Scene*:** Phillips, B. (2016, August 29). Race, Credit, and Hot Chicken. *Nashville Scene.* Retrieved from https://www.nash villescene.com/news/pith-in-the-wind/article/20832025/race-credit-and -hot-chicken

320 **"Do nothing," he said:** Author interview with Semone Jeffries.

BIBLIOGRAPHY

Anderson, Heather Arndt. *Portland: A Food Biography*. Lanham, MD: Rowman & Little-field, 2014.

Bald, Vivek. *Bengali Harlem and the Lost Histories of South Asian America*. Cambridge, MA: Harvard University Press, 2015.

Bourdain, Anthony. *Kitchen Confidential: Adventures in the Culinary Underbelly*. New York: Bloomsbury USA, 2000.

Bourdain, Anthony. *Medium Raw: A Bloody Valentine to the World of Food and the People Who Cook*. New York: Ecco, 2010.

Brooks, Karen, Gideon Bosker, and Teri Gelber. *The Mighty Gastropolis Portland: A Journey Through the Center of America's New Food Revolution*. San Francisco: Chronicle Books, 2012.

Cardoz, Floyd, and Jane Daniels Lear. *One Spice, Two Spice: American Food, Indian Flavors*. New York: William Morrow, 2006.

Chakravorty, Sanjoy, Devesh Kapur, and Nirvikar Singh. *The Other One Percent: Indians in America*. London: Oxford University Press, 2016.

Choi, Roy, Tien Nguyen, and Natasha Phan. *L.A. Son: My Life, My City, My Food*. New York: Ecco, 2013.

Curtis, Wayne. *And a Bottle of Rum: A History of the New World in Ten Cocktails*. New York: Three Rivers Press, 2006.

Davis, Timothy Charles. *The Hot Chicken Cookbook: The Fiery History and Red-Hot Recipes of Nashville's Beloved Bird*. Nashville: Spring House Press, 2015.

Drummond, Ree. *The Pioneer Woman: Black Heels to Tractor Wheels*. New York: William Morrow, 2011.

Edge, John T. *Hamburgers and Fries: An American Story*. New York: G.P. Putnam's Sons, 2005.

Edge, John T. *The Potlikker Papers: A Food History of the Modern South*. New York: Penguin Press, 2017.

Edge, John T. *Southern Belly: A Food Lover's Companion.* Chapel Hill: Algonquin Books of Chapel Hill, 2007.

Freedman, Paul. *Ten Restaurants That Changed America.* New York: Liveright Publishing Corporation, 2016.

Friedman, Andrew. *Chefs, Drugs, and Rock and Roll: How Food Lovers, Free Spirits, Misfits, and Wanderers Created a New American Profession.* New York: HarperCollins Publishers, 2018.

Jacobs, Jane. *The Death and Life of Great American Cities.* New York: Vintage Books, 1992.

Jaffrey, Madhur. *A Taste of India.* New York: Atheneum, 1988.

Kamp, David. *The United States of Arugula: How We Became a Gourmet Nation.* New York: Broadway Books, 2006.

Kaplan, David, Nick Fauchald, and Alex Day. *Death & Co: Modern Classic Cocktails.* Berkeley: Ten Speed Press, 2014.

Lee, Edward. *Buttermilk Graffiti.* New York: Artisan, 2018.

Lohman, Sarah. *Eight Flavors: The Untold Story of American Cuisine.* New York: Simon & Schuster, 2016.

Moss, Robert. *Barbecue: The History of an American Institution.* Tuscaloosa: University of Alabama Press, 2010.

Packer, George. *The Unwinding: An Inner History of the New America.* New York: Farrar, Straus and Giroux, 2013.

Prashad, Vijay. *The Karma of Brown Folk.* Minneapolis: University of Minnesota Press, 2001.

Ray, Krishnendu. *The Ethnic Restaurateur.* London: Bloomsbury, 2016.

Rucker, Gabriel, Meredith Erickson, Lauren Fortgang, and Andrew Fortgang. *Le Pigeon: Cooking at the Dirty Bird.* Berkeley: Ten Speed Press, 2011.

Rushdie, Sameen. *Indian Cookery.* New York: Picador Cookstr Classics, 2018.

Simonson, Robert. *A Proper Drink: The Untold Story of How a Band of Bartenders Saved the Civilized Drinking World.* Berkeley: Ten Speed Press, 2016

Vaswani, Suneeta. *Complete Book of Indian Cooking.* Toronto: Robert Rose, 2007.

Vaughn, Daniel. *The Prophets of Smoked Meat: A Journey Through Texas Barbecue.* New York: Ecco, 2013.

Wondrich, David. *Imbibe!* New York: Perigee, 2007.

Wondrich, David. *Punch: The Delights (and Dangers) of the Flowing Bowl.* New York: Perigee, 2010.

IMAGE CREDITS

INDEX